Laws Relating to Sex, Pregnancy, and Infancy

Laws Relating to Sex, Pregnancy, and Infancy

Issues in Criminal Justice

Carmen M. Cusack

palgrave
macmillan

First published in 2015 by PALGRAVE MACMILLAN® in the United States—a division of St. Martin's Press LLC, 175 Fifth Avenue, New York, NY 10010.

Where this book is distributed in the UK, Europe and the rest of the world, this is by Palgrave Macmillan, a division of Macmillan Publishers Limited, registered in England, company number 785998, of Houndmills, Basingstoke, Hampshire RG21 6XS.

Palgrave Macmillan is the global academic imprint of the above companies and has companies and representatives throughout the world.

Palgrave® and Macmillan® are registered trademarks in the United States, the United Kingdom, Europe and other countries.

ISBN: 978-1-137-50518-7

Library of Congress Cataloging-in-Publication Data

Cusack, Carmen M., author.
  Laws relating to sex, pregnancy, and infancy : issues in criminal justice / Carmen M. Cusack.
      pages cm
  Includes bibliographical references and index.
  ISBN 978-1-137-50518-7 (hardcover : alk. paper)   1. Sex crimes—United States.   2. Parent and child (Law)—United States—Criminal provisions. 3. Sex discrimination in criminal justice administration—United States. 4. Pregnant women—Legal status, laws, etc.—United States.   I. Title.
  KF9325.C87 2015
  345.73'0253—dc23

                                                                2014044459

A catalogue record of the book is available from the British Library.

Design by Amnet.

First edition: May 2015

10 9 8 7 6 5 4 3 2 1

This book is dedicated to YC, W, M, RY, P, B

Contents

Introduction

The role of children, mothers, and pregnancy in the criminal justice system is varied and wide ranging. The presence of infants in legal environments may illustrate that the criminal justice system functions successfully. For example, Justice Ruth Bader Ginsburg was one of the only women to attend Harvard and Columbia law schools. She ranked first in both her classes while caring for her first child, who was a toddler at the time. Yet, society has brutalized and ignored babies. Because the system works, many babies have been defended and protected using the criminal justice system. *Laws Relating to Sex, Pregnancy, and Infancy: Issues in Criminal Justice* describes some of the laws, anecdotal evidence, science, history, and policy dealing with pregnancy, babies, and sex in the criminal justice system.

Sex, pregnancy, and babies are not necessarily correlated. Sex does not necessarily lead to pregnancy; pregnancy does not necessarily result in babies; and babies are not necessarily the result of sex or pregnancy between intimate partners. Babies and motherhood may be the products of rape, fertilization treatment, adoption, and other anomalies or unique experiences; and yet, since the beginning of human history, sex, pregnancy, and babies have shared a biological, and often sacred, relationship. *Laws Relating to Sex, Pregnancy, and Infancy: Issues in Criminal Justice* discusses family law, criminal codes, case law, policy, politics, history, behavioral science, social science, current events, and anecdotal evidence to demonstrate how varied and, at times, unpredictable the relationships may be between the criminal justice system; sex; babies; and pregnancy. The criminal justice system is not a singular entity; it is a concept describing numerous organized responses to problems in society; but, practically, philosophically, and legally, it is anchored together by a single root, which is the U.S. Constitution. Despite its history and ability to evolve, the criminal justice system must consistently respond in a manner that demonstrates fairness, fulfilment of duty, equality, and best practices. Yet, facts between parties and changes in culture constantly require the system to adapt; create new standards; respond to emergencies; and accommodate vulnerable populations (e.g., children and women).

Women and children are not always accommodated by criminal justice responses. For example, women may be electro-stunned by police or placed in isolation in prison; they may be ignored by jailers when they are hungry; and they may be discouraged from exercising their rights. Children may be placed in physically and psychologically uncomfortable situations by criminal justice system branches (e.g., state custody). However, the system, at large, attempts to regard these special populations with the requisite level of sensitivity. The system should act in the best interest of children; and at times, in the best interest of fetuses. Sometimes, this interest countervails pregnant women's interests or lifestyles. Protections for vulnerable populations have increased in recent years; but great work remains to further develop them. *Laws Relating to Sex, Pregnancy, and Infancy: Issues in Criminal Justice* discusses a history of laws' progression; gaps in protection; and future directions for policy changes. This interdisciplinary text includes analyses of foreign policies, laws, and cases, which may be compared to the U.S. criminal justice system.

CHAPTER 1

Sex

Morality

The government regulates sex, sexuality, morality, and family structure. Legislation and regulation of morality have been traditional state powers. Under the Constitution, the state is authorized to use police power to enforce morality laws. Morality laws affecting sex include laws prohibiting consensual harmful sex (i.e., bondage and sadomasochism). The government regulated non-harmful consensual sodomy prior to 2003. However, following *Lawrence v. Texas* (2003), police power can no longer be used by the state to prevent homosexuals or heterosexuals from non-harmful private sexual relations.

Numerous fetishes (e.g., exhibitionism) are banned. Some fetishes are banned because they harm individuals or society. For example, the City of Sandy Springs, Georgia bans adult toys because it believes they are offensive and obscene (Dixon, 2014; Ordinance No. 38–119, 2009). Thus, obscenity is not protected under *Miller v. California* (2003). The city also claims to have a substantial interest in protecting itself from crime (i.e., secondary effects) caused by adult establishments (e.g., prostitution and vagrancy). Secondary effects may not be limited to increased crime associated with vice. They may possibly also include domestic violence correlated with pornography. For example, research indicates that women who are coerced to watch pornography with their partners are significantly likelier to be victims of domestic violence (Cramer, 1998). Thus, stores selling pornographic materials may be linked to domestic violence, even though, according to the Rational Choice Theory, adult establishments are not the proximate cause of domestic violence. Yet fetishes, like exhibitionism, are illegal even when those crimes are victimless, because decency laws are designed to prohibit sexual immorality. For example, indecent exposure inside a vehicle may be illegal even if no one witnesses the crime.

Family structure was traditionally regulated under morality-based laws. For example, criminal law, civil law, and family law were traditionally used to prevent homosexual couples from marrying and adopting children. As Constitutional law has been newly interpreted by the courts, use of police power to regulate family structure has shifted in some jurisdictions. Shifts reflect judicial activism; contemporary attitudes toward homosexuality; and evolved understandings of family. For example, some jurisdictions currently permit same-sex marriage under the Fourteenth Amendment and Fifth Amendment. Adoption by same-sex couples has been permitted under best-interest-of-the-child standards (*In re Gill*, 2008). States conclude that despite traditional morality, children in foster care would not likely experience adverse consequences from being adopted by same-sex parents; and, the state and children would benefit from increased adoption rates.

Consent

Consent is freely given assent and agreement (Cusack, 2014). Legally cognizable consent is both a complicated area of law and a facet of interpersonal relationships. Non-consent is discussed further in Chapter 15. Conditions that void consent in some jurisdictions include minority, intoxication, and incapacitation because they cause consent to lack legal force or knowledge. Incapacitation could include sleep and unconsciousness.

Consent must be knowing; thus, implicit consent apparently granted during incapacitation may not be knowing. Most jurisdictions define incapacitation to include sleep, but sleep is not necessarily an incapacitated state. Generally, defendants may defend by claiming that they did not know that a victim was sleeping or incapacitated (10 U.S.C. §920b. Art. 120b, 2014).

Intoxication may make consent void or voidable in some jurisdictions. Intoxication may be considered to be a victim's state of mind. Since intoxication changes or clouds a victim's mind, intoxication may void or make assent voidable when a victim cannot freely and knowingly consent. Mental incapacitation voids consent. If an intoxicated victim is considered to be mentally incapacitated (e.g., blacked out), then that victim will not have consented. However, intoxication does not necessarily result in mental incapacitation. Degree and voluntariness of intoxication, as well as *stare decisis*, will influence whether intoxication constitutes mental incapacitation or vitiates consent.

Some jurisdictions provide heightened protections for victims by distinguishing mental incapacitation from intoxication. One difference may be the force required to demonstrate an absence of freedom. Distinctions may become relevant when intoxicated victims can remember consenting but do not believe that their consent was voluntary. A victim's state of mind is always relevant; thus, intoxication could impact victim credibility (Stone, 2013). Statutes may potentially create strict liability for intoxication or permit any amount of intoxication to meet legal elements; however, in some jurisdictions, intoxication may not have any effect on the validity of consent. In jurisdictions without intoxication provisions, victims' credibility may be doubted because they were intoxicated. Evidence of intoxication could become relevant when parties dispute whether consent was express or implied. Express and implied consent are discussed in Chapter 15.

Future laws may benefit from more-precise definitions about the legal effect of intoxication on incapacitation because, one, women are more likely to be raped while intoxicated and, two, approximately half of sexual assaults involve alcohol. Intoxicated women are more likely to be victims of sexual assault than sober women, sober men, or intoxicated men. Yet, legislatures must protect each gender equally from sexual assault. Laws protecting individuals from predatory or opportunistic crimes involving alcohol can be precarious because perceptions of and relationships between alcohol and sex may be relative to culture, gender norms, education, gender rules, age, environment, and rape myths (Cowley, 2014). Thus, predatory or opportunistic behaviors may be normalized in some environments. Researchers have found that women who consume alcohol were more likely to associate alcohol use with sex, but women who did not consume alcohol were more likely to associate alcohol consumption with coercion (Untied, Orchowski, and Lazar, 2013).

Legislatures may help reduce risk of sexual victimization by increasing deterrence, especially by deterring sexual victimization of children (Walsh, 2013). Researchers sampled 546 female college students. They found that childhood sexual abuse correlated with revictimization. Respondents' expectations for relationships between sex and alcohol correlated with risky sexual activity; perceptions of low sexual control; alcohol-related revictimization; and childhood sexual abuse. Legislators could consider providing child victims with programs designed to reduce risk of substance use and revictimization.

Minority voids sexual consent. Voluntary sexual intercourse with a postpubescent minor who is younger than the legal age of consent is described as statutory rape. Statutory rape would be consensual sex except for legally imposed age limits on consent. This is discussed further in Chapter 15. In most states, age of consent is delimited between 16 years old and 18 years old. For certain kinds of charges (e.g., unlawful sexual activity), age limitations may be relevant to partners' ages and to the difference in years between the victim and the offender (Fla. Stat. § 794.05, 2014). For example, elements may not be met if one partner is 17 years old and one partner is 20 years old. In some jurisdictions, minors may lawfully engage in sexual encounters with peers of the same age. However, in other jurisdictions, minors have no right to consent to any sexual activity. Thus, a minor may be a victim and an offender (*Womancare of Orlando v. Agwunobi*, 2006). In almost every jurisdiction, prepubescent children may not engage in any sexual contact. Thus, children younger than twelve, for example, could potentially be held culpable for voluntarily participating in sexual contact with one another in some jurisdictions. Engaging in sexual contact with a prepubescent child is a serious criminal offense and a felony.

Parents possess a fundamental right to raise their children and to direct children's moral upbringing; however, parental assent does not legally grant sexual consent to children. Children may be removed from their parents' home if parents permit children to be statutorily raped. Some violations seem merely to bend cultural norms in favor of harmless sexual deviance, but other violations are patently egregious. For example, a 19-year-old partner dating a 15-year-old partner would be distinguishable from the case of *In the Matter of Martha A.* (2010). In that case, a mother began having sex with a 25-year-old man after that man twice impregnated her 14-year-old daughter. He also smoked marijuana with her daughter; and he slept in the same room as another of her children, a 12-year-old daughter, on whom he created a hickey mark. The court said that the mother "show[ed] such poor judgment and flawed understanding of the mother's role as a caretaker over a period of years as to place the children at risk of imminent harm" (*In the Matter of Martha A.*, 2010, p. 478). That mother's children were removed. Removal is discussed is Chapter 12.

Parents and the court can consent to marriage, which emancipates minors and makes statutory rape laws irrelevant between spouses. Thus, emancipation may be a complete defense (*State v. Plude*, 1993). However, minors who were emancipated through marriage, but not through court order, may potentially revert to being minors under statutory rape laws if they divorce before turning 18 years old (Fla. Stat. § 39.01, 2014). For example, under the Uniform Code of Military Justice (UCMJ) "[a] child not legally married [at the time of the offense] to the person committing the sexual act, lewd act, or use of force cannot consent to any sexual act, lewd act, or use of force" (10 U.S.C. §920b. Art. 120b, 2014). Emancipation is discussed further in Chapter 14.

In some jurisdictions, minority may create strict liability; or, a defendant's knowledge of a victim's age may be required to satisfy the elements. Some jurisdictions hold any defendant culpable for engaging in voluntary, nonconsensual sex with minors. Jurisdictions may only hold defendants culpable if they should have or could have reasonably known a victim's age. For example, a victim who appears to be a young teen may be presumed to be lying about being an adult if the defendant knows that the child attends middle school. Defendants will be prosecuted for production and transmission of child pornography if they knew a minor victim's age (*U.S. v. X-Citement Video*, 1994). In some jurisdictions (i.e., California) emancipation and marriage may provide a defense to child pornography prosecution, but in other jurisdictions (e.g., Missouri) they will not (*U.S. v. Stringer*, 2014). In some jurisdictions, defendants may be strictly liable. Defendants charged with sexual contact with minors have argued constructive emancipation when minors live without parents and provide for themselves; however, these defenses often fail when a defendant knew or should have known a victim's age; or in jurisdictions that hold defendants strictly liable (*People v. Perry*, 2012). Thus, legal emancipation by court order is distinguishable from constructive emancipation under many statutory schemes (*Feliciano v. State*, 2006; *Womancare of Orlando, Inc. v. Agwunobi*, 2006).

Voluntary and Involuntary

Relationships between consent and voluntariness are somewhat circuitous. Consensual sexual activity is sanctioned under the law. Involuntary sexual contact is never consensual; but, it may be legal in jurisdictions that define force, but not consent, as an element of sexual assault. Consensual sexual activity is always voluntary; however, voluntary sex acts may be nonconsensual under the law. Involuntary sex acts are further discussed throughout Chapter 15. Voluntary sex may include incest or violent sex; but those acts are typically considered to be nonconsensual (i.e., illegal). Incestuous sexual activity is illegal. Definitions of incest may include step-relatives and distant cousins, or may include only immediate family. Each jurisdiction defines incest. Many definitions include biological first cousins, aunts and uncles, grandparents, and relatives of similar familial proximity by marriage, consanguinity, or adoption.

Voluntarily incestuous sex between adults is illegal. Parents may be held culpable for violating children even when children are older than 18 years old (*U.S. v. Vigil*, 2003). In one case, minors between the ages of 18 years old and 21 years old were held to be vulnerable child victims because of the special position of authority held by a parent, stepparent, or adopted parent. This is because young adults may feel coerced by parents; fear the consequences of noncompliance with sexual requests; or trust that parents will not harm them *(U.S. v. Hargrove*, 2005; *U.S. v. Martinez-Carillo*, 2001).

Adults cannot consent to violent sexual activity (Cusack, 2015). Right to Privacy under the Fifth Amendment and Fourteenth Amendment protects private consensual sexual activity between adults. However, sexual activity must be non-harmful (*Lawrence v. Texas,* 2003). In many jurisdictions, people who knowingly and voluntarily engage in self-harm may be charged with battery, aggravated battery, or other crimes. More likely than not, people who self-harm may be institutionalized, which is a civil remedy. In some jurisdictions, people can consent to be harmed because battery laws only apply when an actor harms another person (Spindelman, 2013). In some situations (e.g., sports), consent may be a defense for committing a battery upon another; but it is not a defense when batteries occur during sexual activity (Rapp, 2008). Harmful sex acts vitiate consent for sex and participants can be charged with sexual assault, battery, aggravated sexual battery, and other violations (Cusack, 2014).

CHAPTER 2

Birth Control

History of Birth Control, Planned Parenthood, and Women's Privacy Rights

Birth control has been controversial for more than two centuries. Early attempts to create birth control made by Charles Goodyear included vulcanized rubber for condoms; syringes for douching; diaphragms called "womb veils"; and intrauterine devices (PBS, n.d.). Early in the 1900s, the government began persecuting Margaret Sanger and others for providing information about birth control and contraceptives (*Message Photo-Play Co., Inc. v. Bell*, 1917). Sanger opened the first birth control clinic in 1916 (*People v. Sanger*, 1917). Her sister and friend assisted her to distribute information about birth control to women in New York. After little more than one week, the New York City vice squad, led by an undercover police officer posing as a patient, searched and seized the clinic, along with patients' records, diaphragms, and condoms; and they arrested Sanger (Wardell, 1980). Ethel Byrne, Sanger's sister, was convicted of selling literature about birth control in contravention of New York Penal Law § 1142 (*People* v. *Byrne*, 1917). Byrne claimed that the law violated the Constitution because it unreasonably interfered with women's rights not to bear children. The court noted that the unlawful literature sold by Byrne, "What Every Girl Should Know," depicted female sex organs; was distributed to minor males and females; and allegedly contained text that promoted non-procreative sex. This literature allegedly diminished an important deterrent for premarital sex (i.e., fear of unwed pregnancy). Thus, Byrne was convicted. In *New York v. Sanger* (1917), Sanger was found guilty of violating New York Penal Law § 1142, which mirrored some portions of the federal Comstock Act designed to eliminate use of the U.S. mail to transport obscenity. It was a misdemeanor to advertise; inform the public about; or sell birth control. Sanger argued that the law was overbroad because it prevented doctors from dispensing medical advice to married patients. On appeal, the judge accepted Sanger's rationale; but, affirmed her conviction because she was not a doctor. The court held that doctors may treat married women seeking medical advice about birth control.

> This exception in behalf of physicians does not permit advertisements regarding such matters, nor promiscuous advice to patients irrespective of their condition, but it is broad enough to protect the physician who in good faith gives such help or advice to a married person to cure or prevent disease (*New York v. Sanger*, 1917, p. 195)

The landmark shift, known as "the Crane decision," opened the door for a new interpretation of the Comstock Act (PBS, n.d.). It exempted doctors from the ban on obscene materials, which included material about birth control. The Crane decision permitted Sanger to open medical clinics throughout the country.

Margaret Sanger began to publish *Birth Control Review* in 1917 (Wardell, 1980). Sanger published 136 issues by 1928, and wrote more than 600 articles and speeches. Sanger and other editors of *Birth Control Review* discussed academic philosophy, social justice, and scientific information. She distributed literature to persuade the public to reform birth control legislation and to inspire women to liberate themselves from the patriarchal control that banned birth control contraptions, medicine, and information. *Birth Control Review* delineated arguments for reproductive rights and policy demands. These materials discussed women's freedom as well as issues such as selective breeding and overpopulation (i.e., eugenics and neo-Malthusianism). Because she related eugenics and neo-Malthusianism to birth control, and because various social and political movements during this era supported her, Sanger's literature helped unify and fortify the movement to legalize birth control.

Despite feminist victories, courts assisted members of the criminal justice system to continue harassing and unlawfully arresting members of the Birth Control League (*In the Matter of Michael Martin Dolphin*, 1924). Many defendants were convicted or pled to the charges. In *Davis v. U.S.* (1933), the Sixth Circuit Court of Appeals dismissed violations of 18 U.S.C. §334 and 18 U.S.C. §396 relating to the use of mail and interstate commerce to distribute birth control information. A rubber wholesaler was charged after selling goods to druggists, but successfully defended its actions because rubber products could legitimately be used to treat and prevent disease. In 1936, the Appellate Court for the Southern District of New York heard *U.S. v. One Package* (1936). In that case, a doctor imported vaginal birth control devices from Japan. The government alleged that the contents of the package violated section 305(a) of the Tariff Act of 1930 (i.e., 19 U.S.C.S. § 1305[a]). The appellate court affirmed the lower court's dismissal of the charge. The package's abortive contents were exempted because they could be used to save a mother's life. Lifesaving procedures were legal and the law only criminalized importation of objects to perform unlawful abortions. The court held that conscientious physicians were permitted to import, sell, and transport objects through the mail that could competently be used to save a patient's life.

Many doctors continued to adhere to traditional morals and associate best practices with morality (Murhree and Gower, 2013). Although some doctors became informed about birth control, they refused to participate in political reform. However, other doctors, as well as corporations, researchers, venture capitalists, and activists, realized the market for birth control. Still, contracts regarding experimentation with and production of birth control products (e.g., rubber tampons and diaphragms) were invalidated by the Comstock Act and state laws (Ill. Crim. Code § 223, 1937; Ill. Rev. Stat. ch. 38, 1937; *Lanteen Laboratories, Inc. v. Clark*, 1938). This increased the risks associated with funding and developing birth control. Parties risked unenforceability and loss; and agreements could be used as evidence of criminal activity.

During the early 1950s, Margaret Sanger and Planned Parenthood had begun to fund scientific development of birth control. The Food and Drug Administration (FDA) granted limited approval to test a birth control pill on human subjects in Massachusetts, but by the mid-1950s larger clinical trials were moved to Puerto Rico because anti-birth-control laws in the United States excessively restricted administration of birth control to the population. President Dwight Eisenhower stated that birth control use should not be a political issue or governmental problem. Birth control production then increased, after receiving FDA approval and President Eisenhower's apolitical endorsement; millions of women began using birth control pills. However, the federal Comstock Act and state laws could still ban dissemination of information discussing birth control. Birth control activists (e.g., Bill Baird) continued to be arrested during this time (*New York v. Baird*, 1965). In *Griswold v. Connecticut* (1965), the court held that the right to make procreative choices was a Constitutionally protected right that could be asserted by a doctor for his or her patients. In that case, a Planned Parenthood doctor was convicted under a Connecticut statute as an accessory for giving a woman medical advice about contraception and prescribing a contraceptive device. The well-known holding in *Griswold* expanded reproductive rights for women and men. "[T]he *Griswold* decision can be rationally understood only as a holding that the Connecticut statute substantively invaded the 'liberty' that is protected by the Due Process Clause of the Fourteenth Amendment" (*Roe v. Wade*, 1973, p. 168). The *Griswold* court said,

> The present case . . . concerns a relationship lying within the zone of privacy created by several fundamental [C]onstitutional guarantees. And it concerns a law which, in forbidding the *use* of contraceptives rather than regulating their manufacture or sale, seeks to achieve its goals by means having a maximum destructive impact upon that relationship. The very idea is repulsive to the notions of privacy (*Griswold v. Connecticut*, 1965, p. 485–486).

The U.S. Supreme Court held that the Planned Parenthood League in Connecticut could not be prevented from counseling or distributing information about contraception to married people because marriage was protected under the penumbra of the Fourteenth Amendment and Fifth Amendment. The right to privacy protects marriage and guarantees that the government will not interfere with marital relations (*Griswold v. Connecticut*, 1965).

Despite worldwide support for birth control pill sales, the Pope of the Catholic Church declared opposition to the pill in 1968. Even so, one-third of Catholic women in the United States used a pill form of birth control (Murhree and Gower, 2013). In spite of its popularity, or perhaps due to the popularity of birth control, the government continued to oppose its distribution. In 1972, Bill Baird was charged with a felony because he provided contraceptives to an unmarried couple; but, he was not a medical doctor (*Eisenstadt v. Baird*, 1972). The Massachusetts law under which Baird was charged was stricken by the court as a violation of Constitutional right to privacy, which must protect married and unmarried people equally from governmental intrusion. *Eisenstadt* stands for the proposition that reproductive decisions are fundamental matters that are outside the realm of governmental interference. Due to controversy surrounding abortion, history of birth control seems most impacted by *Roe v. Wade* (1973). *Roe* held that the right to privacy legalizing abortion was a fundamental right. However, the state's interest in women's health and fetal life needed to be balanced against the Constitutional fundamental right to privacy. Thus, abortion in the first and second trimester was legalized in *Roe*.

Pregnancy, Abortion Laws, and Politics

Roe v. Wade and *Planned Parenthood v. Casey* are two cases that guide first and second trimester abortion law. More than simply a right to abort a fetus, the history of birth control demonstrates that a woman has a right to impede or end reproduction without undue burden placed on her by the government. Access to medical advice, medical devices, and birth control should not be regulated unless they pose harm to mothers or fetuses. Abortion is one method of birth control protected by the right to privacy, as stated by the Fourteenth Amendment and Fifth Amendment. A woman's right to privacy is balanced against the state's interest in fetal life. The state's interest seems to increase as gestation progresses. Spouses have some limited interests in fetuses; but, gestational week does not increase parental or spousal interests in abortion. These interests are discussed in Chapters 12, 13, 14, and 15.

The court considered the government's rational or important interest in defending potential fetal rights in several cases, including *Planned Parenthood v. Casey* (1992), *Webster v. Reproductive Health Services* (1989), and *Gonzales v. Carhart* (2007). "With respect to a state's important and legitimate interest in potential life, the 'compelling' point is at viability, since the fetus then presumably has the capability of meaningful life outside the mother's womb. State regulation protective of fetal life after viability thus has both logical and biological justifications" (*Roe v. Wade*, 1973, p. 163).

Following *Roe*, *Planned Parenthood v. Danforth* (1976) set the groundwork for the contemporary undue burden standard elucidated later in *Planned Parenthood v. Casey* (1992). *Danforth* holds that married women are not required to obtain spousal consent to receive abortion services. Married women cannot be relegated to the position of children; thus, abortions cannot require spousal consent. *Bellotti v. Baird* (1979) held that the Constitution cannot permit all abortive procedures for minors to be conditioned upon parental consent. Judicial waiver, parental abuse, and other contingencies must be contemplated by legislatures that require parental consent. In *Planned Parenthood v. Casey* (1992), the court held that the undue burdens (e.g., consent or notification requirements) could not pose a substantial obstacle to a female's right to abortion. However, restrictions may be placed on abortion services, as long as they do not unduly burden pregnant women. For example, restrictions may require that doctors have admitting privileges at local hospitals; or that patients have any opportunity view sonograms (*Whole Woman's Health v. Lakey*, 2014). Many abortion providers lack admitting privileges; thus, some clinics in operation prior to restrictive legislation have been closed after legislation is passed. Pro-choice activists claim that patients are unduly burdened by such restrictions because closures force them to drive long distances to be treated at compliant clinics. Yet, driving distance may not present a substantial obstacle in some jurisdictions. Requirements that patients view sonograms may be circumvented when patients close their eyes. Thus, a substantial obstacle may not limit women's right to privacy and reproductive freedom. Patients are not required to acknowledge the sonogram; thus, free speech and right to privacy may be upheld.

Following political discord between abortion rights activists and fetal rights activists, *Roe* and *Casey* were further defined in *Gonzales v. Carhart* (2007). *Roe* specified that post-viability abortion could be proscribed in circumstances that were not threatening to a mother's life; and the undue burden test is not disturbed by limits on partial-birth abortion because pre-viability restrictions do not prevent access to abortive services.

> A state criminal abortion statute that excepts from criminality only a life-saving procedure on behalf of the mother, without regard to pregnancy stage and without recognition of the other interests involved, is violative of the U.S. Const. amend. XIV. For the stage prior to approximately the end of the first trimester, the abortion decision and its effectuation must be left to the medical judgment of the pregnant woman's attending physician. For the stage subsequent to approximately the end of the first trimester, the state, in promoting its interest in the health of the mother, may, if it chooses, regulate the abortion procedure in ways that are reasonably related to maternal health (*Gonzales v. Carhart*, 2007, p. 163–164).

Historically, maternal safety, well-being, and health have been central to both the development of birth control rights and the maintenance of restrictions on birth control. Concern about maternal health appeals to both pro-life and pro-choice activists. *Carhart* reiterates that mainstream pro-life and pro-choice advocates believe that the law should permit a mother's life to take precedence over a fetus's life. Therefore, political consensus is achieved when pregnancy may be lawfully terminated at any stage of gestation if a mother's life can be saved by a terminative procedure, including partial-birth abortion during the second and third trimesters.

In addition to rights to be counselled, to be prescribed medication, and to use contraception, it seems that the right to an abortion during the first trimester cannot be abridged; and a licensed doctor, who meets jurisdictional requirements, has a right to supply a woman with access to a terminative procedure during the first trimester (Silverberg, 1994). Pregnancy in zygote, embryo, and fetus stages can be terminated under the right to privacy during the first trimester. The meaning of "trimester" is as fluid as the gestative process itself. The first trimester extends from week one through week 12 (Kid's Health, n.d.). The second trimester runs from week 13 to week 26, and the third trimester begins at week 27. So, while the public or activists may discuss partial-birth abortion in terms of trimesters, legislatures often discuss pregnancy in terms of weeks. Laws that solely refer to gestative weeks and viability demonstrate that women have the right to abort zygotes and embryos. However, fetuses have rights that may escalate and eventually outweigh a healthy woman's rights as the gestation process nears birth (Rovner, 2006).

During the first week of gestation, the zygote is microscopic, but by the sixth week of gestation, the embryonic nervous system, the heart, and the arms just begin to form a two-millimeter glob of tissue (Kid's Health, n.d.). Between the sixth and twelfth weeks, the embryonic stage has ended, a few weeks prior to the conclusion of the first trimester. During this time span, several options for abortifacients and abortion are available under the Fifth and Fourteenth Amendment. However, birth control options become limited as pregnancy gestation progresses. By the eighteenth week, the fetus develops sensory organs necessary for hearing and sight, and the fetus's bones begin to ossify. At this stage, though, most forms of abortion are still guaranteed under the right to privacy.

The court in *Roe* cut off abortion rights at approximately 27 weeks, and drew a bright dividing line at the end of the second trimester, at around 24 weeks. Experts in *Roe* believed that a fetus's life could be sustained by the use of medicine outside the mother's body. Fetuses' lungs develop rapidly during the third trimester, which is what makes

viability possible. Thirty weeks into the pregnancy, with the third trimester almost over the fetus weighs about three pounds, and begins
to gain fat rapidly before birth at 36 weeks. At this point, abortion is
only permitted as a lifesaving procedure. The court specified, at the time
Roe was decided, that viability was "placed at about seven months (28
weeks)," but the court acknowledged that it "may occur earlier, even at
24 weeks" (*Roe v. Wade*, 1973, p. 160). Before the twenty-fourth week,
but after viability, some states may limit abortion to situations in which
a woman requires a lifesaving procedure. In some jurisdictions, viability is believed to begin at 20 weeks; several babies have been delivered
early in the second trimester; and partial-birth abortion restrictions may
begin as early as the fifteenth week (Collins, 2011; Hofstetter, 2010;
Telegraph, 2011; *Webster v. Reproductive Health Services*, 1989). Thus,
women have the right to exercise their rights to privacy before fetuses
become viable and are capable of surviving outside the womb. Viability
is not delimited by number of weeks or months; and due to scientific
advancements, fetal viability may occur sooner than at the beginning of
the second trimester.

Pro-life and pro-choice demonstrators have been visible within local
and national politics. Demonstrations outside abortion clinics were unrestricted speech under the First Amendment until 2000, at which point
the U.S. Supreme Court upheld a key Colorado statute. That law required
demonstrators to stay at least 100 feet from entrances to abortion clinics when intending to distribute information to patients or approach
patients no closer than eight feet to discuss abortion (*Hill v. Colorado*,
2000). The court held that the law was a time, place, manner restriction
that was Constitutional because it did not restrict the content of speech
and left adequate alternative means to communicate with patients. Demonstrators could hold signs, use loudspeakers, place leaflets or pamphlets
on cars, or discuss abortion with patients while remaining an adequate
distance from clinics. In 2009, this policy was challenged in *McCullen
v. Coakley* (2014). Massachusetts' legislature required a 35-foot buffer
zone protecting all entranceways to abortion clinics. Pro-life counselors
seeking to discuss abortion with patients claimed in federal district court
that the law violated free speech protections under the First Amendment.
The district court upheld the law as a valid time, place, manner restriction. The appellate court upheld the district court's ruling. However, the
U.S. Supreme Court granted *certioriari* and unanimously distinguished
this case from other valid time, place, manner restrictions because the

law was not narrowly tailored. In the past, the court has held that time, place, manner restrictions should be scrutinized at an intermediate level. Intermediate scrutiny requires that laws have an important purpose that substantially relates to the government's regulatory scheme. In this case, the court required that the law be narrowly tailored. This level of scrutiny has generally been reserved for Due Process violations and race-based classifications.

> To meet the narrow tailoring requirement, however, the government must demonstrate that alternative measures that burden substantially less speech would fail to achieve the government's interests, not simply that the chosen route is easier (*McCullen v. Coakley*, 2014).

This analysis is consistent with *stare decisis,* but conservatively interprets Constitutional requirements. The court held that the content neutral act does not permit close, consensual conversations necessary for pro-life counselors to exercise their speech rights. Pro-life counselors must stand at a distance with political demonstrators, where their particular approaches and messages are likely to be washed out.

Illegal Abortions and Late Term Abortions

Morality surrounding preservation of human life was the basis for a Nebraska law prohibiting partial-birth abortion (*Stenberg v. Carhart*, 2000). That law was found by the U.S. Supreme Court to violate Due Process. Many pro-life advocates believe that life begins at conception. For the most part, though, first trimester pregnancy does not resemble human life. During the embryonic stage, which lasts until about week 12, there is no visible human identity in the tissue. All the matter that is excreted during a termination procedure has the appearance and quality of thick menses (Cusack, 2011). Allegedly, during the fetal stage, the semblance of a human is first possible (Greenwood, 2010).

In *Gonzales v. Carhart* (2007), the court upheld the federal Partial-Birth Abortion Ban Act of 2003. Abortion post-viability (i.e., approximately 15 weeks) is considered to be a late-term abortion, also known as partial-birth abortion (Rovner, 2006). Partial-birth abortion restrictions are prohibited under moral, ethical, and medical rationales (Lim, 2008). Restrictions are not necessarily limited by viability or trimester; however, viability may be a guide (*Webster v. Reproductive Health Services*, 1989).

Stare decisis does not indicate that states are required to protect late-term fetuses from partial-birth abortion.

Legislatures may pass laws that do not place an undue burden on pregnant women who are seeking to abort. In *Gonzales v. Carhart*, the court stated (2007):

> The *Casey* Court reaffirmed what it termed *Roe*'s three-part "essential holding": First, a woman has the right to choose to have an abortion before fetal viability and to obtain it without undue interference from the State. Second, the State has the power to restrict abortions after viability, if the law contains exceptions for pregnancies endangering the woman's life or health. And third, the State has legitimate interests from the pregnancy's outset in protecting the health of the woman and the life of the fetus that may become a child . . . Though all three are implicated here, it is the third that requires the most extended discussion (*Gonzales v. Carhart*, 2007).

The third part is discussed in Chapter 13 and Chapter 16. A state may express profound respect for all life, even life that begins at conception, as long as laws do not create an undue burden. Despite the court's recapitulation of *Roe* in terms of the state's legitimate interests in protecting mothers' health, a mother's fundamental privacy interest outweighs the government's legitimate interest in fetal life pre-viability. Post-viability, only threats to a mother's health outweigh governmental interests. However, late-term abortions allegedly increase risks to a woman's health. Thus, doctors must weigh the seriousness of health risks against the risk of pregnancy to determine whether late-term abortions are medically necessary (Mills, 1998).

Medications such as RU486 are contraceptives and an abortifacient that may be prescribed to terminate pregnancy during the embryonic stage (Cusack, 2011; Morris, 2001; Silverberg, 1994). Generally, they are legal. However, women who use them to terminate during late stages may be arrested. For example, Jennie Linn McCormack was arrested in Idaho for buying abortion pills online and terminating a late-stage pregnancy (Hartmann, 2011). She was charged under a fetal pain statute prohibiting self-induced abortion after 20 weeks. She sued and a court enjoined the law prohibiting self-induced abortions, but did not enjoin the fetal pain law. Because she aborted sometime after five months, she was charged with feticide. Before her case was dismissed for lack of evidence, she argued that she was placed under an undue burden because so few doctors provided abortion in her state. Feticide is discussed in Chapter 4.

A British study surveyed 883 women who had chosen to abort during the second trimester (Abortion Review, 2007). Half of the women were past the thirteenth week of gestation when they finally sought an abortion. Researchers asked women why they delayed, and participants selected reasons from a checklist; they were unrestricted in the number of reasons they could choose from the list. Overall, the list reflected common events that coincide with abortion and with the timing of a woman's abortion. Researchers found that many reasons were quite common; and approximately 20 percent of the respondents selected 13 reasons. Forty-one percent of women cited needing more time to make a decision. Thirty-eight percent cited ignorance of pregnancy due to biological or medical reasons. And 20 percent continued menstruating. Thirty-six percent believed that they were in the early stages of pregnancy when they elected to abort. Thirty-two percent were uncertain about how to carry a child to term. Slightly less than one-third said that they used contraception; thus, they did not realize they were pregnant. Thirty percent cited failure to react before the end of the first trimester. Slightly more than one-quarter were too worried about their parents' reactions to decide early on; and 23 percent cited emotional breakdowns with their parents. Almost one-quarter disclosed that they had missed appointments that would have led to early-term abortions; and 20 percent said that they had to wait too long for an appointment. More than one-fifth were reportedly worried about having an abortion and wanted to avoid it. In most instances, first term abortions were accessible, but women voluntarily delayed.

CHAPTER 3

Fakers

Unlicensed Medical Practices

Unlicensed medical practitioners and midwives may claim to deliver phantom babies; attempt to fraudulently provide fertility treatments; and perform other duties that endanger patients and children (*People v. Odam*, 1999). When licensed practitioners falsely claim to have administered fertility treatment or fraudulently claim to have delivered phantom pregnancies, criminal charges may result. Offenders may be convicted of criminal negligence, criminal fraud, battery, sexual assault, aggravated battery, and other relevant charges. Similar to unlicensed abortions, unlicensed fertility treatments can be risky and unsafe. Vulnerable women who knowingly or unknowingly turn to unlicensed fertility doctors may risk unscrupulous practices and unsanitary conditions.

Reproduction is a rite of passage in Indonesia (Yeung, 2014). Couples who cannot conceive may feel vulnerable and desperate. Thus, they may feel too pressured to question suspicious practices. One unlicensed doctor offered 14 sessions of fertility treatments over a seven-month period for approximately $25. He provided women with capsulized pills intended to create weight gain in cattle. The pill allegedly contained an anti-inflammatory steroid, Oradexon, which was allegedly consumed by prostitutes in the region to create inflammation in their secondary sex organs. The unlicensed doctor's fertility treatments included hands-on energy channeling, and orders that patients abstain from certain foods that are normally associated with fertility and health during early pregnancy (e.g., bananas). Women were fooled into believing in false pregnancies. The practitioner asked women to close their eyes and pray. While their eyes were closed, he would switch urine samples that tested positive for pregnancy. He lied to patients about the dangers of obtaining sonograms at legitimate hospitals; and most patients believed him. Through fraud, he earned approximately $1,500 per month until patients began to realize the scam when they received treatment from a licensed doctor and tested pills through a local laboratory.

In Nigeria, an established lecturer and popular obstetrician and gynecologist routinely scammed patients into believing that they received In Vitro Fertilization (IVF) and became pregnant (Salako, 2012). He used hormonal therapy to cease menstruation and presented positive pregnancy tests. Patients were likely desperate to conceive; excited to be pregnant; trusting toward their doctor; and relieved to satisfy African cultural expectations to reproduce. After paying approximately $6,000, patients were tricked into believing for nine months that they were pregnant. Under hormonal therapy, patients exhibited the psychological and physical symptoms of pseudocyesis. The doctor recommended Cesarean delivery to patients and pretended to deliver stillbirths. On some occasions, the doctor presented dead fetuses as evidence of stillbirth. However, one couple attempted to lynch the doctor after he told them that their baby had disappeared as the result of voodoo. Several other women reported similar experiences; and the doctor was arrested and charged. The doctor blamed his pseudocyesis scam on incompetent sonologists. One patient, who could not conceive with her husband, claimed that the doctor advised her to secretly secure another man's sperm to covertly receive artificial insemination. Thus, his scams may have been multitiered, involving multiple victims. The doctor is also suspected of murdering one of his staff nurses who refused to participate in his pseudocyesis scam.

Hidden Contraband

Offenders attempt to smuggle contraband using fake baby-bumps, baby diapers, baby formula, and other related objects. In some instances, the crimes are petty, but others involve massive crime syndicates trafficking millions of dollars. Use of infants demonstrates callousness and disguising drugs inside baby products demonstrates cunning. The government is aware of these tactics. In recent years, authorities like the Transportation Security Administration (TSA) have been criticized for administering full body pat-downs to infants, yet law enforcement, corrections officers, U.S. Drug Enforcement Agency (DEA) agents, and TSA officers (TSO) continue to discover contraband inside babies' diapers, baby bags, and baby formula. Infant formula and black markets are discussed in Chapter 17.

Occasionally, inmates' intimate partners attempt to smuggle small amounts of drugs into prisons (Chang, 2011). Drugs are intended for intimates' consumption and to sell on the prison black market. In one case, police received a tip that a young woman was going to attempt to smuggle sedatives into a prison. They observed that when she visited her inmate boyfriend, she placed a baby on the inmate's lap. The inmate extracted from the child's diaper a rubber glove containing pills. The inmate and the girlfriend were charged. In other instances, intimate partners involve their children in substantial drug operations. In Germany, a young woman visited her husband in prison to deliver 46 ecstasy pills and 15 grams of amphetamines (*The Local*, 2009). She transported those drugs in her daughter's diaper, and 12 additional grams of amphetamines in her clothing. Following her arrest, more than one dozen K-9 officers searched the couple's mobile home where they found 60 grams of amphetamines, 166 ecstasy pills, and 530 grams of amphetamine paste.

Inmates use baby diapers not only to smuggle drugs, but also cash, cell phones, weapons, and other contraband (Farrington, 2014). Cell-phone possession in prison is a serious problem. Florida's Department of Corrections alone reports that it confiscates 11 cell phones each day. K-9 units are trained to detect cell phones inside prison cells because they can be used to deal drugs; conduct phone scams; maintain prohibited relationships on social media; plan escapes; and disturb prison safety. In some jurisdictions, cell phone possession can be a felony (Cusack, 2015).

Some mothers endanger their infants beyond involving them in drug trade (*Inquisitr*, 2014). One woman, who was driving under the influence, hid heroin drug paraphernalia inside her infant's diaper bag. After she collided with an 18-wheeler, police discovered other serious violations. She possessed ecstasy; her license was suspended; and she failed to secure her infant in a car seat.

Offenders have faked late-term pregnancy and motherhood to smuggle drugs. A woman from Georgia attempted to smuggle drugs inside a fake baby-bump (The Smoking Gun, 2011). She packed 34,000 ecstasy pills into the baby-bump and attempted to enter Canada riding a Greyhound bus. The baby-bump, containing 33 ziplock bags that weighed a total of 21 pounds, was discovered to be fake during a pat-down. Another woman, carrying four pounds of cocaine, attempted to evade detection by smuggling the drugs under a fake latex belly (*Daily Mail*, 2013). Colombian police who administered a pat-down noticed her belly seemed cold to the touch and unusually hard. She was searched and arrested. Another example finds an offender crossing through a border checkpoint in California, attempting to enter with what appeared to be six infants but were actually six bundles of cocaine (Manning, 2012).

Major drug busts reveal that drug dealers sometimes package drugs inside baby products (Fidrus, 2012). In one case, Indonesian authorities discovered that baby-powder bottles imported from Nigeria contained 532 grams of crystal methamphetamine worth $74,885. Another gang smuggling heroin from Pakistan to Britain was sentenced to a total of 109 years in prison for attempting to smuggle approximately $15 million of heroin inside baby-powder bottles (Edwards, 2013).

The DEA reported in 2004 that a crime syndicate used infants and infant formula to mask drug-running (DEA, 2004). Millions of dollars' worth of cocaine and heroin were smuggled between New York, Chicago, Illinois, and the United Kingdom (UK) between 1996 and 1999. Dealers hid drugs inside baby formula containers. To avoid raising suspicions, the crime syndicate paid female couriers to travel with infants, who they rented from postpartum parents. Parents rented their children to travel internationally on at least 45 occasions. Twelve of the 22 babies used by the gang had been rented for cash or exchanged for drugs. The crime syndicate also commissioned women to travel from Panama and Jamaica into the United States with liquidized cocaine. They injected liquid cocaine with a syringe into baby formula cans so that the cans appeared to remain sealed. The gang forged passports and defrauded airlines over $500,000 with fake tickets. Shutting down this operation involved Immigration and Customs Enforcement (ICE); the Chicago Police Department; the New York Police Department; British Customs; the National Police Department of Panama; Royal Canadian Mounted Police; the U.S. State Department's Passport Office; and local police departments throughout the suburbs of Chicago.

Escapes

Labor, labor pains, and pregnancy complications have been faked during attempted escapes from custody, incarceration, court appearances, detention, correction facilities, mental institutions, and other related criminal justice locations. Some inmates' attempts may be cunning; others are rudimentary. For example, one pregnant inmate splashed red Kool-Aid and convinced guards that the stain was blood (WJBK, 2013). Hospital staff confirmed that she faked fetal distress. The inmate, who planned to break out of the hospital, was charged with attempting to escape.

Prison officials have attempted to avoid escape attempts by taking extreme measures. Constitutionally, when inmates are a high flight risk they may be shackled to a hospital bed during labor. However, several inmates have been falsely accused of faking labor or experiencing false labor when actual labor began. Some inmates have been labeled medium risks because they missed court appointments; but not because they have attempted to escape or pose a danger to themselves or others. Women in labor being transported to hospitals have been placed in full restraints, including waist restraints and shackles. Women who pose little threat of flight have also been shackled during labor (*Journal of Obstetric, Gynecologic, and Neonatal Nursing*, 2011). Prison policies are often contravened when waist restraints are used on a woman pregnant in her third trimester. Restraints and prison policy are further discussed in Chapter 11. Shackling a prisoner throughout labor may interfere with serious medical needs (*Brawley v. State*, 2010). This interference may increase risks to inmates' health and pregnancy. Many times, shackling cannot be justified because it is a penological aim designed to minimize flight risk. Courts have held that unjustifiably shackling women contravenes common sense, departmental policy, and Eighth Amendment proscription against cruel and unusual punishment. If officers illegally shackle women during labor, they may be immunized from charges if their actions were not deliberately indifferent to the risks of harm under those circumstances.

In one case, an inmate was placed in full restraints as she was transported to a hospital (*Brawley v. State*, 2010). Restraints were removed when she arrived at the hospital; a male guard stood by during her examinations; and an ankle cuff was placed on her to attach her to a hospital bed. The ankle cuff was only removed briefly for an epidural, and then it was reattached. Because the inmate had been forced to wait several hours at the prison before being transported to the hospital, her amniotic sac contained no amniotic fluid when she arrived at the hospital. Cesarean surgery was required. Immediately prior to surgery, her ankle cuff was removed. After surgery, the plaintiff could barely ambulate. While she bonded with her son, she was chained to the hospital bed. At one point, her son had been placed out of reach so that he could receive medicine. Hospital staff were not present when he began to choke. The inmate called for help and attempted to reach her son, but the restraints bound her in place. At another point, hospital staff required her to perform exercises (e.g., walk around her room). She was forced to wear leg restraints and could not adequately perform the exercises required to help her recover.

The pregnant inmate brought a claim under the Eight Amendment, arguing that shackling a nonviolent inmate who posed no flight risk unnecessarily, unjustifiably, and wantonly inflicted pain and cruelty (*Brawley v. State*, 2010). Under the Eighth Amendment, prison officials must treat inmates humanely, ensuring that they are adequately fed, clothed, sheltered, and given medical care. Inmates must be kept in safe conditions (*Farmer v. Brennan*, 1994). Guards may not deliberately act indifferently toward inmates' serious medical needs (*Estelle v. Gamble*, 1976). The court held that an objective standard demonstrates that labor is a serious medical condition; however, prison officials who shackle inmates may or may not act with deliberate indifference (*Brawley v. State*, 2010). The second prong is a subjective determination. In this case, the inmate was not faking contractions. She experienced unnecessary pain because her chains restricted her movement. She could not adjust her body to find a comfortable position; yet, changing positions is central to coping with labor pain. However, the guards may not have acted with deliberate indifference even if their actions were purposeful and failed to satisfy any penological aims. A guard's subjective state of mind about the necessity of the shackles may be relevant. Also relevant is whether a guard could have inferred that shackles created a substantial risk of harm. In this case, guards knew that they were violating prison policy by shackling the inmate during labor. However, one guard's testimony indicated a belief that the inmate was not in labor. That guard cited several examples where the inmate stated that she may not be in labor. Even after receiving an epidural, guards continued to believe that the inmate was experiencing illness or false labor. Thus, guards were mistaken about whether the inmate's medical condition was serious; and in their belief, her labor was false. The guards who shackled the inmate would be immunized if policy had been unclear, or if they made a good-faith mistake about the law; but on this occasion, courts had already held that shackling inmates during labor violated the Eighth Amendment (*Brawley v. State*, 2010; *Hope v. Pelzer*, 2002; *Nelson v. Correctional Medical Services*, 2009; *Women Prisoners of D.C. Dept. of Corrections v. District of Columbia*, 1994).

Guards who falsely accuse inmates of faking labor or who mistake actual labor for false labor are not necessarily culpable under the Eighth Amendment (*Smith v. Kankakee County*, 2013). In 2011, an inmate was in her second trimester of pregnancy with twins. Early in the morning on September 11, she experienced severe pain. At 5:00 a.m. she used an intercom in her cell to call for help, but an unidentified male corrections officer replied that she should "mind her own business" (*Smith v. Kankakee County*, 2013, p. 3). Around 8:00 a.m., another inmate found the expectant mother in a fetal position in her cell; and at about 8:30 a.m. the inmate asked a corrections officer if she could go to a hospital. Around 9:30 a.m. prison staff likely learned that the inmate believed that she was going into labor; and other inmates reported to prison staff that the expectant mother was experiencing contractions. Prison officers contacted a nurse who did not describe the inmate's contractions as an emergency medical situation. At times, the inmate was mobile and did not appear to be in distress. Two hours later, the inmate called her mother crying. The inmate's mother called the prison to inform them that her daughter was in labor and required hospitalization. Prison officials told officers in contact with the inmate that "she can stop calling her mama because her mama can't do nothing up in here" (*Smith v. Kankakee County*, 2013, p. 8). Prison staff and officials said also said that the inmate "thinks she's having contractions," and "she's—in my opinion, a lot of times she's full of shit. She don't even want to take her prenatal vitamins for the baby. You know what I'm saying?" Then they said,

> And now you talking about she having stomach cramps. You can go eyeball her and call me back if you want. She's probably full of shit. But you can let her know that she can see the doctor tomorrow if she'd like. Actually, she was scheduled to see him, but refused. So if she doesn't—take her blood pressure. If she doesn't appear to be in any serious distress, she's going to wait until tomorrow (*Smith v. Kankakee County*, 2013, p. 15).

The inmate complained about pain in her back and genitals; but, when the inmate complained about pain in her butt, prison staff joked that the inmate was "not going to have the baby out of her ass" (*Smith v. Kankakee County*, 2013, p. 15). At 2:45 p.m., the inmate began screaming while sitting on the toilet bleeding. Around 3:00 p.m., officers on the next shift were ordered to transport the inmate to the hospital. She was not given a wheelchair, but was forced to walk down stairs. By the time she arrived at the hospital, ten miles from the prison, she was fully dilated. The twins that she delivered around 5:20 p.m. died. The inmate alleged that guards' conduct violated the Fourteenth Amendment and Eighth Amendment because it was deliberate, reckless, and wanton. She claimed that the guards knowingly and willfully ignored her serious medical needs, which resulted in substantial risk of serious injury, and ultimately, the death of her twins. The court denied summary judgment but permitted the case to go before a fact finder to determine whether deprivation of care was objectively sufficient; and whether the prison staff subjectively intended to deliberately behave indifferently toward the inmate's safety. Juries would likely find that an inmate who is pregnant with twins in the second trimester is at greater risk and in serious medical need. Thus, the objective component will be met. To determine whether guards were aware of and deliberately indifferent to excessive risks, juries must find that guards had a culpable state of mind (*Holloway v. Delaware County Sheriff*, 2012; *Johnson v. Doughty*, 2006). Criminal recklessness, not civil negligence, is the required state of mind. A jury could find either that the inmate did give or did not give sufficient notice of excessive risk; thus, the subjective component was a matter for the fact finder.

Pseudo Pregnancies

Pseudocyesis is false pregnancy, also known as imaginary pregnancy, phantom pregnancy, hysterical pregnancy, and spurious pregnancy (Gaskin, 2012). Traditionally, pseudocyesis was thought to affect newlywed men or women or older women who are close to being menopausal. In most cases, a person suffering from pseudocyesis wishes to be pregnant even if they believe that pregnancy is unlikely. False pregnancy primarily afflicts women who present with swollen abdomens and breasts and pigmented areolae. In some cases, urinary tract infections and urine retention, or other conditions, can present as pseudocyesis in patients who suffer from severe mental illness (Yeh, 2012). In rare cases, men who have false pregnancies may suffer similar symptoms. Symptoms may include morning sickness; sensation of fetal kicking; and cessation of menstruation (i.e., amenorrhea) (Gaskin, 2012). Men are likely to understand that they are experiencing false pregnancy; but for women, pseudocyesis, can be extremely saddening or humiliating when they discover that pregnancy was false. Some feel that they will be perceived by others as being delusional, which further stigmatizes pseudocyesis. Women are likely not delusional if they have no way of knowing that pregnancy was false; for example, receiving false-positive results on a pregnancy test.

Mental illness may relate to pseudocyesis in some cases (Simon, Vörös, Herold, Fekete, and Tényi, 2009). Hypochondriacal delusion results in extreme preoccupation with contraction of diseases or infections. It may correlate with psychosis and postpartum symptoms following false pregnancy. Symptoms could include belief that babies are absent because they have been stolen by culprits such as hospital staff or relatives. Pseudocyesis typically describes delusional beliefs about pregnancy that contradict factual evidence (Rosch, Sajatovic, and Sivec, 2002). Some patients with false pregnancy who suffer from postpartum delusions may have family histories of pseudocyesis (Simon, Vörös, Herold, Fekete, and Tényi, 2009). Patients with phantom pregnancies or postpartum delusions may have family histories of schizoaffective disorder; however, they may not have personal histories of psychiatric illness. Positive pregnancy tests may be false positives or may merely be delusions (Bianchi-Demicheli, Lüdicke, and Chardonnens, 2004).

In one case, a 51-year-old female patient reported a positive home pregnancy test after demanding urgent care at a hospital. She claimed that she was in labor even though two gynecological visits demonstrated that she was not pregnant. She presented no symptoms of pregnancy. She had not menstruated for a year, but had experienced hot flashes for the past two years. Doctors discovered that she was infertile as a result of voluntary tubal ligation ten years prior. Doctors believed that her medical history, including an abortion, combined with perimenopausal hormone changes may have played a role in her pseudocyesis. In another case, a young woman's uncle attempted to fondle her four years prior to her presenting with pseudocyesis (Manoj et al., 2004). Before presenting, but after being incestuously attacked, the young woman attended a religious meeting in which premarital sex was admonished. Thereafter, she began to experience delusions that a test-tube baby was growing inside her. She also believed that someone would attempt to murder her. Her prior victimization and fear of future victimization likely correlated with pseudocyesis.

Pseudocyesis may correlate with increased likelihood for encounters with the criminal justice system. Comorbidity or risk factors include postpartum psychosis; increased levels of hostility; greater likelihood of polypharmacy and antipsychotic medications; frontotemporal dementia; motor neurone disease; mania; past trauma; and higher resistance to treatment (Larner, 2013; Moselhy and Conlon, 2000; Rosch, Sajatovic, and Sivec, 2002). These factors could potentially correlate with increased risk for victimization; deviance; criminality; depression; self-medication; risky behavior; violence; suicidality; or problems with medication. Biologic, medical, and psychotherapeutic treatment could successfully intervene by addressing emotional factors, including hostility, and resistance to treatment. Psychotropic agents, cognitive therapies, and behavioral modifications may help to shift belief paradigms. In some cases, women may deny being pregnant (Walloch et al., 2006). Emotional, therapeutic, and social interventions may also benefit patients.

Men who present with false pregnancy may be intimately involved with pregnant women. In these cases, symptoms may be physical, but unaccompanied by belief. However, delusions likely correlate with true belief in the possibility of male pregnancy or persistence of belief after scientific evidence of impossibility has been presented to the patient (Tényi et al., 2001). Though it is somewhat normal for patients who develop physical symptoms to attempt to self-diagnose, when males conclude that they are pregnant it may demonstrate problematic or abnormal thinking. Delusional pregnancy in males may relate to trauma, posttraumatic epilepsy, retardation, or better-than-average intelligence. To some extent, doctors should investigate and be sensitive to patients' cultural backgrounds and exercise sensitivity. For example, some cultures believe in "puppy pregnancy," which could result when any human has been bitten by or has come into close contact with a dog (Chowdhury, 2003). "Puppy pregnancies" may present with psychological and somatic symptoms. Nevertheless, these strong cultural beliefs can correlate with obsessive-compulsive disorder, anxiety, phobia, and pathological thinking. Rural cultural beliefs must be contextualized within modern medical and criminal justice contexts because patients are subject to dominant culture and laws. Thus, their thinking and behavior to some extent must be normative and must conform to modern norms to avoid criminal justice entanglements.

In some situations, people may fake pregnancies to commit fraud. These cases may begin as phantom pregnancy, but then offenders accept scientific evidence that pregnancy is false. They may continue to behave as if they are actually pregnant to avoid shame and humiliation, or to continue benefiting financially. In either case, they may perpetrate fraud or attempted fraud if they accept or request money for assistance with fake pregnancies. Some offenders never truly believe that they are pregnant. They pretend to be pregnant to bilk donors, friends, or relatives. A couple in Tennessee faked a pregnancy with twins (Bobo, 2013). The also faked the twins' deaths to fraudulently obtain donations for fictitious funeral expenses. To induce donors, the wife showed prenatal ultrasounds. The wife also contacted the mother of an ex-boyfriend to claim that he was the father. The ex-boyfriend's mother donated $100, but then contacted the authorities. The husband showed photos of dead babies at work, and bilked approximately $900 worth of paid time and donations. The wife was sentenced 30 days in jail. The court ordered two years' probation; a $100 fine; and 192 hours of community service in exchange for a plea to the charge of creating a false impression of death. The husband pled to the same charge and to theft of under $500 by fraud. The husband was sentenced to just less than one year of probation and fined $100. The wife claimed that her husband did not know that she faked the pregnancy and miscarriages. The offenders repaid all of the victims, around $500, which did not include a few hundred dollars in bereavement time the husband collected at his job. Their pleas to creating a false impression of death raise interesting legal and theoretical issues about the "death" of unborn children or harm to fetuses. Fetal "death" is discussed throughout Chapter 15.

Fake Surrogates

Sometimes, surrogates and surrogate agencies commit fraud, forgery, and other crimes. These crimes defraud would-be parents of money and may inflict severe emotional damage. Scams may involve asking clients to put down nonrefundable deposits (Wood, 2006). Agencies pretend to search for surrogates, and charge a fee, but then fail to locate any. They may also pretend to have found a surrogate who required medical costs throughout the pregnancy, but then became unwilling to give up the baby. Scams may also involve surrogates taking money and pretending to be pregnant (Vorzimer, 2011). Some surrogates steal tens of thousands of dollars from each victim. Most surrogacy involves little government oversight; thus, fraudulent surrogates may attempt to forge contracts, receive stolen property, and commit theft (Jensen, 2014).

The Uniform Status of Children of Assisted Conception Act (USCACA) outlines rules for surrogacy. It specifies requirements for surrogacy contracts and legal parenthood. However, few states have adopted it. Allegations of fraud may be raised in civil court, family court, and criminal court (Spivack, 2010). Generally, the elements of civil fraud and criminal fraud are the same or similar throughout each state. The elements of fraud in surrogacy contracts may be met when (1) an agency or surrogate knowingly and intentionally makes a deceptive statement; (2) the statement is of material importance; (3) the victim is justified in relying on the statement; and (4) as a result of relying on the statement the victim suffers damages.

States may prohibit surrogacy contracts under certain circumstances. Some states prohibit surrogacy contracts for embryo implantation only when embryos are unrelated to the surrogate; legislatures may prohibit artificial insemination; and some jurisdictions forbid natural means of conception if surrogacy is the goal (A.R.S. § 25-218, 2014). Parties may avoid involving the justice system if they entered into fraudulent surrogacy contracts in jurisdictions that prohibit surrogacy or void surrogacy contracts or provisions.

In states where surrogacy is prohibited, natural mothers are considered to be legal mothers who are entitled to custody (A.R.S. § 25-218 (2014). Husbands of natural mothers are presumed to be legal fathers. When surrogacy contracts are entered into illegally, contracts can raise issues about human trafficking, abandonment, and child endangerment. Legal provisions regulating surrogacy often deal with contract law, not criminal behavior. However, sale of children is prohibited in all states; and parties who contract for surrogacy in an illegal manner could potentially be charged under certain circumstances. For example, a few legislatures specify that surrogacy amounts to child trafficking if any money is paid to a broker, not including nonprofit adoption agencies; or if any money is paid for services beyond living expenses and medical care for approximately one year total (La. R.S. 14:286, 2013).

In some cases, individuals pretend to be surrogates so that they can participate in child trafficking (Gecker, 2014). They may participate in small-scale or large-scale trafficking operations. Child trafficking may be a form of unregulated adoption; or it may be motivated by sexual exploitation of children. Sexually exploited children may be undocumented and enslaved. Surrogacy is a convenient cover for human trafficking operations because it may be used to explain numerous births and infant relocation. Infants may be sold to enslavers, who don parental roles or enslave children. Chapter 4 and Chapter 17 further discuss surrogacy, adoption, and human trafficking.

Reborn Dolls

Reborn babies are dolls that appear lifelike. Details may include lifelike head weight, milk spots, ethnic features, birthmarks, wrinkles, skin tags, acne, sonograms, "warm to the touch" bodies, heartbeats, and latching mouths (BBC, 2008). Children, teens, adults, and seniors own these dolls. Many invest considerable amounts of money on related designer clothes, carriages, car seats, feeding tools, changing products, and nurseries. Some treat reborns as dolls, but others treat reborns as children. Adults who treat dolls as children or adults who play with dolls may face ridicule (Fitzgerald, 2011). Social constructions of motherhood and child's play may be too narrow to classify ownership of reborns as either motherhood or play. "Motherhood" may be defined as a strategic, laborious, or loving effort exerted by a woman to raise and protect a minor under her care. "Play" is an activity during which a child uses imagination to participate in fictitious events or to create an atmosphere of enjoyment. Ownership of reborns may cause ridicule because in many cases, it is neither motherhood nor play. Reborn "babies" may be criticized because they are not protected by "real mothers" or society; and adults' dolls may be criticized because they are disconnected from the innocence. For example, a documentary about reborns noted that commenters on Internet websites often discuss reborns using violent sexual innuendo. Violent sexual innuendo violates normative discussions about babies and innocent childhood activities. Thus, feelings and skills involved in caring for a reborn doll may be marginalized by the public.

Some people may be aware of and socially accept reborn dolls and attendant ownership. Yet, because of the dolls' lifelike appearances, many members of society and the justice system are unlikely to be aware that "babies" are actually dolls; and they may respond to reborns as if they are children. The reborn community may play into gray areas, and may enjoy blurring the boundaries between motherhood and play. For example, a reborn doll maker in England solicits clients at grocery stores by shopping with a reborn in a basinet; she approaches shoppers by asking, "Would you like to buy a baby?" (BBC, 2008). At first, customers are engaged by the odd question, which implies solicitation for human trafficking; but then, the doll maker quickly dismantles their concerns by discussing reborns, but only after using gray language to insinuate human trafficking.

The lifelike quality of the dolls occasionally insinuates that abuse or neglect are afoot. A few criminal justice system events have transpired after concerned citizens, who confuse reborn dolls with actual children, report child abuse or neglect. For example, police have attempted rescue after tipsters report reborn dolls locked in hot cars (*Daily Mail*, 2011). Babies left in hot cars have died; thus, police likely do not anticipate that alleged "babies" in hot cars are actually dolls (McLaughlin, 2014). When dolls are located where babies normally would be, police may likely believe that dolls are babies. Police should not derogate doll owners, who lawfully leave dolls in cars or other situations that cause police to mistakenly initiate rescue operations. Even if some police could differentiate between toys and babies, social conscience may not encourage individual officers to exercise discretion without 100 percent certainty because the risk of failing to rescue an actual infant would be too serious. Society expects police to rescue infants in crisis. When police are aware that reborns are in fact dolls, they may choose to be sensitive to owners who view reborns as children. For example, Memorial Reborns may resurrect deceased children (BBC, 2008). Police who encounter these simulacrums may respect emotional bonds that people have with these dolls; yet, some may not choose to assume risks associated with protecting or rescuing dolls.

CHAPTER 4

Baby Snatching

Child Custody

Most often, child custody is a civil matter. However, it may become a criminal matter when children are kidnapped. Nonviolent, familial kidnapping is the most common form of kidnapping. Often, noncustodial parents defy court orders and move, with a child, from a ruling jurisdiction. Violating court orders can carry criminal sanctions in addition to kidnapping charges (FBI, n.d.; U.S. Department of State, n.d.). The International Parental Kidnapping Crime Act (IPKCA) of 1993 permits issuance of an arrest warrant for international kidnapping; and the Unlawful Flight to Avoid Prosecution (UFAP) law permits federal authorities, at states' request, to issue a federal arrest warrant for a parent who abducts a child from a state. Internationally, interagency collaboration facilitates investigation and enforcement.

Children are often relocated to foreign jurisdictions where their custodial parents may be either unable to locate them or unable to enforce domestic custody orders without significant effort and financial expenditure (Gorman, 2014). Many children are abducted to jurisdictions that will not enforce custody orders from the United States. Occasionally, children may be flagged by local, federal, or international authorities when parents attempt to travel outside a foreign jurisdiction or enter the United States. Seventy-four countries have partnered under the Hague Convention permitting parents to file an Application for Return. Central Authorities in each nation help locate children and encourage civil resolutions between parents. Custody orders are relevant, but not necessary. Thus, court orders need not be violated for signatories' Central Authorities to become involved.

Fetus Theft

Offenders may cut out babies from expectant mothers' wombs. Some women and fetuses have survived, but many have not. Offenders are generally mentally ill and may suffer from delusions. Mentally ill men may attack women and remove fetuses, although in such cases male perpetration often relates to domestic violence. For example, a man was accused of stabbing his wife in the stomach (Malm, 2012). She was pregnant when the accused attempted to cut the fetus from her womb. He was charged with feticide and second-degree attempted murder.

Mentally ill offenders are often women who desire to be mothers or believe that they are mothers. Pseudocysis is discussed in Chapter 3. Sometimes, offenders have histories of sexual trauma or may have been sterilized (*U.S. v. Montgomery*, 2011). They may convince others, including their families, that they are pregnant. In one case, a woman who abducted a child was sexually traumatized and had been sterilized (*U.S. v. Montgomery*, 2011). As a teenager, she had been sexually abused by her stepfather, and she married her stepbrother when she was eighteen. She was forced by her spouse to be sterilized. On at least four separate occasions prior to her crime, she told people that she was pregnant. Various experts provided theories about her being malingering, calculating, severely defective, or delusional.

Some defendants may be charged with kidnapping or homicide for actions relating to the mother or fetus. In one case, a defendant abducted and strangled an expectant mother (*U.S. v. Montgomery*, 2011). When the victim lost consciousness, the defendant cut open her abdomen with a kitchen knife. The victim regained consciousness while the fetus was still inside and struggled with the offender, but the victim died thereafter. The defendant argued that the victim was killed before abduction could be completed; thus, she should not be charged with kidnapping. However, the court found that murdering the mother facilitated the kidnapping.

Human Trafficking

Human Trafficking is a billion-dollar business. It is discussed in Chapter 3 and Chapter 17. Fertile women, babies, and expectant mothers are trafficked for various reasons. Depending on the jurisdiction and circumstances, surrogacy may or may not be a form of trafficking (Iowa § 710.11, 2014). Some victims will be adopted, but others will be sexually exploited or enslaved. One common way to traffic infants without suspicion is to falsify birth records (i.e., lie about the biological father's identity). In one case, a woman became pregnant with an unwanted child. She drank alcohol throughout her pregnancy and the child was allegedly born addicted to opiates (*Daily Mail*, 2012). The woman's grandmother reported to authorities that the woman sold her infant to a homosexual couple for $15,000 to pay for her bills and a trip to Disney World for her other children. The woman falsified a birth certificate by falsely claiming that one of the men who paid her was the child's biological father. She claimed that she was mentally ill, and that she did not want to give the child up for adoption because she wanted to remain in contact with the child. As a result of selling her child, the state took custody and placed the child into foster care. The mother and the buyer pled to the charges, and faced up to five years in prison with a fine of up to $100,000. In these kinds of cases, trafficking effectively kidnaps children from the biological father.

Stealing Babies

Offenders have kidnapped babies from hospitals and homes. In some cases, infant victims have not been recovered. In other cases, authorities have investigated and located the victims. A major kidnapping conspiracy was alleged to have begun in Spain under General Francisco Franco (Dunbar, 2011). More than 300,000 infants were allegedly stolen over the course of five decades. Following delivery, rogue churches, nuns, doctors, priests, and nurses would allegedly tell mothers that their babies were stillborn. Sometimes, they told them shortly after delivery, but other times they waited several hours or days. Responsible parties sometimes showed frozen stillborn infants to postpartum mothers; or they failed to present any child to the mother. Often, victims were vulnerable because they were typically unmarried. When questioned about why pregnant women failed to place their names on birth certificates and why children and infants were available for adoption, those priests, doctors, and other officials responsible could claim that the women chose to adopt infants into other families, and that the birth mothers had chosen to remain anonymous. However, many women later believed that they were targeted because they were undesirable parents to the church. They were unwed, which made them vulnerable and an affront to traditional establishments. Rogue nuns, priests, doctors, and nurses may have been paid thousands of pesos to sell children illegally to families who could not adopt. Some families were alternative families (e.g., same-sex couples), which refutes claims that all babies were stolen to enforce traditional morality.

Switching Samples

Criminal offenders have purposefully contaminated sperm samples or other biological materials at reproductive clinics. These cases have been rare but their impacts are far-reaching. Some offenders have fathered numerous children by replacing sperm donors' samples with their own semen. Tom Lippert's case is a notable example because he had a criminal record and psychiatric history prior to working at a fertility clinic (Foy, 2014). His background was not checked prior to employment. Lippert first encountered the criminal justice system when he allegedly kidnapped, threatened, and tortured a woman to force her to love him (Lippert's Children, 2014; Witt, 1975). He accepted a plea deal to reduce his charges from kidnapping to conspiracy and received psychiatric treatment for 90 days. Lippert then worked at the fertility clinic for approximately ten years beginning in 1986; but he began making semen donations in 1983. He allegedly processed his own samples and could have switched or intentionally mislabeled numerous samples. At least one victim received confirmation through DNA testing that Lippert fathered her child; and more than one dozen other families suspected that their samples may have been switched by Lippert. The U.S. Food and Drug Administration regulates fertility clinics, but it mainly focuses on sanitation, disease control, and quality control protocols. Yet, semen samples are required to be clearly and accurately labeled. The U.S. Clinical Laboratory Improvement Act (CLIA) regulates registered clinics, but Lippert's actions were criminal because he acted in bad faith beyond professional negligence; thus, the laboratory was not held liable (CLIA, 1967; WJLA, 2014). Furthermore, labs are not required to register with CLIA, but they must comply with requirements to submit samples to the Centers for Disease Control and Prevention and to be certified by the Society of Assisted Reproductive Technologies (Davidson and Andersen, 1992).

In another case involving fraud and bad faith, an infertility doctor used his sperm to impregnate as many as 75 patients; and he falsified positive pregnancies to defraud patients (WJLA, 2014). Denying criminal culpability, the doctor characterized his actions as mistakes. He said that he misread sonograms; yet he substituted his own sperm samples on several dozen occasions and lied to at least one patient about using her husband's sperm sample. The doctor lost his license; was ordered to pay $77,805 in fines and $39,000 in restitution to at 15 least victims that he fathered; and was sentenced to five years' incarceration without parole.

Surrogacy

Surrogacy laws may be complex; and, yet, many jurisdictions are criticized for minimalistic or nonexistent surrogacy laws. This is discussed in Chapter 3. Surrogacy disputes are usually resolved in civil court, but some cases have criminal implications. Occasionally, criminal charges have been brought against couples who kidnapped pregnant surrogates or forced women to become surrogates. In some cases, surrogates absconded with fetuses or infants; yet, due to surrogacy laws, this may not necessarily be criminal (Soda Head, 2010). For example, a couple purchased egg and sperm; and they paid a surrogate to carry twins for them. The couple met with the surrogate in family court for the purpose of being granted custody. While in court, the surrogate became uncomfortable after learning that the would-be mother had a criminal history of drug use and had used medication to treat a mental disorder for the past ten years. The surrogate asked the court to permit her to retain custody of the twins, who were not biologically related to any of the parties. Because the State of Michigan does not recognize surrogacy contracts beyond compensation for medical expenses, the agreement was void and the contracting parents could not exercise parental rights. The surrogate retained custody of the infants, although they were in the couple's physical custody.

Surrogacy may become criminal when it overlaps with human trafficking or sexual exploitation. After Australian surrogate parents allegedly abandoned one twin born with Down's Syndrome, Interpol in Thailand began investigating a Japanese businessman who impregnated several surrogates and fathered 16 surrogate children (Rawlinson, 2014). Interpol raided his apartment and discovered nine infants and nannies; investigations revealed that he had traveled to Thailand 41 times in four years; and had traveled to Cambodia on several occasions to deliver babies. His goal was to produce between 10 to 15 children each year, and freeze sperm for the future. The man claimed that he wanted a large family who could vote for him in elections; but authorities believed that he was trafficking children for adoption or sexual exploitation. Chapter 17 further discusses surrogacy and the law.

CHAPTER 5

Animals

Emergencies

Sometimes, the criminal justice system becomes involved when animals attack humans. For example, in one South African town, two babies were attacked and eaten by giant rats (Newling, 2011). One of the infants' teenage mothers was arrested for culpable homicide and negligence. Emergency situations involving animals are further complicated in remote areas (e.g., national parks) where cell phones have no reception and dialing 9-1-1 would not result in an immediate emergency response (Brisman and Rau, 2009; Simon and Pasternak, 2008).

Babies and pregnant women have been rescued from crime and danger by animals, including dogs, horses, cats, and pigs (Barness, 2014; Nation News Agency, 2008; Ochs, 2013). Many animals are trained to dial 9-1-1, and others spontaneously dial 9-1-1 during emergencies. Sometimes, before the criminal justice system can respond to such emergencies, animals have already responded, physically rescuing mothers and children. For example, in Indiana, a man and his dog witnessed four dogs attacking a pregnant woman (Held, 2011). The attacking dogs punctured the pregnant woman at least 50 times below her waist. The man fought off two of the dogs and his dog rescued the woman from the other two attackers.

Feral Children

Some babies have been abandoned by humans and cared for by animals for brief or even extended periods of time. Several examples of feral children were the result of willful desertion; yet other examples involve neglect and isolation with animals. Often, children who are abandoned and isolated suffer from parallel problems and exhibit similar behaviors (e.g., quadruped locomotion and difficulty ambulating) (McNeil, Polloway, and Smith, 1984). In one study of 31 cases, approximately 10 percent of the children were reportedly covered in fine hair. Of 46 cases reviewed in another study, 78 percent of recovered children were unable to articulate intelligible words.

Feral children and isolated children present similar difficulties. For example, an eight-year-old girl and a toddler were raised by wolves; and two boys and one girl were isolated and confined with animals. Each of the children lacked language skills, socialization, and human-coping skills. They demonstrated fear of new environments. All of the children required training to unlearn animal skills, reactions, and emotions. Successful rehabilitation may relate to the children's exposure to human society prior to living with animals. The girls were young when they began living with wolves. When discovered by humans, they were described as hunched over and their appearance was described as hideous (McCrone, 2003). Unlike children who were isolated with farm animals, the girls ate only raw meat and tore off human clothing. They had superior night vision and could smell meat from a distance. Unlike children who were raised in isolation, girls raised by wolves never observed human society while in the wild. Mentally and psychologically, they were so different from humans that they were not attuned to human voices. After recovery, the girls never learned to be normal humans.

The idea of unlearning animalism and learning humanism raises philosophical and neurocriminological questions about human nature and the influence of human mentality at birth. One possibility is that some such children, who do not adapt to human society early on, are abandoned and become feral. They are abandoned by their parents in nature because they seem predisposed to be wild. This could suggest that some humans may naturally be less capable of conforming to tame social norms. This idea may presuppose that infants are born with such mentalities or that some have human psychological traits that resemble or are more compatible with animal societies than human societies. The effect and fairness of the law could be called into question because some people may be inclined to behave wildly. However, feral children may develop animal instincts, survival skills, and traits after being immersed in animals' environments and isolated from humans (Candland, 1993). Deprivation of human contact and care provided by animals early on may create permanent impressions that limit assimilation into human society later (Dennis, 1941). This possibility suggests that children are born without human perspectives; and that, mentally, they are unarranged. Often, when feral children are discovered, caretakers and researchers expect them to learn to speak, identify with humanity, and use human perspectives to explain feral childhood (Whiten, 1993). However, this presumption may be ill conceived. Many feral children reject human society and fail to become articulate. Feral children may only mirror or adopt human morality when caretakers or researchers punish them for bad behavior and reward them for good behavior (Gibbons, 2004).

Willful abandonment and isolation demonstrate extreme psychological and physical abuse (*The Week*, 2012). Authorities may not be capable of locating feral children's biological parents. Parents may abandon children in the wild or disappear once children have been rescued. However, some feral children simply go missing or are carried away by animals. Thus, parents may not be abusive in these cases. Isolated children may be confined to live with goats, dogs, or other animals at a residential property. Several relatives may willfully isolate children or be complicit, participating in the abuse. In these cases, children who are rescued may be unlikely to have relatives who will raise them as human. Isolated children may be placed in state custody or foster care. Children who are young, such as a one-year-old boy cared for by eight wild cats, may be easier to reintroduce into human society and place with a foster family. In cases where children were missing, but not neglected or abandoned, reunification with legal parents may be possible and beneficial. However, if abusive parents can be located, then their parental rights would likely be terminated, and they may likely face charges for child maltreatment or torture.

Costumes

The criminal justice system encounters people dressed as animals. For example, nude pregnant animal rights activists have posed mostly nude to depict pregnant pigs restricted on farms. They attract a significant amount of press and public attention to their message, which is intended to raise awareness of animal mistreatment. They may notify police of their demonstration in advance in order to secure permits to block sidewalks. Generally, using public sidewalks for demonstrations does not require a permit unless large crowds gather that pose a threat to order or safety; or walkways are blocked by immovable objects (e.g., displays or seated bodies) (ACLU, 2012). Crates containing pregnant women are positioned on the sidewalk, which likely requires permitting (*The Telegraph*, 2009).

Without a permit, blocking a public walkway could be an arrestable offense (*PETA v. Grace*, 1983). Demonstrators have been arrested for blocking sidewalks with displays. When demonstrators do secure permits to block public walkways, they may have to choose a sidewalk that does not serve a large amount of pedestrian traffic. Municipalities' granting of permits implicitly guarantees that demonstrators' rights to protest on that sidewalk will be protected. Municipalities may provide police presence to protect nude and pregnant demonstrators (Cusack, 2015a). Demonstrators who do not require permits may notify police of their presence in advance so that vulnerable pregnant activists are protected from members of the public who may sexually harass or assault them.

Another example concerns an alleged sex offender in Orlando, Florida who dressed as a dog and collected child pornography (Pacheco and Curtis, 2007). Plushophilia is a victimless fetish involving animal costumes; in this case, the man dressed professionally as Disney character the Beast at the Magic Kingdom (Cusack, 2014a; Cusack, 2015; Pacheco and Curtis, 2007). Thus, this man, who fetishized children, interacted with thousands of children on a regular basis. When police searched his home, they discovered over 1,000 pornographic depictions of young children. The accused was the father of a one-year-old child whose mother was 16 years old at the time she conceived. He was charged with 51 felony counts of child pornography.

Working Animals

Working animals cannot consent to sex or impregnation. Thus, human-animal sexual relations are considered to be cruel (Cusack, 2013). Furthermore, sexual intercourse and object penetration with animals is illegal because it is immoral. However, breeding is not classified as sexual contact because of tradition; commercial purposes; and potentially, industry standards (A.R.S. § 13-1411, 2014). Object penetration, however, performed to artificially inseminate animals, is considered to be neither immoral nor harmful. Generally, artificial insemination of working animals is legal when it conforms to industry standards and is performed for commercial purposes. Animals' compliance with insemination is irrelevant to breeders' legal right to inseminate them, who have a quasi-property status in this context.

It is likely that most animals working in K-9 and mounted units are surgically altered (i.e., spayed and neutered) (Cusack, 2015b). Though many will not be bred after retirement, a few may be. Breeding is usually performed by contracted breeders, but some police departments breed dogs in-house. For example, over a six-year period, the Winnipeg Police Service bred 42 pups; 90 percent of their dogs were purchased by police forces and passed training courses for street work (The Winnipeg Police Service K9 Unit, n.d.). Some pups began working at 13 months old and may continue working for nine to ten years before retirement.

Many canine and equine officers are bred; and yet, in recent years, numerous working animals have been donated to or adopted by police units (Cusack, 2015a). For example, the New York State Police Division Canine Unit receives donated canines from Humane Societies, breeders, and private citizens (New York State Police, n.d.). Almost all working animals are adopted from the government after they retire. More than 90 percent are adopted by their handlers, while some are adopted by the public (Department of Defense Military Working Dog Adoption Program, n.d.). Robby's Law was passed in 2000 to ensure that adoptable military working dogs are not euthanized after retirement (H. R. 5314, 2000). When young working animals fail training standards, then they may also become available for adoption. Failing training standards does not necessarily indicate that animals lack sociability. To the contrary, the animals typically have been housebroken, but may lack the best temperament, physique, or requisite skills for their jobs.

CHAPTER 6

Freedom of Religion

Male and Female Circumcision

Parents have a fundamental right to raise their children (Seldin, 2013). Parents have a right to provide children with religious upbringing, but they cannot exploit children through religious practice (*Pierce v. Society of the Sisters*, 1925; *Prince v. Massachusetts*, 1944). Though the government is obligated to act in the best interest of children, the court cannot substitute its judgments for parents' judgments. The government may intervene into families when children's health or safety is at risk.

Parents are typically prohibited from consenting to elective cosmetic surgeries on infants' genitals (Seldin, 2013). Yet, the government makes general exceptions to applicable abuse laws made for ritual circumcision on male infants. Religious freedom, including faith-healing exemptions, and parental rights seem to result in a quasi-hybridized right to circumcise. Furthermore, some studies indicate that circumcision may correlate with health benefits; and long-standing tradition supports rationales for legalizing circumcision, generally. Orthodox religious procedures for removing male foreskin have been questioned by a couple of jurisdictions in recent years, but have not been widely criticized even though criminal charges could arise from religious ceremonies involving *bris milah* (i.e., circumcision). Orthodox Jews participate in ritual circumcision procedures called metzizah b'peh (MBP) that require ritual circumcisers (i.e., *mohels*) to orally suck blood off infants' penises after foreskin is removed. Several infants have died from the procedure after being infected by *mohels* (e.g., contracting herpes). Yet, the majority of jurisdictions have refused to contemplate either health concerns related to MBP or sexual implications arising from oral-genital contact between *mohels* and infants.

Female Genital Mutilation (FGM) is a term used to describe various forms of circumcision, including clitoral amputation (i.e., clitoridectomy), clitoral amputation and labia minora removal (i.e., excision), and labial removal and vulva closure (i.e., infibulation). It is a cultural and cosmetic procedure aimed at improving females' sexual status that is alleged to reduce sexual pleasure; cause shame; and perpetuate patriarchy. Like the majority of male circumcisions, FGM is performed without anesthesia. FGM is usually performed without surgical tools, and it is performed in groups, which could spread HIV (Seelinger, 2010). It is mainly practiced in Africa. FGM performed on children is criminalized throughout the United States; and it is illegal to travel outside the United States to perform FGM (18 U.S. Code § 116, 2014). Several U.S. states criminalize performance of FGM on adult women (Equality Now, 2014; Center for Reproductive Rights, 2004). However, the same jurisdictions may not interfere with other elective procedures (e.g., vaginal rejuvenation) that potentially reduce pleasure, and arguably, relate to patriarchal influence (Cusack, 2012). Every jurisdiction permits routine episiotomies during labor even when they are not medically necessary (Cusack, 2011). Some legal theorists claim that FGM is unfairly targeted because it relates to Islam, whereas male circumcision is accepted because it relates to Judaism. Yet Muslims practice male circumcision in far greater numbers than Jews; and some people practicing FGM are not Muslims (e.g., Christians in Africa). One major difference between male and female circumcision is that FGM amputates portions of a female's sex organs while male circumcision removes skin. Yet, male circumcision is performed during infancy, before foreskin has retracted and forceful removal causes trauma and pain; the procedure can result in amputation, scarring, reduced sensation, disease transmission, and death (NoCirc, n.d.). Critics of FGM claim that it is a crime against women with historical roots in male dominance; yet, male circumcision targets males, and is rooted in a belief that God made a pact with Abraham to rule many nations (Genesis 17: 1-27). All males, including slaves, in Abraham's home had to be circumcised at eight days old so that Abraham could increase his power and wealth. The story is the foundation of patriarchy in Judaism (i.e., the first patriarch); and circumcision signifies that patriarchy continues. This narrative is also the basis for male circumcision in Islam because Ishmael was circumcised as a result of Abraham's patriarchy.

Satanic Rituals

Satanism is a religion and secular philosophy that upholds and instructs members about Satanic values and ritual. Anton Szandor LaVey, author of *The Satanic Bible,* founded Church of Satan in 1966. Church of Satan delineates rules and principles for Satanic individualism. Rituals, psychodramas, ethical codes, and church membership are available to anyone wishing to follow Satanism. Convicted felons are not permitted to be members of Church of Satan, though they may practice independently. The public may believe that Satanists sacrifice humans and animals; drink blood; become demon-possessed; rape women; and mutilate babies. However, Church of Satan disavows any rituals that involve harming animals or humans. In 1988, LaVey officially addressed misconceptions about Satanism in "Pentagonal Revisionism: A Five-Point Program":

> In recent years, we've wasted far too much time explaining that Satanism has nothing to do with kidnapping, drug abuse, child molestation, animal or child sacrifice, or any number of other acts that idiots, hysterics or opportunists would like to credit us with. Satanism is a life-loving, rational philosophy that millions of people adhere to (LaVey, 1988).

LaVey's statement is consistent with "The Eleven Satanic Rules of the Earth" established by Church of Satan in 1967 (LaVey, 1967). Satanic ritual practice is not required for membership in Church of Satan or belief in Satanism; rituals are considered to be a tool.

Generally, Satanism may be lumped together by traditional Christian religious communities with Wicca, pagan religions, and nonconventional religions (e.g., Scientology, Branch Davidians, UFO religions, and Heaven's Gate) (French, 2003). On one hand, thousands of religions are linked by a common thread (i.e., that they are non-Christian). Historically, Christian Europeans labeled people "witches" if they practiced other, nonconventional religions (Elder, 1991). Poor people who served as scapegoats were also labeled "witches." Impertinent women who rejected patriarchy could also be labeled "witches." Demonologists worked with courts to create a stereotype about female witches and their evil rituals. On the other hand, Church of Satan is unrelated to witchcraft, Wicca, paganism, voodoo, other forms of Satanic practice, and other non-Christian religions.

Unlike Christian and non-Christian traditions that acknowledge faith in false gods, demons, and spirits, Church of Satan believes that beliefs in supernatural attacks and demonic oppression are psychological delusions that require professional mental health treatment. Black Masses, and other traditional rituals that stem from Church of Satan rituals, do not invoke or communicate with spirits, demons, or supernatural beings. However, Satanism may be associated publically with demons, mental illness, and child murder because some offenders have claimed to hear or have spoken to Satan prior to murdering their children (*Pouncey v. State*, 1983).

Defendants have suddenly experienced delusional beliefs about Satan during sporadic manifestations of psychosis. They may have believed that they are killing Satan or exorcising Satan from their children. People who are mentally deranged or experience psychotic reactions may not be able to appreciate the nature of their conduct; and may not be able to conform their behavior to the law during delusional religious ideation. If these people kill their infants during a delusion, then they may become suicidal. Infanticide is discussed in Chapter 15 and Chapter 17 (*People v. Littlejohn*, 1986). Andrea Yates, who drowned all of her children in a bathtub, suffered from severe postpartum psychosis (Leblanc, 2007). She killed her children during a delusional episode because she believed that Satan possessed her, and that the only way to save her children from infernal suffering was to kill them. Postpartum psychosis is discussed in Chapter 16.

Child abuse and neglect have been associated with Satanism and mental illness. Neglect may be established when, without malicious intent, a parent's mental illness causes children to believe that their parent has ritualistically abused them (*Matter of William O.*, 1995). In one case, a mother frequently experienced psychotic delusions about her children's father perpetrating Satanic ritual sexual abuse on her children. The children adopted this belief and experienced delusions about Satanic ritual child abuse. The children's symptoms abated after they were removed from her custody.

Antisocial personality disorder, which may or may not relate to mental illness, has afflicted offenders who may also be Satanists (*Alvarado v. Dretke*, 1995). Antisocial personality disorder significantly correlates with violent crime. Satanists who suffer from antisocial personality disorders and commit crimes may cause misconceptions about Satanism. In one case, an institutionalized juvenile offender confessed to raping a woman to become initiated in a Satanic cult that mutilated and tortured infants. Therapists said that he suffered from antisocial personality disorder, a reading disorder, and narcissism. He was charismatic and manipulative. He had no conscience, used drugs, obtained weapons illegally, and bragged about possessing powers sufficient to avoid consequences for his actions. Due to his narcissistic personality and absent conscience, he may possibly have been a psychopath (Cusack, 2014c).

Victims may report alleged Satanic abuse to therapists while under treatment. One patient reported that her parents forced her to participate in Satanic rituals (*Jones v. Lurie*, 2000). She reported that cult members physically and sexually abused her. Her father allegedly impregnated her. The patient could remember babies being murdered and cannibalized. She reported having over 100 alternative personalities, who informed her about past abuse. She described those personalities as inner children who would fight and dominate her. While alternative personalities spoke to her, she would mutilate herself and attempt suicide; and she medicated her problems with alcohol addiction.

Some doctors have been skeptical of patients' allegations about ritual Satanic abuse (*Althaus v. Cohen*, 1998). Allegations may become increasingly eccentric as treatment progresses. Memories may implicate an increasing number of people leading to unfounded arrests. In one case, a doctor feared being implicated by a patient who continued to make false allegations about her family, her father's coworkers, and strangers. Physical evidence did not support the patient's allegations that she had been ritualistically tortured. She also claimed that several babies that she delivered through C-section had been murdered. Though the doctor believed that the patient had been sexually abused, and as a result, suffered from Post-Traumatic Stress Disorder and depression, the doctor exercised professional discretion by avoiding the patient possibly because the doctor feared the patient's escalating claims and blame on those around her.

Defendants and victims may be pressured to have false memories about participating in sexual abuse and Satanic rituals. Memories may be suggested by police or therapists (Cusack, 2014c; Kisch, 1996; Knox, 2013). The psychological effects of Satanic rituals have been documented by courts; however, cases have also documented implantation of false memories of Satanic abuse. In one case, a psychologist may have been the proximate cause of damages suffered by a patient who was made to believe that she was sexually abused during Satanic rituals. The psychologist also misdiagnosed the patient with multiple personalities.

Childhood memories of incestual abuse may be obscured by recovered memories of Satanic abuse, alien encounters, and other improbable events that are suggested and implanted by therapists (Leo, 1997). Some recovered memories may be negligently implanted, but some may be intentionally implanted (Bannon, 1994). Therapy patients may experience false memories of Satanic abuse inflicted by teachers and neighbors; and they may envision high priests or priestesses and cults. Some patients have recovered false memories of drinking blood, sacrificing fetuses, and rape. The Federal Bureau of Investigation (FBI) acknowledges that innocent parties have been incarcerated for allegations of Satanic ritual abuse even though very little evidence of cults with these practices exists. In one case, over the course of four years, children in therapy recovered false memories of sacrificial human bones, murdered infants, and fetal remains. However, after hearing the evidence a jury reached a not guilty verdict in one day.

False accounts of Satanic ritual child abuse are not unheard of. In 1983, a mother alleged that her two-year-old son was ritualistically and Satanically sodomized by a preschool teacher. Suddenly, seven adults were implicated for ritualistically molesting numerous children. Animal sacrifices and child pornography were some of the 208 counts of alleged abuse. Children told investigators that they had seen flying Satanists; walked through underground tunnels; been drilled; seen mutilated corpses; been attacked by lions; seen goat men; exhumed coffins; and suffered sexual abuse from Chuck Norris (McNeill, 2014). The spectacle became known as the McMartin trial. It lasted seven years and cost $15 million. While awaiting trial, one defendant was incarcerated for five years. Only two of the accused were tried and neither was convicted.

Famously, false memories were produced using a few faulty methods during the McMartin trial investigations (McNeill, 2014). Interviewers who worked with McMartin children praised or rewarded them for disclosing abuse. Negative comments and behavior discouraged noncompliance. For example, interviewers may have repeated questions if children failed to admit some kind of abuse. Interviewers prompted children to develop false memories by telling them what other children had admitted. This induced conformity and stereotyping. Once stereotypes were established, interviewers could also invite children to speculate about whether abuse was possible. Interviewers also introduced information to children that they had not previously discussed, encouraging them to incorporate it into their own narratives. The town in which the children were living was struck with Satanic panic. This sort of sensationalistic fear of Satanic abuse was not atypical of the 1970s and 1980s (Galanter, 1998). In some circles, fear flourished about Satanic kidnappers, predators, and abusers.

Some defendants admit to Satanic rituals and membership in Satanic cults. For example, a music teacher committed self-serving Satanic sexual abuse and battery on students; and he admitted that he belonged to a Satanic cult (*Doe v. Robinson*, 2010; *Duyser v. School Bd. of Broward County,* 1991). In other cases, an adult victim remembered that as a child she was subjected to sexual abuse during a Satanic cult ritual. Among the participants, she remembered one hooded man who had evil eyes; one fat, hooded man; her brother; and her brother's friends. Each of the accused admitted to committing sexual and Satanic ritual abuse in a cult environment.

In numerous cases, the authenticity of the rituals allegedly performed is not investigated, and offenders' bona fide beliefs are not at issue. For example, an offender was convicted of false imprisonment because he tied a victim inside an abandoned barn and performed a Satanic ritual; he also made death threats to silence the victim (*Commonwealth v. Enders*, 1991). Alleged Satanic rituals in this case were not linked to organized practices. In another case, a teenage father's rights were terminated because he seriously injured his two-week-old son (*In re A.S.*, 2002). He ignored his treatment plan for chemical dependency and was incarcerated. While incarcerated, he committed assault. The teen father failed to comply with the terms of his parole. These facts are enough to support the court's decision; however, the court included other facts to illustrate the offender's character and potential dangerousness. In incarceration, the offender created violent images depicting Satanic overtones, hatred, mutilation, and death. He also recited lyrics from Marilyn Manson's music, which has been linked to several high profile murder cases, including those of Amanda Knox and Raffaele Sollecito, the Columbine murders, Jodi Jones, and others (Knox, 2013). However, the court did not indicate that the drawings or recitation of lyrics related to the offender's personal philosophies or beliefs.

Perhaps due to legitimate fears, but possibly due to Satanic panic, some states outright impinge on freedom of religion by claiming that psychological protection of children is compelling; however, other states are silent about the use of minors in Satanic rituals that are not physically harmful (*Hall v. Miller*, 2001). Abuse inflicted through any religious practice is illegal, but ceremonial aspects of Satanism involving children are targeted in some jurisdictions. Montana Code (MCA) 45-5-627 (2013) prohibits ritual abuse of a minor if during ritual abuse an offender knowingly and ritualistically engages in sexual intercourse with a minor younger than 16 years old, assaults in any way a minor younger than 16 years old, or kills a minor younger than 16 years old. This statute is consistent with statutes in all states that prohibit battery, murder, and sexual assault, and that may add or aggravate charges for particularly heinous acts against certain victims. However, the statute also punishes simulations of torture, mutilation, or sacrifice performed in the presence of a child. Simulated victims may be animals or humans. Yet, in the case of *Church of the Lukumi Babalu Aye v. Hialeah* (1993), the U.S. Supreme Court prohibited jurisdictions from implementing laws that unfairly target religious practices of animal sacrifice. The ruling stands for the proposition that jurisdictions cannot use pretext to single out religious practices. Jurisdictions cannot unfairly target religious rituals that are harmless under the pretext that they relate to harmful rituals. *Wisconsin v. Yoder* (1972) and *Pierce v. Society of the Sisters* (1925) permits parents the authority to choose the religious upbringing of children.

Rituals in Christianity expose children to simulated torture. For example, Easter plays performed in Christian churches may reenact the stations of the cross, during which a character playing Jesus may be whipped; beaten; humiliated; stripped; pierced with spears and thorns; nailed to a cross; crucified; or buried in a tomb. Montana's statute prohibits adults from dissecting, mutilating, or incinerating any portion of a corpse in the presence of a child. However, children may dissect hunted and farmed animals and children may participate in rituals that involve scattering human ashes. Laws, codes, and best practices may not prohibit all children from being present when human corpses are incinerated or autopsied at a licensed business or a government morgue. The statute prohibits anyone from forcing a minor of any age to participate in or witness application of human or animal excrement; secretions; blood; bone; drugs; or chemical compounds. During Christian communion, children witness others ritualistically consuming wine and wafers, which represent blood and flesh. Even if these are symbolic, and not literal as required by the statute, children are often forced to handle bones and consume flesh during Judeo-Christian rituals. For example, a child may be forced to handle a shank bone or eat animal meat during Thanksgiving, Christmas, or Passover dinner as part of a ritual. The statute also criminalizes placing a child in a coffin or grave; or any person in a coffin or grave in the presence of a child. Yet minors are not prohibited from playing the role of or watching a performance of Jesus, Lazarus, or any other characters that are entombed in Christian dramatic productions. The statute, which includes threats of bodily harm and murder, when taken as a whole, may seem to indicate that entombment must intentionally frighten or psychologically torture a child. Yet, on its face, each prohibition seems to describe widely accepted religious practices. Jurisdictions may be unlikely to prosecute mainstream Christian practices under this statute. The statute does not include lawful activities, so it becomes a matter of interpretation as to which religious practices are lawful. Offenders face between two and 40 years in prison, a $50,000 fine, restitution, and counseling costs for the victim.

Many Christians use a rosary cross for prayer, celebrate virgin birth, and consume Jesus symbolically or actually. However, not all Christian denominations focus on virginity or the virgin miracle; symbolically use flesh and blood; or believe in transmogrified flesh and blood (Stewart, 2011). Courts often view Christian religious practices and faith favorably under best-interest factors in family proceedings and as character evidence in criminal proceedings. Satanic rituals are often viewed disfavorably in family and criminal proceedings. Despite the fact that Church of Satan rituals do not necessarily harm children psychologically, and Satanic use of sex and infants may be symbolic, several factors likely play a part in criminalization of non-harmful and non-sexual Satanic rituals. Those factors may include traditional religious prejudices against Satanists; historical witch hunts of Satanists falsely accused of crimes against children; and the cultural affiliation of some rock music with violent crimes.

Historically, legislators, judges, and the public have punished or ostracized Satanists for practicing Satanism. Courts characterize Satanic values as possibly leading to and explaining self-centered behavior; self-focus; desire-driven motives; disregard for others; individualism; taking advantage of relationships; impatience; rejection of criticism; lack of remorse; and being demanding. Satanism prioritizes self-preservation, grants entitlement, permits practitioners to view themselves as God, and promotes materialism (*In re Dominique K*, 2010). Satanists may break social mores and disregard social values at their convenience. In the Christian tradition, Satan is God's enemy; and Satan is the source of evil, suffering, and godlessness. Members of the government may believe that Judeo-Christian values underlie U.S. law. A parent's Satanic practices and values may be presented in family court as evidence of a parent's faulty morals or unwillingness to be a responsible parent; or as a reason to modify visitation or custody (*McDowell v. McDowell*, 1994; *Troop v. Troop*, 1996; *Troxel v. Granville*, 2000). Satanic worship may be one reason that courts terminate parental rights when parents neglect work; fail to stabilize a home environment; fail to formulate positive bonds with children; and neglect children's medical issues (*In re Interest of Deziree k. v. Richard K.*, 2012). However, parents have made false criminal allegations of Satanic ritual abuse to gain custody of children (*McClelland v. McClelland*, 1992). Their plans backfire when courts find that false allegations about such a serious matter create a dangerous environment for their children.

Some defendants deny that crimes are Satanic rituals or argue that Satanic rituals have been unfairly linked to crimes. Evidence that Satanism relates to a particular crime has been controverted by experts at trial (*Clark v. O'Dea*, 2001). Unrelated facts, such as Satanic poems, handwritten spells, and sacrilegious drawings, may be undermined by evidence that a crime was committed in a manner that seemed personal or passionate, not calculated and ritualistic. However, Satanic prayers, drawings, and participation in rituals could be used to demonstrate a motive or modus operandi even if none of those objects were involved with the murder (*McIntyre v. Williams*, 2000). For example, Satanic writings may become relevant to a crime if they express a desire to fulfill Satan's work by murdering and mutilating people (*Hardin v. Kentucky*, 2013). Evidence consistent with ritual abuse has supported confessions of ritual abuse; yet, some defendants have been acquitted (*Wright v. Illinois*, 1994). For example, in one case, scars on children's genitals and anuses, shallow graves, and testimony about postmortem rape corroborated a confession that the offender committed ritualistic child abuse and murdered a child. Two devil-like masks, bone fragments, a mattress stained with blood, and knives used to dismember children supported the confession and witness testimony. Child victims alleged that their parents and grandparents molested and tortured them with unknown people during Satanic rituals. Yet, private occult investigators physically restrained the children during interviews and suggested answers. Child Protective Services was critical of investigators' holding techniques. Adults interviewed by the investigators recanted their testimony and claimed that answers had been suggested to them. Furthermore, child witnesses are notoriously unreliable (*Brown v. Lyford*, 2001; *Doe v. Johnson*, 1995; *Jones v. San Francisco*, 2013).

Some children experience Satanic child abuse as infants or toddlers, and then continue to be abused throughout their lives. One child suffered ritual abuse at 15 months and was removed to foster care, where she continued to be physically and sexually abused. Another child claimed that he had been forced to participate in Satanic sexual abuse (*In the interest of Emma Hair*, 2000). He blamed his foster parents and employees at the Office of Child Services. He said that while at a Satanic church, cult members worshiped Satan and abused him (*State v. Towery*, 2003). Stories about Satanic abuse may become conflated with later episodes of abuse that are not rituals (*In Re: Chrystal and Tasha*, 1994). Even though Church of Satan does not have programs designed for youth, many allegations of Satanic ritual abuse involve teenagers (*J. P. v. Carter*, 1997).

A defendant may attempt to defend or mitigate by claiming a history of ritual abuse. One defendant claimed several incidents of abuse, including one during which his grandfather and several adults wore hooded robes; beat and dismembered an infant; and attempted to force the defendant to eat some of the corpse (*People v. Hawes*, 2008). Generally, history of abuse is insufficient for acquittal, but severe abuse could possibly mitigate crimes. Sentencing may also be influenced by whether an offender worships Satan or merely believes in Satan. At sentencing, offenders have attempted to deny or play down Satan worship (*People v. Kerbs*, 2006; *Simmons vs. Nevada*, 1996; *State v. Howell*, 2000).

Some courts hold that Satanism, Satanic paraphernalia, or discussions about Satan may be unrelated to motives or crimes (*Slaughter v. Oklahoma*, 1997). Satanism should not be used as character evidence to demonstrate that a defendant had a propensity to commit a particular crime on the occasion in question (*State v. Wyatt*, 1996). Satanist practices may be protected by the First Amendment unless the practices are illegal. Highly prejudicial evidence may outweigh any probative value. It is improper to present evidence that defendants who commit crimes unrelated to Satanism are the kinds of defendants who would be guilty of crimes because they believe in Satanism. In one case, the state argued that a defendant would be more likely to willfully kill a small weak infant because he was a Satanist. The defendant claimed that his girlfriend secretly gave birth to their child in her parents' bathroom; and that his girlfriend smothered the infant while the defendant cleaned the bathroom to hide the pregnancy and birth. The defendant concealed the corpse. The court erred in permitting the state to enter evidence about Satanism to prove the defendant's motive, because the defendant's beliefs in Satanic worship were unrelated to the crime. Thus, the evidence was improper and prejudicial, especially because the defendant had no history of committing crimes in connection to his beliefs in Satanism (*State v. Stensrud*, 2006).

A prison inmate complained that his First Amendment rights were violated because he was denied access to Satanic books and paraphernalia. Valid penological aims may relate to reasonable measures taken to deny access to Satanic books (*McCorkle v. Johnson*, 1989). Four factors were considered by the court: (1) whether a valid connection between restrictions and legitimate governmental interests were rational and justifiable; (2) whether regulations left alternative means for practicing Satanism; (3) whether practicing Satanism in prison would significantly impact allocation of prison resources, including use of guards and maintenance of prison safety; and (4) whether alternative forms would be more cost effective. The court agreed with the state that Satanism is not a bona fide religion protected under the First Amendment; but even if it were to be a bona fide religion, the inmate did not have a sincere belief in Satanism. Furthermore, access to Satanic books and a medallion threatened prison security. *The Satanic Book of Rituals* discussed Christian female virgin sacrifice as an initiation ritual. This ritual also included mutilation; blood drinking; and eating human fingers. The ritual could possibly involve murder. Candles used during the ceremony were to be made of fat from an unbaptized infant. Other inmates had witnessed the complainant slicing his wrist or drawing blood with a needle; burning paper; requesting blood from other inmates; and worshiping Satan. The prison found that *The Satanic Bible* condones self-serving actions, including murder, rape, and theft; and disregards moral and legal consequences. Thus, the prison felt that other inmates would be threatened by these sorts of practices in prison.

The State of Kentucky systematically banned Satanic practices inside prison (Elkins, 2004). Previously, Satanic worship was perceived to be safer if it was regulated and monitored by prison officials. Then officials changed their positions, citing security risks recognized by other prison systems (e.g., Texas Department of Criminal Justice). The court considered whether Kentucky's policies interfered with Satanists' right to freely exercise religion. Even though Kentucky's policies were not neutral, the rules were designed to protect internal institutional order and security. Alternative means of practice and impact on prison resources to maintain order must be considered. Prisons cannot accommodate traditional Black Masses, involving a nude woman; two black candles composed of fat syphoned from an unbaptized infant; and a chalice filled with urine excreted by a prostitute. Yet, *The Satanic Bible* admonishes harm to others, including the acts of actual or symbolic rape, animal abuse, and child molestation. Thus, prisoners may potentially be permitted to read *The Satanic Bible* in prison and perform modified rituals.

Church of Satan promotes pleasure moderated by self-discipline for inmates; and it claims that ritual (i.e., Greater Magic) is like therapeutic release (Information for Prison Chaplains, n.d.). Modified rituals in prison would require a fully dark room, black candles, and possibly, white candles. They could necessitate a bell, gong, cup, and sword, which can be substituted for an outstretched arm. Rituals may require masturbation, a phallic symbol, a bowl of water, and fire; and an altar bearing a goat face pentagram symbol, medallion, black robe, and incense (Cusack, 2014b). Inmates are not entitled to full Constitutional rights in prison due to safety concerns (e.g., fire hazards). Inmates may be denied violent Satanic literature or religious items necessary to practice Satanism (e.g., candles). In prison, any occult interests, Satanic literature, or Satanic paraphernalia may demonstrate continuing dangerousness to society, resulting in a threat to safety and denial of parole (*Davis v. State*, 2010).

Constitutional freedom of religion is protected by the First Amendment. Satanic worship and practice is protected insofar as it does not require practitioners and adherents to break the law. Satanic doctrine prohibits inflicting harm on others, even though it advocates selfishness. Thus, Satanic practices should be fully protected. However, members of society and the criminal justice system may believe that Satanic rituals involve sexual abuse, physical abuse, and murder. Numerous statutes and cases prohibit and punish ritual abuse that is allegedly associated with Satanic practices. Statutes may not specify Satanism, but case law and legislative history indicate opposition to occult rituals. Cases may not directly outlaw Satanism, but they raise Satanism as a criminal motive or modus operandi. Slowly, Satanism that is disconnected from the notions of baby sacrifice, candles made of infants' fat, rape, and child sex abuse is demanding equal rights to place symbols in public places (Abcarian, 2014; Prager, 2014; *Town of Greece v. Galloway*, 2014). For example, at governmental meeting places where Christian prayers are permitted and nativity scenes are displayed, Satanists are requesting Satanic prayers be allowed and statues to be displayed.

Medical Care

Religious exemptions for free exercise of religion may exist under state law, the First Amendment, and the Religious Freedom Restoration Act (RFRA) (42 U.S.C. § 1996a(a), 2004; 21 C.F.R. § 1307.3, 1990; *City of Boerne v. Flores*, 1997; *State v. Mooney*, 2004). Laws may not be designed to restrict such free exercise. Some federal and state laws prohibit governments from creating certain laws that abrogate religion. In her dissenting opinion in *Burwell v. Hobby Lobby Stores* (2014), Justice Ruth Bader Ginsburg stated that "[n]o tradition, and no prior decision under [Religious Freedom Restoration Act] RFRA, allows a religion-based exemption when the accommodation would be harmful to others". This may include withholding necessary medical treatment from children through either the practice of religion or in favor of faith healing. Parents have a fundamental right to raise children, as well as a right to exercise religion (Carpenter, 2012). Educating children in religion may be a hybrid right; however, hybrid rights are not unlimited. For example, parents can withdraw children from compulsory public education, forgoing secular education, so that the children receive religious education; yet religious parents cannot break child labor laws for religious purposes (*Pierce v. Society of Sisters*, 1925; *Prince v. Massachusetts*, 1944; *Wisconsin v. Yoder*, 1972). Hybrid rights may underlie exemptions for medical treatment, or they may end when medical treatment is necessary.

Parents have a fundamental right and duty to act in their children's best interest. Seeking and following medical advice may be in a child's best interest; yet, some religions require the faithful to avoid certain medical practices or even all health treatment other than faith healing. Courts will not substitute their values for parents' values; however, children may not be neglected, abused, or abandoned. In *Parham v. J.R.* (1979), the court decided whether parents had a right to make medical decisions on behalf of their children in their children's best interests. The court held that parents' control over medical decision-making is not unlimited. Neutral authorities (i.e., physicians) may report medical decisions or lack of decisions to the state that are not in the best interest of children. Any person may place an anonymous tip about abuse or neglect; but physicians are obligated to report abuse and neglect to the state. Furthermore, religious practice cannot be a pretext for neglect or abuse.

Religious freedom and the right to parent may trump the state's interest in children's welfare to an extent. For example, newborns with medical conditions may not receive medical treatment due to their parents' religious beliefs. Christian Scientists, Seventh-day Adventists, Orthodox Jews, and Jehovah's Witnesses are some religious groups that may opt out of some or all medical procedures (Lonon, 2014). Many states provide that use of spiritual or religious healing is not sufficient to prove neglect or abuse (Ala. Code § 26-14-7.2, 2013; Ark. Code Ann. § 9-30-103, 2012; Colo. Rev. Stat. §19-3-103, 2012). The District of Columbia, Guam, and 37 states provide some exemptions or affirmative defenses for parents or guardians who refuse or fail to provide their children with medicine or medical procedures pursuant to religious beliefs (NDAA, 2013). Most statutes specify that religious exercise alone is insufficient grounds for findings of abuse or neglect. Yet the wording of many statutes suggests that religious practices could potentially be one factor in abuse and neglect.

The U.S. Supreme Court has not decided whether exemptions to neglect and abuse statutes for religious exercise are required under the First Amendment or under hybrid protections; are valid uses of state power; or violate the Establishment Clause (NDAA, 2013). However, in many states parents cannot willfully place their children in life-threatening situations. Parents who willfully refuse to provide children with lifesaving treatment will not likely fall under religious exceptions. Courts may intervene when parents make decisions that threaten a child's life or jeopardize well-being. Courts have been most willing when HIV-positive mothers fail to take medicine that reduces risk of HIV transmission (*A.D.H. v. State Dep't of Human Res.*, 1994). This is discussed in Chapter 16. States may investigate whether children are old enough to decide whether to seek treatment or independently practice faith for healing. Whenever the state believes that it should act on behalf of children who require medical treatment, the government may order medical evaluation. If doctors believe that treatment is necessary to avoid serious injury or death, then children will receive treatment despite parents' and children's religious beliefs. In the past, cases have turned on whether children were of sufficient age to decide whether to seek medical care, but several jurisdictions may place into state custody minors of any age or religion if they require medical care (*In re Jensen*, 1981). Some statutes are broader than others (Hamilton, 2009; Plastine, 1993). For example, some states may permit parents to defend children's death using religious exemptions for spiritual healing and religiously motivated conduct. Statutes in Idaho and New Jersey indicate that parents who willfully cause a child's death, injury, or suffering by praying for or spiritually treating a child may not be prosecuted for violating his or her parental duties to care for a child (Idaho Code Ann. § 18-1501, 2013; N.J. Stat. Ann. § 9:6-8.21, 2013). Yet inclusive language may be narrowly interpreted by courts if children die (Mayes, 2013). Governments have indicated that religious exemptions do not extend to decisions that lead to death; and legislatures have revised or eliminated exemptions and defenses after faith healing leads to death (ORS 137.712(2)(a)(A), 2011).

Employment Division v. Smith (1990) stands for the proposition that parents seeking to give their children peyote to teach them about religion may be exempted from child welfare laws (Daniels, 2009; Peyote, 2003). Though peyote consumption cannot be prohibited under the Religious Freedom Restoration Act (RFRA) of 1993 and the Religious Freedom Act Amendments (1994), those pieces of legislation were responses to *Smith*. *Smith* held that unemployment benefits could be withheld from Native Americans who used peyote for religious purposes (42 U.S.C. § 2000bb-1(a), 1993; 42 U.S.C. § 1996, 1994). Though *Smith* is not guiding law, it elucidates an important point. The court held that hybrid situations involving peyote could receive greater deference if the government's drug laws "attempt to regulate religious beliefs, the communication of religious beliefs, or the raising of one's children in those beliefs" (*Employment Division v. Smith*, 1990, p. 882).

Children must likely be of sufficient age to learn about religion and not be harmed by peyote (Daniels, 2009). In *People v. Woody* (1964), the California Supreme Court found that religious use of peyote was safe because

> [t]he evidence indicates that the Indians do not in fact employ peyote in place of proper medical care; and, as the Attorney General with fair objectivity admits. . . . Nor does the record substantiate the state's fear of the 'indoctrination of small children'; it shows that Indian children never, and Indian teenagers rarely, use peyote. Finally, as the Attorney General likewise admits, the opinion of scientists and other experts 'is that peyote . . . works no permanent deleterious injury to the Indian.'

Thus, religious use of peyote may be exempted, in part, because the government believes that young children will not consume peyote (Brownstein, 2006). Some evidence shows that the government may feel that children younger than five may be too young to consume peyote (Peyote.com, 2003). Young children may be permitted to take drugs under religious exemptions even if they cannot make those decisions for themselves (*Parham v. J.R.*, 1979). The justification may be analogized to young children sipping wine during a religious ceremony or meal; but not if peyote is administered in much more potent doses than a sip of wine (Dussias, 2012).

Women are not obligated to seek prenatal care. Thus, religious beliefs that affect prenatal care are not required to be exempted. Religious use of peyote is optional among natives, and may not be required during pregnancy (Meyer, 2011). Peyote is a Class C drug, which means that harmful effects may be possible. Therefore, while peyote used for ritual practice is not known to harm fetuses, it is not recommended during breastfeeding. Though legal exemptions for peyote consumption do not exclude pregnant women, women who consume drugs (e.g., *hoasca,* or peyote*)* in harmful quantities may be charged with harming or killing fetuses. Thus, women potentially may be charged if they knowingly use drugs during religious activities that are the proximate result of fetal death and injury (*Gonzales v. O Centro Espirita*, 2006; Religious Freedom Act Amendments of 1994). This is discussed further in Chapter 13. The government has shown some interest in protecting fetal life; but Congress has mandated that no state or federal government can criminalize use of peyote in bona fide religious practices. State laws that protect fetuses from drug addiction and overdose are not aimed at religious practices (*Employment Division v. Smith*, 1990). If laws are generally applicable and pose a substantial burden to religious practice, then RFRA will exempt adherents. However, fetal and infant well-being may be a compelling government interest that trumps religious freedom when laws designed to protect fetuses and infants from drug abuse and overdose are narrowly tailored. This area of the law is gray because laws may be applied either to prosecute or to exempt pregnant women who harm fetuses or infants pursuant to religious rituals.

Cults

Freedom of religion is protected by the Free Exercise clause in the First Amendment and the Religious Freedom Restoration Act of 1993 (RFRA) (*Burwell v. Hobby Lobby Stores,* 2014; 42 U.S.C. § 2000bb, 2014). Religiously motivated conduct may not be substantially burdened by the government unless a narrowly tailored law restricting religious exercise is necessary to protect a compelling government interest; and the law is the least restrictive means for protecting that interest so that it leaves alternative means for practicing religion.

Right to marriage is a privacy right protected by the Fifth Amendment and the Fourteenth Amendment. States and the federal government define marriage individually, but all definitions limit a marriage to two people. Bigamy and polygamy are illegal (*Reynolds v. U.S.*, 1879). In some jurisdictions, professing to be married to more than one person may be illegal if the public believes that spiritual ceremonies are marriages (Cusack, 2013b). However, single adults may participate in polyamory or cohabit with multiple partners simultaneously. Polyamorous households have the right to bear and raise children. Married adults may potentially have the right to cohabit with multiple partners or participate in open marriages depending on the jurisdictional criminalization of adultery and other factors; however, prosecution of adultery is scant within the few jurisdictions that criminalize it.

Children may marry if they meet the legal minimum age requirement, have parental consent, or have judicial waiver. Judicial waiver will never be granted to prepubescent children, and is unlikely to be granted to immature minors. Adults who have sex with minors younger than the legal age of consent must be legally married to minors to avoid committing statutory rape. Spiritual unions, professed relationships, parental consent, and cohabitation may be insufficient, though some minors may be emancipated or constructively emancipated. Emancipation and sex are discussed in Chapter 1.

Some religious cults and sects may generally deviate from normative, traditional, monogamous, adult, marital coupling. They may engage in polygamous "marriages" that are not legally sanctioned, but are recognized by their communities as spiritually and socially binding unions. In some cults, leaders and older men conscript young brides and lovers. Often, teens who are drafted into polygamous marriage become pregnant. Conceptually, polygamous practices may be severable from adult-child marriages. In the first instance, polygamous couples do not legally harm others. Though the parties cannot legally marry or hold themselves out to the public as being married, adult-child polygamous unions circumnavigate the courts in a manner that results in statutory rape. In some cases, children may be so young that relationships result in child sexual abuse.

Mormon Fundamentalists may practice plural marriage (D'Onofrio, 2005). Polygamist families challenge political shifts in legal definitions of "marriage"; and Mormon Fundamentalists have attempted to lawfully participate in adult, polygamist marriages (Richards, 2010). Freedom of religion and right to privacy does not guarantee exceptions to marriage laws or statutory rape laws. Thus, the government has denied their requests to become licensed. Polygamist families are usually ostracized by society, media, and government. One reason is perceived or actual links between polygamy and statutory rape and sex abuse. Governmental investigation and raids of Mormon Fundamentalists' ranches demonstrate that some polygamist cults involve child abuse and unlawful teen pregnancy (Cusack, 2014c).

Fundamentalist Latter-Day Saints (FLDS) depart from contemporary Mormonism, which abolished polygamy; the cult has been linked with sexual violence, domestic violence, and fiscal fraud (Arredondo, 2008; *In re Tex. Dep't of Family and Protective Servs.*, 2008; Kent, 2006; National Geographic, n.d.). For example, cult leader Warren Jeffs settled several civil suits for molesting young children. One litigant claimed that at five years old he was repeatedly and randomly raped by Warren Jeffs. He said, "All these parents put their trust in a man of power to run a school and be the principal of the school over all of these kids but behind closed doors he is this predator who is molesting and raping children, and no one even knows about it." During his tenure as FLDS leader, Jeffs had 60 wives. Before he was apprehended, he fled and was placed on the Federal Bureau of Investigation's (FBI's) most-wanted list for charges of aggravated sexual assault of two minor females (i.e., 12 years old and 15 years old); and he was previously convicted for orchestrating a forced marriage between two cousins (i.e., a 14-year-old female and a 19-year-old male). For committing sexual assault against two female minors, he was sentenced to life in prison. Texas law enforcement seized upon FLDS in 2008, using swat gear and tanks similar to those used on the Branch Davidians in 1993. Child protective services (CPS) were first alerted to abuse at the FLDS ranch when a 16-year-old female minor complained that she was physically and sexually abused by a 50-year-old man to whom she was wed. CPS discovered many underage females were pregnant or had children. FLDS did not feel that fertile females were too young to participate in spiritual polygamist marriages. Sect leaders arranged marriages between men and girls. Approximately 468 children were removed by CPS over several days following the raid. Most of them, unharmed and not imminently at risk, were returned to their families.

FLDS females abandon education to fulfill religious obligations. The Constitution protects religious life and upbringing, including children exiting compulsory education early to participate in religious life. In *Wisconsin v. Yoder* (1972), the U.S. Supreme Court held that Mennonite children could be withdrawn from elementary school to live in religious emersion. However, FLDS females exit education to marry older men and bear the maximum number of children. This practice may be protected if girls lawfully marry, but can be distinguished from practices in which children learn a trade or receive religious education. However, courts should not judge the value of religious beliefs.

Yet, in these cases, incestual marriage and procreation may be forced on girls. Jurisdictions vary in their definitions of incest; thus, some marriages to male relatives may be lawful. However, girls may be forced to share husbands with their mothers and sisters. FLDS females may spiritually conceive each year after marrying. Repeated young pregnancy places additional demands on girls' growing bodies and doubles the mother's mortality rate. Furthermore, reproductive coercion is directly criminalized in some jurisdictions (Cusack, 2013a; Cusack, 2014a).

Polygamist teen pregnancy may be normal throughout the world (Waco, 1995). The majority of nations have polygamist marriages, and evidence demonstrates that polygamist marriages may be several times more prevalent than monogamous marriages worldwide (Price, 2011). In West African cultures, practicing polygamy with girls increases HIV-transmission risk, sex trafficking, female genital mutilation, and domestic violence (Buck, 2012). Boys involved in polygamous families are also more likely to encounter domestic violence and lack education. Boys may feel resentful because another man's polygamous marriage seems to mathematically deprive him of a wife. In the United States and Canada, polygamy more strongly correlates with international human trafficking (Kent, 2006). To take a firm stance against this practice, some U.S. legislatures have specifically outlawed child bigamy. However, numerous cults are virtually insulated from the law. For example, Branch Davidian children were hidden by leader David Koresh. He fathered one dozen children with wives as young as 12 years old. He starved and hit young children to achieve compliance. The government raided their compound to rescue those children; yet the government may be unaware of teen pregnancy, abuse, and sex abuse inside other clandestine cults.

CHAPTER 7

Food

Secretions and Excretions

Sexualization or fetishization of bodily fluids may involve consumption of feces, urine, ejaculate, menses, and breast milk. Consuming bodily fluids is not per se illegal or legal. Private sex acts are protected when they are consensual and non-harmful. Thus, the government could classify consumption of excrement (e.g., urine or feces) as harmful and prosecute it. Pornographication of coprophagia or urophagia is likely to be illegal (i.e., obscene) (Cusack, 2012c; O.C.G.A. § 16-12-80, 2014; *Miller v. California*, 1973). Forcing any individual to consume urine or feces is illegal and may create sufficient contact to constitute an indecent sex act (*People v. Levesque,* 1995; *People v. Pitts*, 1990).

Breast milk consumption between adults is likely to be fully legal as long as it is consumed in private. Informal, non-sexual milk-sharing between mothers is not uncommon; but, the Center for Disease Control and Prevention discourages it. Over one dozen states and the federal government criminalize donation or sale of contaminated bodily fluid by an actor who knows that the fluid is diseased (Ga. Code Ann. § 16-5-60, 2010; King and West, 2012; Va. Code Ann. § 32.1-289.2, 2014; Waldeck, 2002). The penalty may range from one to ten years and a fine of over $10,000. Knowingly donating HIV-positive breast milk to a breast milk bank may be punishable by a prison term of several years. Yet, banks typically serologically screen donors prior to their first deposits.

Every jurisdiction's laws decriminalize public breastfeeding for mothers and babies; yet, as a general rule, adults must breastfeed in private (*Lawrence v. Texas,* 2003). If breast milk is contaminated (e.g., contagious or infected), and breastfeeding is a sex act, then many states could prosecute willful transmission of disease (Cusack, 2012b). Thus, supplying breast milk would be criminal; but consuming it would not necessarily be criminal if the victim was not informed. However, there is no private right to sexually self-harm; thus, some jurisdictions may have an interest in prosecuting individuals who knowingly consume contaminated breast milk (Cusack, 2013). However, states would not likely prosecute unless the breast milk was HIV-positive. Menses may be consumed in private under similar conditions. Thus, knowing disease transmission is likely may be illegal (Utah Code Ann. § 26-6-5, 2014). However, in many jurisdictions *scienter* may be lower, such that an individual may be prosecuted if a likelihood existed that disease transmission was possible.

Placentas, Embryos, and Fetuses

Eating, storing, and buying placentas may be legal or illegal depending on jurisdictional variations and other factors. Anthropophagy (i.e., human eating human tissue or blood) is not specifically criminalized in most U.S. jurisdictions (Cusack, 2011). However, possession of human flesh usually correlates with crime (e.g., grave robbing or murder). Yet, placentaphagia is a form of anthropophagy that does not correlate with crime because hospital policies often permit women to retrieve their placentas following birth. Under these circumstances, consuming one's own placenta, or privately partaking in another person's donated placenta, may be legal as long as such placentas are not contaminated by disease or infection.

Medication abortion permits women to miscarry at home and discard embryos. Medical providers often instruct women to flush embryos because aborted embryos are frequently passed while women are seated on the toilet. Generally, women are not prohibited from handling or keeping embryos. Thus, embryophagia is legal in these jurisdictions because women may lawfully possess their embryos; and laws do not directly prevent them from eating embryos. Purchasing embryos for embryophagia may be illegal in some jurisdictions, but not every jurisdiction. Some jurisdictions completely proscribe the sale of human embryos or ovum; other jurisdictions prohibit the sale of human body parts, but exempt ovum. Sale of aborted fertilized ovum may likely violate health codes; yet privately consuming someone else's lawfully aborted embryo may be legal. Privately consuming semen and secreted ovum in menses during oral sex is likely protected under right to privacy. However, there is no particular right to consume these bodily fluids outside of private, consensual sexual activity (Reich and Swink, 2010). Although consuming embryos is not criminalized, substantive Due Process will not guarantee a right to consume them outside the privacy of the bedroom.

Eating fetuses is different than eating embryos because it raises a reasonable suspicion of feticide. Abortion usually occurs during the first 12 weeks of pregnancy. Embryos are typically aborted using medication abortion; thus, fetuses are usually aborted and discarded at medical clinics. Possession of a fetus may be lawful if it is miscarried before a jurisdiction considers it to be a stillbirth. Stillbirth may occur at approximately 20 weeks. This is discussed in Chapter 2. Women must dispose of stillbirths consistent with jurisdictional requirements (e.g., like corpses or biopsied tissue) (IC 16-18-2, 2014). However, women are not required to report miscarriages. Yet, intentional infliction of harm or death to a fetus may be a crime. Eating a fetus may raise reasonable suspicion about whether a fetus was harmed and the gestational week at which a fetus was miscarried.

Breastfeeding

Each jurisdiction in the United States makes exceptions to nudity laws to allow pregnant women to breastfeed children; several states declare that breastfeeding is a right; and some states specifically decriminalize public nudity related to breastfeeding (18 Pa.C.S. § 5901, 2014; Cusack, 2012a; NY CLS Penal § 245.01, 2014; Tenn. Code Ann. § 68-58-102, 2014; Wyo. Stat. § 6-4-201, 2014). Forty-six states specifically permit public breastfeeding; and breastfeeding is exempted from indecency laws in 29 states. In some jurisdictions, laws are written in a manner that technically permit children of any age to breastfeed from any woman; in other jurisdictions, laws specify that only infants may breastfeed from their mothers. For example, New York's statute says that exposure crimes do not apply to "breastfeeding of infants"; however, Arkansas' statute says that a woman does not commit indecent exposure when "breastfeeding a child" (A.C.A. § 5-14-112, 2014; NY CLS Penal § 245.02, 2014). In a few jurisdictions, women are required to attempt to be discreet or modest; however, other jurisdictions permit women to expose themselves at all times incident to feeding (54 D.C. REG. 10714, 2014; Fla. Stat. § 800.03, 2014; MCLS § 750.335a, 2014). For example, women in North Dakota are exempt from nudity statutes only if they discreetly cover their breasts while breastfeeding; whereas Louisiana permits breastfeeding irrespective of the degree of exposure (La. R.S. 51:2247.1, 2013; N.D. Cent. Code § 12.1-20-12.1, 2014). Some jurisdictions exclude breastfeeding from disorderly conduct statutes, but other jurisdictions could prosecute breastfeeding as disorderly conduct if it is performed in a disruptive manner (R.I. Gen. Laws § 11-45-2, 2013).

The military permits women to breastfeed or express milk at work. For example, the U.S. Navy guarantees service members will have clean and secluded spaces to pump breast milk (Meyers, 2014). Members are guaranteed an area that is not a toilet space. Postpartum mothers are also guaranteed a cold space to store milk. Most postpartum officers and approximately 66 percent of postpartum, enlisted mothers breastfeed; however, approximately one-third finish breastfeeding before returning to their duties (Zannette, 2009). Roughly half of enlisted mothers and more than 30 percent of officers have reported that they lacked a comfortable and secluded area to breastfeed or pump. Thus, more than 60 percent of enlisted mothers and approximately half of postpartum officers reported that work-related reasons led to their decision to stop breastfeeding.

Some women breastfeed baby animals, such as goats and monkeys (The Rehmanshah's Channel, 2011; Wayne, 2011). This activity is rare; but a few women have done it to nurse animals to health. Throughout the United States, this is likely to be legal. There is no right to breastfeed animals; but laws fail to proscribe it directly. Bestiality and cruelty statutes do not seem to prohibit it. For example, bestiality statutes tend to prohibit "any sexual act between a person and an animal involving the sex organ of the one and the mouth, anus, or vagina of the other" (Fla. Stat. § 827.071, 2014). However, oral contact between an animal's mouth and a breast for the purpose of nourishing an animal likely may not constitute a "sexual act" (A.R.S. § 13-1411, 2014; Cusack, 2015; Fla. Stat. § 827.071, 2014).

Crime and Infant Formula

Infant formula is a legal substance that has been involved in some very serious crimes. Formula may be expensive and in demand; it is a billion-dollar business in Asia where lawmakers have attempted to deal with negligent and fraudulent practices among formula corporations (The Milk Code, 2014). Because the product is lucrative, it is attractive for smugglers and shoplifters (Lin and Cruz, 2013). For example, law enforcement officers in Hong Kong arrested hundreds of formula smugglers where smuggling unlicensed formula is an arrestable offense (Lopez, 2014). To date, smugglers have attempted to smuggle more than 20,000 pounds of baby formula into China; one smuggler attempted to personally smuggle 44 pounds of formula. Smugglers may be fined $64,282 and imprisoned for up to two years. The Chinese first became distrustful when tainted formula killed six and poisoned 300,000 children in 2008. As a result of selling fake and substandard products, two dairy industry workers were sentenced to death and a corporate officer was sentenced to life in prison (Yoo, 2010). Investigations revealed that the culprits used melamine to dilute raw milk so that the formula would appear to have higher protein levels and meet nutrition standards. One father began an online support group for parents whose children had been poisoned by formula (CBS News, 2010; CNN, 2010). He demanded compensation for the harm. However, police arrested him for causing a public disturbance; and the government prosecuted him for disturbing social order.

Numerous aspects of infant formula production and sale are regulated in the United States. For example, only certain vendors and locations may lawfully sell infant formula (e.g., flea markets may not sell infant formula in some jurisdictions) (Beckham, 2006; Business and Commerce Code § 35.55, 2014). In *U.S. v. Hanafy* (2002), a jury found defendants guilty for mislabeling individual cans of infant formula, though they were eventually acquitted by the court (Hosch, 2003). The goods conformed to industry standards and were authentic; thus, the defendants were not criminally liable for repackaging retail goods. This case demonstrates that police and prosecutors may view alleged breaches of infant formula regulations as very serious, even though it is the courts that ultimately decide whether actions are criminal.

In the United States, adulteration of infant formula could result in imprisonment and a fine if the product does not meet quality requirements; but this consequence seems unlikely (21 U.S. Code § 350a, 2014). In the past, the Food and Drug Administration (FDA) has sought to prosecute responsible laboratories for failing to market infant formula without a nutrient essential for brain development, but the Department of Justice (DOJ) decided not to prosecute (*Duddleston v. Syntex Laboratories*, 1990; Rustad, 1992). To date, the FDA lacks the power to recall foods other than infant formula (Tennyson, 2012). In 1979, dozens of infants in the United States consumed chloride-deficient soy-based formula (Jacobs, 2009). The infants became physically ill and developed mental retardation and physical-growth retardation. Infants who suffered brain damage were awarded 27 million dollars (Rustad, 1997). In response to this breech, the Infant Formula Act of 1980 was passed to establish standards, quality control, and recall procedures.

Postpartum and pregnant women have been caught shoplifting food (e.g., formula). They may hide items inside maternity clothes or strollers; or use pregnancy as a distraction. Some have received reprieves and goodwill, while others have been dealt with harshly. Social justice scholars have questioned whether shoplifting baby formula ought to be a crime (Matsuda, 1998). Scholars point to the fact that food programs for poor mothers often have long waiting lists; and that infants die of water poisoning each year because their mothers attempt to dilute and ration formula. Some mothers may have so few options that they temporarily resort to shoplifting. In these cases, social justice scholars argue that mothers should be provided with social services, not charged with crimes. Links between infant formula and crime are discussed in Chapter 3 and Chapter 17.

Breastfeeding is associated with crime reduction and reduced health care costs. Breastfeeding is known to protect adults and children from acute and chronic diseases (Va. H.R.J. Res. 248, 1994). Some infant formula has included a protein associated with premature growth, breast cancer, and excessive development of mammary glands in males (Burk, 1997). Breastfeeding is also associated with reduced violent crime. Breastfeeding is less common among urban poor (Crawford, 2000). Some scholars estimate that Black children are more than 300 times likelier than White children to be bottle fed and not breastfed, which makes them likelier to suffer neurotoxic poisoning. Neurotoxicity may contribute to violent behavior.

CHAPTER 8

Pornography

Infant Pornography

Infant pornography is not the most common form of pornography, but it is prevalent. Infants may be explicitly exhibited or penetrated in pornography. The crime is often perpetrated by trusted adults (e.g., doctors, babysitters, parents). Some of the most prolific child pornography producers are babysitters. For example, in one international bust a babysitter was sentenced to 315 years in prison after participating in an international infant pornography ring involving dozens of suspects stretching across Sweden, Serbia, the Netherlands, the United Kingdom, and the United States (News 24, 2012). More often than not, authorities are unable to identify children's identities; but, identifiable children who are abused by their parents will be removed and placed in state custody. Even when pornography distributors do not produce pornography, possessing and distributing such images of infants may be particularly dangerous and offensive to society (*U.S. v. Slinkard*, 2013). Noncontact pornography crimes involving infants may merit an upward variance in sentencing.

Parents sometimes innocently photograph infants' genitals to memorialize their childhoods. These images may be used as pornography (*State v. Aguirre*, 2012). A man developed film at a film lab that depicted an unhappy young boy naked below the waist (*State v. Hamilton*, 2013). The man who developed the role appeared to look at the photos while masturbating in the store parking lot. Police investigated and discovered photos wrapped inside children's underwear in his car. Many of the prints depicted a child wearing a diaper, and the man's storage unit contained thousands of adult and child diapers. Some diapers in the storage unit were inscribed with names and dates. Videotapes were labeled "First Steps," "Potty Training," "Toddlers at Work," "First Six Months," and

"Terrible Twos." The man compulsively stole photos from photo albums, and occasionally burglarized houses to photograph toddlers wearing diapers. He had taken approximately 6,000 photos. Thus, photos stolen from photo albums were not designed to be child pornography, but he was using them as pornography.

Images innocuously posted online may be downloaded and altered by pornographers. If images focusing on a child's genitals are possessed in a collection of exploitative photos, then prosecutors may be able to prove that they were transmitted as child pornography (*State v. Aguirre*, 2012). If innocuous photos are altered (e.g., cropped) to focus on a child's genitals, then they may constitute child pornography. However, even if they do not meet the legal elements for child pornography, they may constitute obscenity (*Miller v. California*, 1973). For example, an image of an infant holding his penis while defecating can be considered obscene if it depicts sexually explicit conduct that appeals to prurient interests in a patently offensive way in violation of local community standards, and the depiction lacks redeeming value using national standards (Cusack, 2012b). Infant pornography is usually downloaded from websites that classify it as child pornography; thus, investigators can determine where depictions were acquired and evaluate whether images were transmitted as pornography or constitute obscenity. For example, a child pornography website may title a message soliciting to rent a child as "Baby White Girl"; or websites may describe depictions as "Pedo Babyshivid Childlover Private Daughter Torpedo Ranchi Lolita" or "Pedo Dad F*cks Toddler Boy" (*U.S. v. Eads*, 2013). Obscenity need not actually depict sexual exploitation or sexual violence to be illegal.

Infant pornography located inside one's home arguably may be in one's constructive possession. In one case, a police located infant and child pornography in two different places in a defendant's apartment (*U.S. v. Sumner*, 2013). The defendant argued that the CDs containing the images had been misplaced by another party inside the defendant's apartment. However, the only other people living in the apartment were the defendant's ten-year-old son and three-year-old daughter. Thus, the government argued that the defendant was in constructive possession.

An offender who views or possesses infant pornography may be a sexually dangerous person (SDP) who should be civilly committed. An offender who completes his or her sentence for a pornography conviction, but is utterly incapable of controlling sexual impulses due to mental and sexual psychopathic personality disorders, may be an SDP if he or she poses a danger to others. Viewing infant pornography alone would not meet statutory definitions for civil commitment; but, it may be one factor considered by the court. For example, in one case, an SDP: downloaded infant pornography; participated in sadomasochism (BDSM); traded thousands of child pornography depictions online; viewed child pornography for up to eight hours daily; fondled two children while working as a teacher; improperly photographed several children's breasts while in class; sexually abused his wife's friend as she slept; molested his wife's young niece while she slept; paid premiums to prostitutes to abuse them; and committed crimes against nature with dogs, a sheep, and a goat. His behavior was extensive and habitual over a long period of time. He repetitively harmed multiple victims.

Pregnant Women

Explicit images may depict pregnant women. Pornographic titles include "World's First Pregnant Orgy," "Mondo Extreme 94: Pregnant & Lactating Xtravaganza," "Mondo Extreme 32: Amber's Pregnant Gang Bang," "Meet The Mother Fuckers," "Make Womb For Daddy," "Keli's Home For Unwed Mothers," "Pregnant & Still Fucking," "Pregnant Cocksockets," "Lesbian Preggos," and "Gynecologist Fucked My Pregnant Wife" (Ramos, 2013). "Erotica" is a term used to describe legal pornography; "obscenity" constitutes illegal pornography (*Miller v. California*, 1973). Fetish pornography may be either artistic erotica or illegal speech. Fetishistic erotic depictions of pregnant women may be legal because they are inoffensive or because they possess artistic, political, or scientific value. However, some fetishistic depictions are illegal because they are offensive and possess de minimis value. For example, fetish pornography of pregnant women expressing milk may be obscene, especially when images are coupled with depictions of other bodily fluids fetishistically being excreted or secreted (e.g., secretion or ejaculation) (Cusack, 2012b). Depictions of breastfeeding are not obscene; however, evidence of child pornography may indicate that breastfeeding was performed to exploit a child or as part of a series of exploitative photos (Fla. Stat. § 847.001, 2014). Thus, actors will be prosecuted for sexual performance of a minor; and, possibly, child pornography or obscenity. In some cases, harmless photos of pregnant or breastfeeding women may be misappropriated online or photoshopped to appear as obscenity (Locke, 2014). In these cases, actors may be investigated and required to prove that the photos were misappropriated or doctored. Defending one's innocence against charges can cost tens of thousands of dollars in some cases (Cusack, 2014).

The issue of whether fetuses are exploited by pregnancy pornography has not been decided. The government has a right to protect fetuses from harm. Fetuses are not usually physically harmed when their mothers perform in pornography; but, they are exposed to increased risk of disease transmission. Critics of pregnancy pornography may argue that society is harmed because pregnancy pornography may involve sexual performance of a fetus; or sexual exploitation of a fetus. While fetuses are not explicitly displayed, some fetish films specifically require women to be pregnant with fetuses who are inherently involved. Yet some titles indicate that fetuses need not be involved to fetishize pregnancy (e.g., *I Skipped Lamaze Class to Suck a Cock*) (Ramos, 2013). Yet, any pornography, including pregnancy pornography, may be banned as obscenity if it offends community standards. Similarly, explicit cartoon pornography depicting pregnant women may also be banned if it is offensive to members of the community, such as police officers, prosecutors, judges, or jurors.

Sonograms

A key difference between child pornography and sonograms is that child pornography is exploitative; sonograms differ from obscenity because they possess scientific value. Furthermore, child pornography laws do not apply to sonograms because fetuses are not children. Generally, sonograms are acceptable and considered to be scientific; however, obscenity laws indicate that displaying sonograms for nonscientific purposes could theoretically constitute obscenity. Sonograms may be detailed enough to depict a child's genitals in detail; thus, displaying detailed sonograms appealing to prurient interests is patently offensive and likely to be obscene.

In *State v. Aguirre* (2012), the court analyzed whether X-rays, MRI images, CT scan images, or other images depicting genitals constituted lewd material even though patients were clothed when the images were created. The statute required a person to be depicted in a state of nudity involving graphic focus on an individual's genitals. An X-ray of a hip socket in which genitals were visible did not meet statutory elements because the image was not preoccupied with sex, wickedness, or indecency, and the genitals were hardly visible. Other X-rays graphically focused on clothed children's genitals; those were prosecuted as "illegal use of a minor in nudity oriented materials or performance." Alone, these images may not have seemed to be criminal, but the offender also possessed images taken in a medical setting of minors in various states of nudity. None of those photos focused on their genitals, but the voyeuristic photos were lewd.

Sonograms have been posted on child pornography websites (Johnson, 2014). One member posted a sonogram photo and wrote, "o man do i have some news i have a new baby about to be added to the game i will share her pics when i get some" (Oosterbaan, 2011). Synthetic sonograms have been posted online. These could be like synthetic pornography, which may qualify as obscenity but not child pornography because children are not harmed by the depictions (Fitzgerald, 2011).

Visible Baby-Bumps

In some jurisdictions, the law may require baby-bumps to be covered by clothing in public because municipal ordinances or morality-based dress codes may require residents to cover their torsos (i.e., no bare midriffs). For example, in the town of Easton, Maryland, males and females in public are required to wear clothing designed to cover the torso. Violators are incarcerated for ten days or fined $100 (§18-9, 2014; Cusack, 2012a). Private establishments may require pregnant women to cover their bellies, but permit nonpregnant women to expose them (Capital Bay, 2014). The government will intervene into private discrimination when it affects suspect or quasi-suspect classes (e.g., women); it is perpetrated by an employer; it affects interstate commerce; or it otherwise falls under governmental regulations (Cusack, 2015). Dress codes disparately affecting pregnant women may or may not be lawful depending on how and why rules are enforced. For example, generally, dress codes cannot prohibit women from breastfeeding (Cusack, 2012a).

During pregnancy, women may paint art on their baby-bumps. Because art is viewed by the public, and may be viewed by children, depictions may not be sexually explicit or profane. Despite First Amendment protections, artistic content may be subject to certain restrictions. For example, some mothers depict fetuses on their baby-bumps. Fetuses drawn or painted on baby-bumps may constitute obscenity if the fetus's genitals are prominently and graphically displayed. Female sex organs depicted may also be obscene, even if they are not lewd, if the content exhibits sexual or graphic themes in a patently offensive way; and the art fails to demonstrate any value using a national standard (*Miller v. California,* 1973;

Rao, 2014). Potentially, artistic symbols such as flowers or caves used to represent sex organs could be obscene, depending on the image when taken as a whole.

Sex Offenders

Under federal guidelines, offenders convicted of child pornography offenses are required to register as sex offenders, though obscenity offenses usually do not require supervised release (Cusack, 2014). Sexual exploitation of children, such as grooming online, sexting, or corruption, may also be registerable offenses. Child pornography accounts for more than two-thirds of total federal child exploitation cases (Carlson, 2010). Offenders convicted of child pornography must register in sex offender registries. Because many sex offenders have been convicted of offenses relating to child exploitation and contact offenses, establishments caring for young children, such as day cares, may be notified if sex offenders reside within a certain distance. Some community control measures (i.e., probation or parole) prohibit sex offenders from being near children; but certain offenses may preclude offenders from contacting children or from having unsupervised contact with children (Channel 3000, 2014; Code of VA § 18.2-370.2, 2014). Each state's requirements differ and each municipality may establish its own rules. For example, in Ohio, sex offenders may not live within 1,000 feet of a school, but they may live near day cares. Offenders who violate the law cannot be prosecuted. Violations are civil, and injunctive relief may be requested by a prosecutor (Cuyahoga County Sheriff, 2014; O.R.C. 2950.031, 2014). In Virginia, sexually violent offenders who wish to enter day cares must notify and receive permission from the circuit court (Code of VA § 18.2-370.5, 2014). In North Carolina, licensed day cares are required to register an email address with the government so that they may be notified when a registered sex offender begins to live within one mile of the day care (G.S. § 14-208.19, 2014).

CHAPTER 9

Pregnant Criminal Justice Employees

Military

Military rules, standards, and protocol for pregnancy may reflect institutional consideration for and misunderstandings about pregnancy within the military. Pregnant and postpartum women are not permitted to join the military. To enter into the military females must take a pregnancy exam; but once women join, they may become pregnant while in the military (USMEPCOM, 2014). Pregnant women may engage in modified duties; however, any strenuous or potentially harmful duties (e.g., flying jets) are prohibited (Lowe, 2014). Pregnant service members are exempted from physical training or duty that would be hazardous if the women were to experience nausea, fatigue, or lightheadedness (Womak Army Medical Center, 2013). Pregnant soldiers may not be exposed to fuel, airborne lead emissions from indoor weapons training, excessive vibrations, riot-control chemicals, or motor pools with poor ventilation, and may not drive military vehicles on unpaved surfaces. Pregnant women serving in the military may wear elastic waistbands with their uniforms, and may not wear load-bearing equipment. Exemptions are modified as pregnancy progresses. Female soldiers who are 20 weeks pregnant are exempt from standing at attention for periods of over 15 minutes; drown-proofing and swimming qualifications; field duty; weapons training; or riding in medium or heavy tactical vehicles. Soldiers at 28 weeks of pregnancy may rest for 15 minutes every 120 minutes; and may not work more than eight-hour shifts. In the U.S. Navy (USN), for example, service members may not remain aboard ships after 20 weeks. Pregnant members will be transferred ashore as soon as pregnancy is discovered. Pregnant members of the USN may not be assigned or travel overseas after 28 weeks of pregnancy (Meyers, 2014). Female service members may engage in lightly strenuous and low-risk work. For example, soldiers who are pregnant may lift up to 15 pounds and carry a rifle (Womak Army Medical Center, 2013). The effects of low-risk work (i.e., standing), repetitive lifting, and noise on antepartum, intrapartum, and postpartum outcomes were measured among 814 active-duty women over four years (Magann et al., 2005). Preterm labor and birth were only associated with standing.

Duty strenuousness, personal physical fitness, leadership, and environmental factors may influence pregnancy and postpartum health in different service branches. Pregnant soldiers are strongly encouraged to participate in Pregnancy Physical Training and Postpartum Physical Training (PSWP). Seventy-four postpartum soldiers, who delivered babies at Womack Army Medical Center, answered a survey about PSWP (Kwolek, Berry-Cabán, and Thomas, 2011). Approximately 66 percent participated in the PSWP; and approximately 60 percent were personally encouraged by their providers to participate. Most participated to achieve required Army weight standards and benefit child health. One study found that postpartum women in the U.S. Marine Corps (USMC) were more likely to be within weight standards within three months after giving birth than women in the U.S. Navy (USN) (Greer et al., 2012). Though weight gain was similar and normal between both groups of women, active-duty USMC were more likely to experience spontaneous vaginal delivery, and their babies' birth weights were significantly lower. In the U.S. Air Force (USAF), active-duty postpartum women are exempt from physical fitness tests for six months (Armitage and Smart, 2012). In comparison to pre-pregnancy performance, at six months USAF women had significantly larger abdomens and could perform fewer push-up repetitions; their sit-up repetitions were the same; and they were able to run for longer periods of time. Overall, their pass rates six months after pregnancy were lower than their pass rates before pregnancy. A study about postpartum soldiers and Army Physical Fitness Test scores (APFT) found that pregnancy complications, amount of weight gain, and exercise practices significantly affected postpartum APFT scores (Weina, 2006). The scores and soldiers' perceived fitness levels indicated that six months was an inadequate time for soldiers to achieve pre-pregnancy APFT scores. Postpartum soldiers may be deployed outside the continental United States six months following labor (U.S. Army, 2010). However, soldiers who qualify may sign a waiver and receive permission to deploy sooner.

Unintended pregnancy can be problematic in the military. Pregnancy and unintended pregnancy are more common among military service members than civilian populations in the United States (Holt, Grindlay, Taskier, and Grossman, 2011). However, contraceptive use may also be higher in military populations. Eighty-two percent of postpartum active-duty singles had unplanned pregnancies; the majority occurred while they were assigned to operational units during their first enlistments (Biggs, Douglas, O'Boyle, and Rieg, 2009). Postpartum active-duty respondents completed surveys within 24 hours of delivery. Singles reported that their commands were unsupportive during pregnancy. Seventy-five percent of single mothers required financial support from The Special Supplemental Nutrition Program for Women, Infants, and Children (WIC); and few of their infants' fathers were involved. In military primary-care clinics, early pregnancy detection correlates with urine tests administration; thus, many women may not know they are pregnant because they are not given urine pregnancy tests at secondary-care clinics (Hochman et al., 2012). Early detection permits women ample time to choose to abort or seek appropriate care. Researchers found that clinicians at military treatment facilities lack knowledge about emergency contraception pills (Chung-Park, 2008; West and Lee, 2013). Thirty-four percent of clinicians at military treatment facilities believed that pills had to be administered within 48 hours of pregnancy; and 60 percent lacked knowledge about timing and doses of the medication (Chung-Park, 2008). Only 54.4 percent reported prescribing emergency contraception. Some clinicians worried about safety and liability; while others reported that service members fail to ask for prescriptions.

Menstruation in austere environments is viewed as decreasing members' readiness and ability; suppression of the menstrual cycle is considered to be essential (Christopher and Miller, 2007). Many female service members elect to take hormonal medications (e.g., birth control medication) to suppress menstruation while deployed. Because women on deployment suppress menstruation using contraceptive medication, they may not realize that they are pregnant before they deploy (Sanghani, 2014). Furthermore, because women suppress menstruation, total contraceptive use decreases during deployment (Holt, Grindlay, Taskier, and Grossman, 2011). A sample of 7,225 female active-duty service members in 2008 found that rates of unintended pregnancy had increased slightly from 2005 (Grindlay and Grossman, 2013). However, younger minority women with lower education levels, who were involved in serious intimate relationships, were at significantly higher risk for unintended pregnancy. Rates were constant between deployed and non-deployed women.

Generally, pregnant female soldiers may not be deployed or assigned to duty outside the continental United States (Womak Army Medical Center, 2013). This policy has mostly succeeded in preventing pregnant women from entering combat zones, even though research demonstrates that participation in war does not seem to be detrimental to fertility or fetal health; it may, however, correlate with slightly premature birth (Haas and Pazdernik, 2006). In some instances, pregnant women have been on deployment. Incident to deployment, servicewomen are required to become vaccinated. Thus, pregnant women are exempt from vaccinations except those for influenza and tetanus-diphtheria (Womak Army Medical Center, 2013). Servicewomen will be asked whether they are pregnant prior to vaccination; however, no pregnancy test is administered (Crossley, 2014). Women who become pregnant may experience four different possibilities (Sanghani, 2014). Women may (1) declare pregnancy prior to vaccination and deployment and be precluded from deployment; (2) intentionally conceal pregnancy to deploy; (3) unknowingly become pregnant and then deploy; or (4) become pregnant while deployed. Being asked about pregnancy may serve to suggest to servicewomen that they ought to avoid becoming pregnant while deployed (Crossley, 2014). However, probably less than 1 percent of deployed servicewomen have returned from deployment in the past decade due to pregnancy (Dury and Gladdis, 2012). For example, in the British military, approximately 100 women have been sent home from deployment since 2006 (Crossley, 2014). Gynecological records of U.S. women deployed to Kuwait between 2003 and 2004 revealed that 77 of 1,737 were pregnant (Albright et al., 2007). Fifty-four percent were active duty, and others were Reserve, National Guard, and governmental employees. Among the soldiers, 77 percent became pregnant in Kuwait while 23 percent arrived pregnant. Almost all, 92 percent, were administratively redeployed. Administrative deployment costs $10,000 per woman (Foster and Alivar, 2013). Thus, the military has a financial interest in detecting pregnancy before deployment and reducing unintended pregnancy on deployment.

Police

Policies for pregnant and potentially pregnant police officers may be handled poorly, be widely misunderstood, and raise contentiousness within law enforcement agencies and departments (Brantner-Smith, 2014; *King v. Pillage of Gilberts*, 2002). Throughout the past 20 years, official discrimination against pregnant officers seems to have subsided, though pressure and gender politics may continue within departments and agencies (Crime Control Digest, 1991; Cusack, 2013; Discrimination, 1992; Moore, 2012; Police Officer Grievances Bulletin, 1992; Police Department Disciplinary Bulletin, 2003; Police Officer Grievances Bulletin, 2005; Przynski, 2006). Medium and small agencies may be the most polarized (Brantner-Smith, 2014).

Many departments have pregnancy policies that outline maternity leave, uniforms, duties, restrictions, and other related matters (Connelly, 2011). Under The Pregnancy Discrimination Act (PDA) of 1978, police departments may not discriminate against pregnant officers or officers who are potentially pregnant (e.g., using fertility treatment) (*King v. Pillage of Gilberts*, 2002). They must treat them similarly to other individuals whose inability to work is comparable (i.e., temporarily disabled officers) (The Pregnancy Discrimination Act of 1978). During pregnancy, officers may transfer to low-risk positions, limited duty, or light-duty status, if departmental structure and agency policy allows; however, pregnant officers may not be required to transfer and may not be allowed to transfer before it is medically necessary unless pregnancy policy permits the transfer (Connelly, 2013; Kruger, 2006). Pregnant officers could be forced to take unpaid pregnancy leave when policies do not require departments to assign light duty. Departments may force pregnant officers to transfer if they fail to properly perform normal duties due to pregnancy or they pose a danger to themselves or other people (Connelly, 2013). However, in this context fetuses are not considered to be persons placed in danger (*Automobile Workers v. Johnson Controls, Inc.*, 1991; Kruger, 2006). Police culture tends to discriminate against female officers; thus, departments may attempt to pressure competent pregnant officers to transfer positions or take leave based on perceived stereotypes about pregnancy. Pregnant officers have been discriminated against; some have been denied the right to take a light-duty position that would be assigned to officers similarly limited by a temporary disability. In some of these discrimination cases, officers have been awarded monetary damages.

Officers are not required to disclose pregnancy status unless they request light duty; female officers are not questioned about or tested for pregnancy (Risk Management Bureau, 2010). Pregnancy policies may require female officers to submit a letter from their doctors verifying their pregnancies when they require light duty (Connelly, 2011; Underwood-Nunez, 2013). Some policies require early submittal, but others may not require verification before the eighth month of pregnancy. Pregnant officers may elect to wear uniform jackets to hide pregnancies whenever possible (Underwood-Nunez, 2013). Female police officers tend to be physically smaller than male officers (Cusack, 2014). Though female officers may view their smaller statures as positive and challenging, civilians and male officers may joke or harass female officers with derisive comments relating to body size. During pregnancy, male officers and civilians may continue to harass pregnant female officers about their smaller statures while also harassing them about weight gain or being larger.

To accommodate pregnancy, female officers may alter their uniform shirts with additional fabric; however, maternity-sized shirts may be required (Underwood-Nunez, 2013). On light duty or in administrative positions, officers are not required to wear gun belts (Underwood-Nunez, 2013). Some pregnant officers on administrative duty may be permitted to wear civilian clothing when standard uniforms are unaccommodating (National Center for Women and Policing, n.d.). However, those who are not reassigned may require larger pants and a new belt. Weapons belts that accommodate pregnancy should be available on the same terms as belts for nonpregnant officers (Risk Management Bureau, 2010). Doctors' orders may be used to excuse pregnant officers from weapons training, especially because range qualifications could expose officers to lead, toxic substances, and excessive noise; but departments may elect not to exclude them. Departments are not required to accommodate or excuse pregnant officers beyond accommodations provided for temporarily disabled officers (Campbell and Kruger, 2010). Critics argue that some departmental pregnancy policies fail to permit women to transfer to light duty, which results in pregnant officers being forced to take unpaid leave during their pregnancies and become adversely affected during promotional consideration. Activists propose that light-duty policies should be flexible; have no time limit throughout pregnancies; and stipulate that women who elect to take light duty will not be adversely affected during considerations of promotion or pay (National Center for Women and Policing, n.d.; Risk Management Bureau, 2010). Despite arguments in favor of administrative duty options, when administrative duties represent lower-ranking positions, pregnant officers inevitably lose opportunities to gain experience (*Glenn-Davis v. City of Oakland*, 2003).

The Women in Law Enforcement Foundation and the International Association of Chiefs of Police produced pregnancy policy guidelines for U.S. federal law enforcement officers (Women Police, 2011). In addition to best practices already established by departments, the guidelines call for federal law enforcement entities to avoid assigning pregnant officers work in which they may encounter toxic chemicals, drug labs, or infectious diseases. Neither traumatic, high-risk, or tactical operations nor riot control should be assigned to pregnant officers. However, these policies should be consistent with treatment given to other employees who are temporarily disabled. If pregnant officers elect to work regular duty that includes risky assignments, then agencies ought to assume no risk for those officers or their fetuses.

CHAPTER 10

Civil-Criminal Crossover

Life Support

Advance directives can be used to declare patients' wishes for medical care in the case that patients become brain-dead, unconscious, or incompetent to make medical decisions. Advance directives may be legally binding if properly executed and filed with doctors or enforced by designated health care surrogates. Pregnant women may elect to be placed on life support (e.g., respirator or feeding tube) treatment or may choose to object to such measures in advance. In some cases, advance directives pertaining to pregnant patients cannot be followed by doctors or enforced by health care surrogates. Some states require that advance directives have no effect when patients are pregnant with viable fetuses, as the state has an interest in maintaining fetal life despite a patient's wishes, while other states only impose this requirement on female inmates (63 Okl. St. § 3101.4, 2013; Ala. § 22-8A-4, 2014; O.C.G.A. § 31-32-4, 2013; Wardle, 2013). In other states, advance directives have no effect throughout the duration of pregnancy. Some states may lack laws on point; may specify that advance directives can be enforced during pregnancy; or may require life to be sustained unless pregnant patients object through advance directives (18 V.S.A. § 9702, 2013; Md. Health-General Code Ann. § 5-603, 2014; N.J. Stat. § 26:2H-56, 2014).

When advance directives are not filed, evidence of a patient's wishes may support a court's orders to either maintain or end life support. However, in certain jurisdictions this may be insufficient when women are pregnant. Families' wishes may also be irrelevant when advance directives are silent or have no effect. Sometimes pregnant women are placed on life support against their families' wishes. Courts may intervene, overturn law, or distinguish certain cases from the law. In Texas, a statute prohibited pregnant women from being taken off life support (Fernandez, 2014; Texas Health and Safety Code § 166.049, 2014). A judge ordered a pregnant patient to be taken off life support in compliance with her family's wishes. Criminal charges could have resulted from taking the pregnant woman off life support before the court order was issued (e.g., killing a fetus); and charges could also have resulted from ignoring a court's order to sustain or end life support (e.g., contempt). The patient's family argued that the patient was brain-dead, thus that she was legally dead. In some cases, patients may require life-sustaining interventions (e.g., feeding tubes); but they are conscious, albeit vegetative (*Bush v. Schiavo*, 2004; *Schiavo v. Schindler*, 2005; *In re Schiavo*, 2001). However, this argument is that a brain-dead woman is legally dead (*Muñoz v. John Peter Smith Hospital*, 2014). Thus, despite pregnancy, a brain-dead woman is no longer a person (Sperling, 2004). A corpse no longer possesses a person's rights, and is not required to follow the law (Cusack, 2011). A judge found that a hospital should follow a family's wishes to end life support. The court considered that life was not assisted because the woman was dead. Though Texas' code did not require fetal viability like some states, the patient's fetus was not viable. Thus, legislators' interests in maintaining fetal life were severely limited. The statute requiring a pregnant patient to be sustained on life support did not apply in this case, particularly because the woman was dead. The law, however, was not declared to lack Constitutionality.

A recent case highlighted crossover between civil and criminal law (Sharp, 2014; Kuruvilla, 2014). An infant, who was shaken by her father, suffered from spastic quadriplegia, blindness, deafness, inability to suck or swallow, pain, neurologic impairment, and inability to breathe on her own. Her father was charged with aggravated assault, but would be charged with manslaughter or murder if the child died within a year of the attack. The child's 18-year-old mother, Virginia Trask, exercised parental rights by signing a do-not-resuscitate (DNR) order for her infant under the guidance of State of Maine child welfare employees. The infant was removed from life support and placed in Trask's arms to die; however, the child unexpectedly began breathing without life support. Trask wanted to void the DNR order, but the child welfare department claimed that she no longer had the authority to do so. A lower court heard Trask's case, claiming that her parental rights entitled her to make medical decisions for her infant. However, the judge found that Trask seldom visited the child and was undependable; thus, the judge granted authority to Maine's child welfare department. Child welfare agreed to abide by Trask's wishes, making the case moot before Maine Supreme Judicial Court.

Hospital Rooms

Women delivering babies possess a right to privacy when babies are delivered within spheres that society is willing to recognize as private (*De May v. Roberts*, 1881). A reasonable expectation of privacy may be possessed in a hospital room and a home (Prosser, 1960). People are often nude in hospital rooms and bedrooms, which is one indicator that a reasonable expectation of privacy may be held in these places. Every U.S. jurisdiction recognizes a reasonable expectation of privacy in bedrooms and, possibly, other similar locations (e.g., nursing homes) (Cusack, 2015). However, a right to privacy guarantees occupants freedom from intrusion even when occupants are clothed. Intrusion is tortious conduct that results when a tort-feasor physically intrudes into a hospital room without consent (*Shulman v. Group W Productions,* 1998). Privacy violations are a matter of degrees. Intruding during labor or birth may be particularly violative conduct. The amount of privacy expected in a hospital room may not be absolute because hospital staff enter a room without notice; yet, an expectation of privacy is recognized as relative (*Sanders v. American Broadcasting Companies,* 1999). Even if a patient can be forced to see nurses or other hospital staff, an adult patient cannot be legally forced to consent to have visitors in a hospital room. When hospital rules authorize visitation, a patient may grant consent to be visited. The mere possibility that any potential visitor could enter a hospital room does not grant consent for all visitors to enter (*People* v. *Brown,* 1979). Thus, an expectation of privacy is relative to consent granted to a particular visitor within a given context.

The identity or conduct of the intruder may determine whether the conduct was intrusive. The guiding U.S. Supreme Court case about tortious intrusion considered whether a pregnant woman was intruded upon when a doctor brought a friend to deliver the birth of her baby (*De May v. Roberts*, 1881). She consented for her doctor's friend to enter her home, but her consent was based on her belief that her doctor's friend worked in the medical field. The court held that her consent was fraudulently obtained because her doctor allowed her to believe that his friend's presence was relevant and appropriate. Thus, consent was not granted and her privacy was violated by their physical and sensory intrusion (*De May v. Roberts*,

1881; *Spinks v. Equity Residential Briarwood Apartments*, 2009). Conduct may be highly offensive in light of the tort-feasors' identity or duty. For example, a pharmaceutical representative was permitted to view a breast cancer survivor's bare chest during an oncological examination because the patient believed that the representative was a medical professional (*Azucena Sanchez-Scott v. Alza Pharmaceuticals*, 2001). The doctor owed a duty to the patient, and the representative's identity was intrusive under the circumstances. When considering whether intrusive conduct was highly offensive, courts should consider the totality of the circumstances, including the degree, context, motive, and setting of the intrusion, in comparison to expectations held by the plaintiff.

In some jurisdictions, biological fathers may attempt to exercise a right to be present in a hospital room during a child's birth. Some women may object to the presence of progenies' biological fathers during delivery. Courts have recognized the importance of women's privacy above a father's rights (*Plotnick v. DeLuccia*, 2013; *Roe v. Wade*, 1973). Courts recognize this right in delivery rooms. Mothers may choose to object to biological fathers being present during delivery (Phillis, 2014). When intruders are not granted consent by a patient to enter a hospital room, and yet refuse to leave, then they may be arrested. The fact that other visitors are present or that an intruder believes he or she has a right to be present does not countervail an intruder's obligation to obey hospital rules when asked to leave (*Cleveland v. Municipality of Anchorage*, 1981; *Kalfus v. The New York and Presbyterian Hospital*, 2012). Trespass (i.e., nonconsensual visitation) committed by fathers could result in court-order violations, trespass charges, breech of peace charges, or other related criminal incidents. Trespassers who are arrested may challenge convictions if sufficient notice was not given to alert intruders to their trespassory activities. For example, a sign forbidding visitors must be prominent to sustain a criminal conviction for trespass, even if the conduct is found to be tortious in civil court. In each case, the totality of circumstances may be considered (*Cohen v. Katsaris*, 1982). A visitor claiming to have a right to be present in a hospital room should seek court orders. However, fathers' requests to be notified prior to birth and to be present during birth without mothers' consent have failed to be supported by the law even when judicial orders are sought ahead of time (*Plotnick v. DeLuccia*, 2013). In addition to the fact that the mother's privacy rights and pre-birth interests in a child are greater than a father's rights, the presence of an unwanted guest in the delivery room could place unneeded stress on a mother in delivery and increase the danger of delivery for her and the child (Phillis, 2014). Furthermore, hospitals owe mothers a duty to protect them from trespass if it is reasonably foreseeable. Hospital protocols and policies are likely to protect women from unwanted intrusion during childbirth; however, traditional attitudes toward fathers' roles during birth may cause some hospital staff to fall below the standard of care and permit intrusion. These breeches are foreseeable and avoidable; and they can be remedied by patients asking intruders to leave or by having trespassers arrested (*Necolayff v. Genesee Hospital*, 1946).

Criminal Procedure

Police may violate suspects' Constitutional rights by deviating from proper criminal procedure. If an officer violates a suspect's rights or department policies, a claim may be brought against the officer under 42 U.S.C. § 1983 (Orovitz, 2012). Theoretically, these claims may serve punitive and compensatory aims. For the plaintiff to prevail, an officer must have acted under the color of law while depriving a plaintiff of Constitutional rights. In this context, late-term fetuses injured in utero during police encounters may not be considered to be persons with rights, but death or loss of a fetus may be a cognizable damage (*AELE Reporter*, 1988; *Security Law Newsletter*, 2011; *Williams v. Anderson*, 2010). Qualified immunity is an affirmative defense that can result in summary judgment. Police who exercise discretion are immunized, but only if they objectively intend to act under the color of law. Exercise of discretion may be called for or result in situations where the law is unclear. Though discretion may be exercised when the law seems unclear, under 42 U.S.C. § 1983 a Constitutional right must be clearly established to give police fair warning. If the law gives police fair warning of a plaintiff's rights and police conduct is unreasonable, then such police conduct will not be immunized.

Many incidences involving babies and pregnant women have resulted in civil rights violation complaints, lawsuits, and judgments against police. Outcomes of incidences and complaints vary widely by jurisdictions, reasonableness of force use, and circumstances surrounding deprivation of rights (*AELE Reporter*, 1982). Many cases involve prisons, and infant death due to negligent custody of inmates. Pregnant inmates may leak amniotic fluid, spot bleed, and cramp for hours or days before being allowed to visit with a doctor (Swift, 2009). Some give birth on toilets, prison ramps, and prison offices; and some have unnecessarily been shackled during labor. This is discussed in Chapter 3 and Chapter 11.

Some violations are less severe. In one case, Portland police were ordered to pay a pregnant woman after they held her for 90 minutes without a bathroom break. Usually, unreasonable detentions in which police deny bathroom breaks span several hours (*Miranda v. Arizona*, 1966). However, this case demonstrates that the system may expect police to be considerate of the effects of pregnancy (e.g., pressure on a woman's bladder). Other cases do not demonstrate that police are required to be considerate of women's pregnant condition. In *Brooks v. Seattle* (2010), the court held that officers who used a Tazer three times on a pregnant woman to achieve pain compliance were entitled to immunity (Johnson, 2010). Police knew that the woman was seven-months' pregnant when she refused to sign a speeding ticket, exit her vehicle, or submit to arrest. Pain-compliance shocks were not excessive under the circumstances because she was noncompliant (*Criminal Law Reporter*, 2010). The offender immediately received medical care and delivered a healthy baby two months after the incident.

Constitutional rights violations could result during search and seizure. For example, police executed a search warrant at a home, but they failed to knock and announce their presence as required by law (Belt, 2014). Under exigent circumstances, police may dispense with knock-and-announce requirements. In this case, the suspect was believed to possess drugs and weapons. A child, who was temporarily residing there, was injured and comatose after police threw a flash grenade into his crib, which detonated on his face. The suspect was then arrested at a different home, which calls into question police's claim that the circumstances were exigent. However, police said that they did not know that an infant was visiting, and there were no signs that any child lived there. Similar cases may turn on what police knew or should have known; exigency of circumstances; and reasonableness of police actions.

Birth Defects

Birth defect cases have played a pivotal role in law and justice (Paltrow and Jack, 2010). For example, in 1993, Merrell Dow Pharmaceuticals was sued by teens with shortened limbs who suffered birth defects relating to their mothers' use of birth control products (*Daubert v. Merrell Dow Pharmaceuticals*, 1993). *Daubert*, a case decided by the U.S. Supreme

Court, set the contemporary standard for the admissibility of expert testimony in civil cases. Although the holding could apply to criminal cases, its reach within the criminal justice system has been limited in comparison to civil cases (Giannelli, 2011). Birth control and birth defects are discussed in Chapter 17.

Birth defects have been studied at length by the criminal justice system. Physiological explanations for crime have persisted in the study of criminology for hundreds of years (e.g., Cesare Lombroso's Positivist Criminology). Some of these theories have been described as racist, classist, or sexist. Some criminological knowledge about birth defects refers to mental defects that cause crime; and recent biological theories explain how hormones, brain shape, and brain function relate to delinquent or criminal inclinations (Rafter, 2001). Certain defects may relate to external conditions affecting children in utero (e.g., maternal intoxication or contamination). Maternal intoxication and criminal liability are discussed further in Chapter 13. Predispositions may be exacerbated by environmental factors, lack of treatment, inappropriate responses to defects, or learned behavior. Other individuals or corporations may be civilly or criminally liable for causing or worsening birth defects.

Birth defects are a private matter, but they are also a matter of public health. The state's interest in individuals' birth defects may be compelling. Parents have a right to privacy, a right to raise children, and a right to make medical decisions for their children, but the state's police power may impinge on those rights to the extent necessary to act in children's best interests and protect public health (HIV Justice Network, 2008; *State v. Neumann*, 2013; *Zucht v. King*, 1922). For example, when treatment is necessary to prevent death, states may intervene into parents' medical decision making (Kaplan, 2010; Seldin, 2013; Srinath, 2012). Parents' medical decision making is discussed in Chapter 6. Birth defects among the general population are a matter of public health, the assurance of which is one of the state's traditional roles enforceable through police power (*Jacobson v. Massachusetts*, 1905). Public health information about birth defects may be gathered to document occurrences and develop research data in case trends are causally related to negligent or intentional activities. The Food and Drug Administration (FDA) recommends that doctors inform them about potential birth defects using a Medwatch form on its FDA.gov website, but they do not require reporting. Hospitals, doctors, midwives, and others who professionally deliver infants may be required to report birth defects to the state (Texas Health

Code § 87, 2014). Departments may conduct epidemiological and toxicological investigations to understand or measure diseases, causes, and controls. Parents may be required to provide medical, toxicological, personal, demographic, and other epidemiological information to the state. Parents and government agents cannot be held liable to children or other entities for collecting this information as required or providing such information during an investigation; however, those who disclose criminal negligence or intentionally criminal acts may be held liable. Records held in a central registry are likely to be confidential and certified for medical and health use only. Criminal, civil, or special proceedings examining government agents in possession of records may require parental consent to disclose records used to monitor individual children's medical histories. However, de-identified records may be released for statistical purposes. If high probabilities of occurrences are identified, then programs may be taken to reduce incidences in certain regions; and potentially, criminal investigations could be conducted. Governmental responses depend on risk factors, causes, strategic practicability, classifications of defects, prevalence, morbidity and mortality rates, costs, and other factors.

Some scholars postulate that incident rates of birth defects may be lowered by moral reprehension toward the environmental or corporate negligence that causes them (Ostas, 2007). For example, even if creating a product or waste product that caused birth defects was cost effective in comparison to criminal liability, most corporations would not choose a course of action that led to birth defects. Corporate agents would find such actions to be reprehensible and public outcry would negatively affect corporate reputation. Others claim that moral reprehension is not a factor, and is unrelated to risk. For example, ongoing animal studies, designed to prevent human birth defects, may be just as morally reprehensible since they may not correlate precisely to human outcomes; and they inflict birth defects on animals (Shuman, 1997). Yet, the level of moral reprehension toward animal birth defects may not be similar to that regarding human birth defects. Even if studies do not directly correlate, corporations may avoid concealing studies that potentially relate to human birth defects. One explanation may be that most individual corporate agents are deterred by criminal justice consequences, which can result in criminal sanctions for individuals and corporations (Shenon, 1985). Individual agents who are grossly negligent or intentionally fall below the standard of care by concealing potentially relevant data may be criminally sanctioned. Corporations and corporate agents may fear jurors' moral outrage in instances of criminal trials or civil trials resulting in massive punitive sanctions (Nagareda, 1998). Incidents have occurred in which medical professionals were encouraged by pharmaceutical corporations to label reports about birth defects as "inquiries" (Green, 1996). These incidents may fall into gray areas that reflect conflicting professional interests and standards, perhaps more so than concealment or immorality. Nevertheless, even the wording could give rise to professional or criminal investigations and sanctions; thus, due diligence may be required (Giles, Hamilton, and Kim, 2011).

CHAPTER 11

Criminal Justice Environments

Babies in Corrections

Some female inmates are pregnant while incarcerated; and numerous women deliver while in state custody (Babies Behind Bars, 2011). For example, some babies live behind bars at Wee Ones Nursery in Indiana Women's Prison. Advocates argue that Wee Ones Nursery lowers incarceration rates for inmates and children. Officer Morton at the prison says, "We have to show the ladies we believe in them, and we believe that they can change and make a difference for their babies; and that would make it worth it." Yet, there is only room for ten infants at any one time, while sixty inmates deliver at the hospital each year. Most inmates give birth with only hospital staff and a prison guard present. Relatives rarely attend births to support the women. Inmates support, advise, and comfort each other. Officer Morton at the prison says, "If you're pregnant and in prison, you pretty much gotta feel like you failed something really badly. [Other female inmates' support] is not changing the facts, but it's making them a whole lot better." Infants living behind bars receive medical and safety care. Women with short sentences (e.g., 18 months), who have never been convicted of a violent crime, are ideal candidates for the program.

Many inmates enter prison not knowing that they are pregnant. Many use drugs and may feel grateful that they served time during pregnancy, so that their infants were healthy throughout gestation and infancy. Prisons encourage mothers to breastfeed, but some may express milk. Because many inmates use drugs behind bars, breast milk may be tested; there is no guarantee that it is pure and substance-free. Though grandmothers care for infants living outside a prison's baby dorm, relatives are only permitted to visit once each week for four hours. Toddlers and infants visiting inmates receive full pat downs. Inmates who have good behavior can spend additional hours each month with their visiting children; at Wee Ones Nursery, inmates receive six additional hours.

Another example is the New York State Department of Corrections, where mothers who are nursing at the time they are committed to state custody may continue to nurse while in prison. Children may be born in the facility and reside with mothers until they are one year old; nursing children may accompany mothers for the same amount of time. The main criterion is that an inmate must be physically capable of providing her child with adequate care (N.Y. Correction Law § 611, 2014; 2009 N.Y. Laws, Chap. 411, 2014).

Sterilization, Insemination, and Conjugal Visits

Some prisons, such as the Mississippi Department of Corrections, do not permit conjugal visits (Mississippi Department of Corrections, 2014). The Mississippi Department of Corrections was the first department of corrections in the United States to develop a program permitting conjugal visits, yet one reason cited for recently eliminating the program is birth control (Severson, 2014). Mississippi's program provides inmates with contraceptives, but they cannot enforce that inmates use them. The department feels that babies should not be conceived by and born to parents behind bars. Conjugal programs were implemented in more than a dozen states 20 years ago; but only California, Connecticut, New Mexico, New York, and Washington currently maintain them. In New York and California, inmates must be legally married or in civil unions (i.e., same-sex couples) to participate. Another reason conjugal visits have been eliminated in state penitentiaries is the additional costs incurred when prison staff must escort and clean up after inmates. States providing such visits, such as Washington, may require inmates to pay a nightly fee; but this charge may be less reasonable in penitentiaries that only allot one hour for conjugal visits.

In *Gerber v. Hickman* (2002), an inmate who was ineligible for conjugal visits claimed a civil rights violation because prison officials prohibited him from sending semen in the mail to a hospital where his wife would be inseminated (Cusack, 2014). Both the lower and appellate courts held that procreation is incompatible with incarceration because incarcerated inmates who have been convicted of crimes lose rights to intimate association; cohabitation; sex; conception; and parenting. Artificial insemination could not be permitted to circumnavigate incarceration goals of punishing, deterring, and isolating inmates. In response to strict prison policies, some inmates have nevertheless reportedly smuggled semen to their wives, who have conceived through artificial insemination (*Daily Mail*, 2012).

In some cases, inmates may voluntarily attempt to use sterilization as birth control. However, some sterilization procedures have lacked informed consent; and a few allegedly elective procedures have been considered to be coercive (Howle, 2014). In one case, auditors in California discovered that 39 female inmates were sterilized by the state; but they may not have understood what some 17 doctors and eight hospitals were doing. The State of California prohibits females in prison from electively undergoing sterilization as birth control; but medically necessary sterilization is permitted. A total of approximately 150 female inmates were sterilized without proper consent. Proper informed consent requires that patients appear mentally competent; patients understand the permanent effects; and patients wait between 30 days and 180 days before proceeding with surgery. Informed consent for medical procedures is further discussed in Chapter 16. Over a seven-year period, 144 women cut or tied their fallopian tubes solely to practice birth control. Investigators feared that many of these surgeries were coercive.

Custodial Breaches

Guards sometimes impregnate inmates or become impregnated by inmates. Some sexual activity may be voluntary and other activity may be involuntary; however, inmates cannot legally consent to sexual conduct while incarcerated, and all guards are prohibited from having sex with inmates under their control (Cusack, 2014). In one extreme example, Bulldog, the incarcerated gang leader of the Black Guerilla Family, used several prison guards to courier contraband inside the prison (*The Huffington Post*, 2013). While in business, Bulldog earned over $15,000 each month and impregnated four corrections officers. In another example, one guard planned to conceive with a death row inmate convicted of killing two undercover police officers; she lost custody of her child because she binged on alcohol and cocaine during her third trimester, and she drove while under the influence with her baby in the car (Gregorian, 2013; Marzulli, 2013; Murphy, 2014). She faced a lengthy prison sentence for sexually abusing the inmate; but, she mitigated by citing a history of incest and sexual abuse in the military. She was sentenced to one year and one day in prison.

Sexual misconduct, including unwelcomed and forced contact, between female prisoners and prison staff was alleged in three prisons in Washington D.C. (*Women Prisoners of D.C. Dept. of Corrections v. District of Columbia*, 1994). A court in the case described a high level of tolerance for sexual misconduct and harassment and a sexualized environment that accepted sexual relations between staff and inmates. Abuse included forced kissing, fondling, rape, and sodomy; one inmate was forcibly fondled after receiving prenatal care. Rather than address malicious harassment and abuse, female prisoners were ignored and instructed to avoid guards (e.g., quit their prison jobs to avoid encounters). Officers found to violate sexual misconduct rules would possibly be reassigned, but not fired or prosecuted. In general, female inmates have a higher rate than women in the general population for contracting sexually transmitted diseases (STDs), including syphilis, HIV, AIDS, and gonorrhea, and illnesses from infection, including cervical cancer and sterility. The court held that these consequences are not acceptable forms of treatment or punishment to impose on inmates sentenced to corrections facilities.

Labor

Anecdotal evidence indicates that women experience labor while at police stations, in immigration custody, in incarceration, or in other criminal justice settings. Women are likelier to miscarry while incarcerated, and women in jail tend to have drug and trauma histories that make them likelier to miscarry (Pacillo, 1997). They also have histories of poor health care and are less educated than women in the general population. While in prison they are likelier to continue receiving poor health care and prenatal care. Thus, labor and delivery rates are lower among women prisoners.

Prison staff and police may be required to behave heroically during labor (CBS, 2012). For example, a drunk woman was arrested. After she sobered up, she was released from jail. While being escorted by police, she went into delivery. Her daughter was born a few months premature, and she needed to be resuscitated by jail staff. Because the baby was delivered prematurely to a drunken mother in police custody, Child Protective Services was notified. Another example occurred in Spain. A police officer on the Spanish National Police Force, working as a research officer, filled in for a colleague (Laly, 2004). While beginning her duty shift, she learned that a taxi driver dropped off a pregnant woman. The officer took control and safely assisted the woman through delivery. A final example is of a woman in Iowa who failed to stop when police attempted to pull over her vehicle (Kare 11, n.d.). A male driver led police for several blocks before pulling over their vehicle. She was en route to the hospital, which was two blocks away, when the baby crowned and the driver stopped. Audio from the officer's radio, paired with video from the police-cam in the officer's cruiser, recorded the moment that the newborn first began to cry inside the car while the officer stood by. The mother exclaimed, "Oh my God! He's here! He's here!" as her son was being born.

Dealing with Pregnancy in Prison

Female inmates generally lack gender-specific medical care and counseling, and pregnant inmates often lack prenatal and postnatal care and education. Policies may be unenforced and or completely lacking, while prison resources may fall below the standard of care (e.g., short-staffed). Policies may require prisons to counsel and educate women prisoners about choosing to terminate pregnancies, and to provide religious counseling on request. Written protocol may require inmates to undergo prenatal risk assessment (e.g., Problem Oriented Prenatal Risk Assessment form). Prenatal medical treatment, delineated by a step-by-step process, ensures that providers are not arbitrarily treating women or falling below the standard of care. A physical examination; conversation about breastfeeding; a pelvic exam; sexually transmitted disease (STD) testing; pregnancy and viability tests; and transvaginal ultrasonography are some important steps (Hacker, Gambone, and Hobe, 2009). During the first six months, standard care requires monthly visits; bimonthly visits during the beginning of the third trimester; and weekly visits during the ninth month.

In *Women Prisoners of D.C. v. District of Columbia* (1994), 11 women prisoners failed to receive prenatal care several months after becoming pregnant. This prevented doctors from administering timely treatment for gestational problems, such as anemia, low weight gain, poor infant growth, hypertension, and diabetes. One inmate experiencing vaginal bleeding refused to wait in lock-up as she was instructed because she feared having a miscarriage at the five-month marker of pregnancy. Lock-up would have required her to rest on a metal bed with no mattress for several hours. She did not see a doctor until after the weekend had passed. She requested prenatal treatment, but only received two examinations and one sonogram prior to delivery. On the night before delivery, she was taken to the hospital after she began experiencing labor pains, but she was returned to custody because she was not dilated and her water had not broken. However, her contractions were five minutes apart. She was handcuffed and shackled, and directed to attend her prescheduled appearance in court. Her appearance was cancelled because she suffered severe labor pain and could not walk; but she was only offered aspirin. While in her cell, she delivered her child. Before the afterbirth had passed, guards shackled and handcuffed her, and placed her in an ambulance.

Prisons may fail to offer appropriate treatment (*Women Prisoners of D.C. Dept. of Corrections v. District of Columbia*, 1994). Nutritional needs are to be examined in light of women's weight gain. One inmate was supposed to be placed on a nutritionally balanced diet, including milk and a snack at night; yet, the prison deprived her of a prescribed dietary supplement at least once, and the prison pharmacy failed to sufficiently restock vitamins on several occasions. The prison offered weekly parenting classes; biweekly prenatal exercise classes; and a therapeutic discussion group; but postpartum inmates received minimal time allowances to visit their babies. Furthermore, there was no written policy regarding mother-infant visitation except that mothers were required to hold their children during feeding. Postpartum counseling was available for mothers whose infants were critically ill or died. Postpartum depression and stress were also treated through counseling. Arrangements to place children outside prison were directed to be made as soon as pregnancy was discovered. Thus, counseling to treat separation-related trauma should have begun no later than the second trimester. One inmate claimed that she never received counseling or placement assistance. She was forced to arrange for her child to live with a woman that she met one time briefly. However, several infants were already boarded at the hospital, which indicates that arrangements could not be made. Lack of arrangements was blamed on understaffing, as were missed prenatal appointments and examinations.

Harsh Punishments

United Nations Rules for the Treatment of Women Prisoners and Non-Custodial Measures for Women Offenders (i.e., Bangkok Rules) forbid pregnant women from being placed in solitary confinement (ACLU, 2014). American prisons are not obligated to follow this rule, though corrections departments may devise policies excluding pregnant women from total isolation (e.g., New York State Department of Community Corrections) (NYCLU, 2014). Solitary confinement allegedly emotionally damages expectant mothers (ACLU, 2014). They acutely experience negative psychological consequences of solitary confinement; isolation may deprive them of medical services and prenatal health care (e.g. vitamins). In some cases, lethargy may be cause enough for pregnant women to be sent to solitary confinement. One clinically depressed pregnant woman suffered dehydration and hot temperatures in insolation while guards ignored her requests for water for several hours. Another woman was 34 weeks pregnant when she was arrested on drug charges. She received medical care (Johnston, 2014). However, the inmate experienced severe pain while in solitary confinement, and asked for medical care for several hours before giving birth alone. Her infant was pronounced dead after being transported to a hospital. In North Korea, women prisoners have been placed in solitary confinement and sent to hard-labor camps, allegedly causing miscarriages (Lyons, 2014).

Corrections policies permitting pregnant inmates to be shackled have been criticized even though such policies may call for minimal restraints. (Hershberger, 2014). For example, in Maryland, pregnant women may only be restrained if it is absolutely necessary to prevent harm or escape. Restraints must be the least restrictive available to protect mothers and fetuses while maintaining public safety. The most-restrictive restraints, involving handcuffs with a black box; leg irons; and a waist chain, cannot be used on inmates with medical issues. Moderately restrictive restraints involve handcuffs and leg irons; and least-restrictive restraints may involve flexicuffs or one handcuff securing an inmate to a wheelchair. Pregnant inmates must be secured using the least-restrictive restraints when they are in serious circumstances. If wheelchairs are not available, then flexicuffs must be secured in front using a ten-inch chain. Maryland demands detailed documentation of restraints used on pregnant inmates. In comparison to other policies and policy breeches, Maryland's policies seem progressive. The court in *Women Prisoners of D.C.* (1994) stated that Eighth Amendment violations involving pregnant inmates are not uncommon. In that case, a physician described a prison policy of shackling women during the third trimester of pregnancy and labor, which increases their chances for being injured and suffering pain. Shackling inmates during labor demonstrated deliberate indifference for prisoners' safety. Women were also denied visitation with their children, who were boarded at the institution. The prison was indifferent to inmates' needs for visitation and child placement counseling. The court found that this indifference served no penological purpose. The court upheld policies permitting expectant mothers in their third trimesters to be shackled; but ruled the other acts of indifference to be inhumane.

CHAPTER 12

Parental Duty, Child Maltreatment, and State Control

Duties

Law, justice, and the social contract impose on each person a standard of care. Each person has a duty to behave and perform responsibilities in line with the requisite standard of care expected of an individual in a particular circumstance. Falling below the standard of care results in liability. Criminal liability usually results when a person behaves in a manner that is criminally negligent, reckless, wanton, knowing, or intentional; and that breach causes harm. In general, people have a duty to behave reasonably. Duty changes according to a person's role in a given circumstance. Certain relationships create additional duties; thus, the standard of care is raised.

Professionals must use best practices or a professional standard of care, unless such professionals acting in a particular situation would not expect remuneration. In that case, professionals may sometimes be culpable for exercising a reasonable standard of care, not a professional standard of care (Lake, 1999; *McIntyre v. Ramirez*, 2003). However, volunteers who willfully take on the role of professionals during routine duties may be held to a professional standard of care. In one case, a volunteer firefighter responded to a call where he found, abandoned in a cemetery, a newborn infant covered in blood with her umbilical cord attached (AOL, 2014, May 23). She was unharmed, and was adopted five days later. Eighteen years later, he was reunited with that girl and he gave her the fleece blanket that he wrapped her in when he found her. At first, the volunteer fireman who responded to the call was given an address to the wrong cemetery. By taking the call, he committed to rendering aid; but, after failing to find the infant in the wrong cemetery, his duty to render aid likely concluded. However, his gut instinct led him to a nearby cemetery. Once he discovered the infant there, his duty to aid her resumed. A volunteer gardener at a park across the street, for example, may not have been under any duty to report the infant. The gardener could watch the infant languish and perish. However, once the infant died, the gardener may have a duty to report the location of a corpse.

A minority of states impose a duty to call police if a serious crime is occurring (*Anderson v. Atchison*, 1948; *Cornell v. State*, 1947; *Dove v. Lowden*, 1942; *Hollinbeck v. Downey*, 1962; *Johnston v. De La Guerra Properties*, 1946; *Jones v. U.S.*, 1962; *Martin v. Jones*, 1953; Osbeck, 1985; *Palmer v. State*, 1960; *State v. Benton*, 1936). In some jurisdictions, the duty only arises if parties share a special relationship. For example, employees may be owed a higher duty by employers that they will not be harmed at work. People in a few states may have a duty to assist civil servants (e.g., police officers or firefighters) when requested to do so in an emergency. This duty is likely very limited and would not harm the volunteer.

Generally, there is no duty to aid infants, pregnant women, or rape victims during emergencies. Aid includes calling police or reporting crime (*Bemis v. Edwards*, 1995). However, the law in this area is nuanced. Certain individuals may have a duty; certain crimes may create a duty; and certain victims may be owed a duty depending on the circumstances. For example, in Minnesota, reasonable assistance must be rendered by a witness who knows or has reason to know that a person has been wounded by gunfire (Minn. Stat. § 609.662, 2014). The duty requires that a witness investigate a victim's injuries and immediately render reasonable aid. When a person harms another in self-defense, the person performing self-defense may be required to render aid after injuring the attacker (*Pope v. State*, 1979). Aid may be required if it can safely be performed. Victims and witnesses are not required to place themselves in harm's way to perform these duties. Placing oneself in significant risk of harm is unreasonable. If an attacker has not been incapacitated, those who render aid may be placed in unreasonable risk (*Kuntz v. District Court*, 2000; *State v. Bier*, 1979). Attackers may be incapacitated with deadly force by bystanders who witness attacks, but bystanders are under no obligation to render aid (*People v. Bowman*, 1971; *People v. Williams*, 1965). One of the most common exceptions to the general rule that there is no duty to aid victims arises after automobile collisions. In most jurisdictions, people involved in car accidents have a duty to render aid (*Karl v. C. A. Reed Lumber Co.*, 1969; *People v. Monismith*, 1969). The degree of aid required varies by jurisdiction. In some jurisdictions, motorists may be required to notify police or may be required to render reasonable aid. "Reasonable" may be defined by case law.

The U.S. Supreme Court has held that the government does not have a duty to protect citizens from private violence (*Deshaney v. Winnebago City Social Services Department*, 1989; Klein and Orloff, 1993). When the state took custody of a young boy, and failed to prevent him from being exposed to his father's violence pursuant to a modified visitation order, the boy brought a civil action. The court held that it was a not a substantive Due Process violation for the county to permit visitation. Taking custody of the boy with the desire to protect him from violence did not create a "special relationship" that created an additional or heightened duty. The state does not have to protect children from dangers that it did not create. The court reasoned that perhaps if the state had limited the child's ability to protect himself from his father, then perhaps a greater duty would have been owed.

Even though pregnant mothers do not owe a high duty to fetuses, they owe some. This is discussed in Chapter 14 and Chapter 16. Mothers may have a duty to receive assistance during childbirth that is adequate to ensure safe delivery. If neglecting to receive proper care and medical attention during delivery results in a child's death during birth, then a mother may be held culpable for involuntary manslaughter. In one case, an eighteen-year-old mother may have known that she was pregnant; but, she never sought care and lived in a state of denial for several months during her pregnancy (*U.S. v. Riley*, 1997). Late in her pregnancy, she went to a hospital emergency room because she was experiencing excruciating pain. While doctors were waiting for lab results from her pregnancy test, the woman delivered a child in the hospital waiting room. She said that while on the toilet she experienced an instinct to push and a child "squirted out" and hit the floor (*U.S. v. Riley*, 1997, p. 606). The child immediately died from head fractures; and the woman left the corpse covered in blood and paper towels in the bathroom. Because a doctor had already initiated a pregnancy test, and hospital staff knocked on the door during delivery, the court found that the woman behaved negligently by not accepting medical assistance. She was culpable of disregarding foreseeable consequences and negligently impeding assistance.

Parents always owe the highest duty to their children. Parents have a duty to render aid to their children. The degree of assistance required varies according to circumstance and jurisdiction. In *Romley v. Dairman* (2004), the court held that a representative could be appointed for a minor victim if a minor's parents or guardians did not act in a child's best interest. Parents who fail to believe that a defendant injured their child may not be acting in their child's best interest, even though a defendant is not at fault for their child's injury. Thus, parents may owe their children a duty to believe that they were injured.

A parent-child duty exists when children cohabit with adults who are not their legal guardians, if a relationship between the adult and child is similar to a parent-child relationship. Psychological parents or people entrusted with care over a child may have relationships that are similar to child-parent relationships. At common law, these relationships raise a duty to protect a child; and if duty is breached, then a cohabiting adult may be convicted of criminal endangerment (*State v. Hocter*, 2011). In *State v. Kuntz* (2000), a defendant was convicted of criminal endangerment after he swung his girlfriend's baby headfirst into a crib. The six-month-old baby sustained serious bodily injury. The court found that children who live with cohabiting adults are owed a duty. At common law, wives were not obligated to report husbands' felonies; however, witnessing felony child abuse obligates mothers to render aid (e.g., inform the authorities). Mothers who fail to render aid may be convicted of abuse or aiding the defendant (Hanson, 2014).

Once a person begins to render aid, assistance must be administered in a safe and reasonable manner. Behaving reasonably under the circumstances (i.e., duty) may require people to respond to and be aware of many factors. People "acting in loco parentis . . . [are liable for] creating a substantial risk of harm to [a child]'s health or safety by violating a duty of care, protection, or support" (*State v. Johnson*, 2009, p. 1). They may be liable for other charges when "the violation . . . result[s] in serious physical harm to [a child]" (*State v. Johnson*, 2009, p. 1). In several cases, defendants have been charged with criminal endangerment for failing to call for emergency assistance for infants; and excessively attempting to treat or resolve medical issues without emergency care. Sometimes courts hold defendants responsible for poor responses only after defendants cause injuries to infants and then attempt to treat them or take them to a hospital. Failing to take an infant to the nearest hospital and opting for a more distant hospital in another state may be a factor in a conviction for child endangerment.

Defendants may choose to delay emergency responses when they believe that it will minimize evidence of their crimes. For example, fractures to an infant's bones may begin to heal after one week. People who delay more than a week to bring infants to the hospital may be hiding evidence.

However, failure to call immediately for emergency care may not be sufficient evidence of gross negligence demonstrating reckless disregard for an infant's life (*Davis v. Commonwealth*, 2012). In one case, a defendant observed unusual spit-up. The defendant patted the child's back and swept the child's airways. He changed the child's diaper twice and bathed the child. He called and consulted with the child's regular caregiver. He attempted to administer CPR for approximately 15 or 20 minutes to the child, who appeared to be distressed. Finally, he called 9-1-1. His actions may have demonstrated that he did not ignore the child. He did not avoid calling 9-1-1 because he was grossly negligent or wanted to hide evidence of abuse.

Gross and wanton reckless disregard for human life is judged under an objective standard. A defendant must know or should have known that his actions would probably result in an infant's death or injury (*Ferguson v. Commonwealth*, 2008; *Kelly v. Commonwealth*, 2004; *Mosby v. Commonwealth*, 1996). Negligence is generally a civil matter. Thus, criminal negligence requires recklessness that demonstrates callous disregard for human life and probable injury or death (*Bell v. Commonwealth*, 1938; *Keech v. Commonwealth*, 1989; *Wright v. Osborne*, 1940). Failing to call 9-1-1 immediately is not necessarily heedless shirking of legal duty, especially if a defendant sought advice and rendered emergency aid (*Tubman v. Commonwealth*, 1986). Wantonness is manifested by arrogant, merciless, inhumane, reckless, or unjust violation of others' rights or feelings.

In some jurisdictions, those who render aid that results in harm may be excused civilly and criminally. These are known as Good Samaritan laws. People may be discouraged from attempting to render aid if they believe they would be held liable. Thus, Good Samaritan laws are policy-based. However, aid must be rendered in a reasonable manner. It cannot be grossly negligent or reckless. Once assistance begins, a rescuer may be obligated to continue rendering aid if the victim will be in a worse position because of the initial attempts. If charged with criminal endangerment or criminal recklessness, a defendant may only claim a Good Samaritan defense by admitting to the elements of a crime (*Shaw v. Texas*, 2007). The elements include the physical acts (i.e., *actus reus*) and the mental state (i.e., *mens rea*). The law provides a defense for good faith, reasonable attempts to administer emergency medical care. A Good Samaritan defense is a justification that follows a confession. The conduct and mental state are not negated by the defendant who invokes the defense. If a defendant denies intent to injure a child, then the defendant may not be able to use a Good Samaritan defense.

In *Shaw*, a grandmother could not claim a Good Samaritan defense of shaking her grandchild if she shook her grandson and hit his head against objects. The government argued that, in fact, she shook and struck her grandson because she was angry. His injuries led to his death. She administered CPR to resuscitate him after inflicting the injuries. She claimed that CPR inflicted the injuries. She did not believe that these actions were the only way to administer CPR; yet, she knew that she might cause head injuries. Therefore, she was not entitled to a Good Samaritan defense. Yet, attempting to render aid or administer CPR may be considered a mitigating factor when a person cannot claim a Good Samaritan defense and is convicted of criminal endangerment (*Cathey v. State*, 2010).

Criminal Abuse

Child abuse is a serious crime. Scholars and legislatures have analyzed whether corporal punishment, humiliation, and other severe forms of discipline constitute child abuse. In some jurisdictions they may. However, allegations of abuse must be determined on a case-by-case-basis; and often, facts are considered under the totality of the circumstances (Fla. Stat. § 827.03, 2014). Clear instances of abuse may involve intentional physical or mental injury to a child. An actor need not be a parent to commit child abuse. Intent may be determined by the reasonable likelihood that a child would be injured. Individuals who actively encourage others to mentally or physically harm children are also culpable of child abuse. Some intentional abuse may be legally justifiable. For example, a mother was beaten and shot to death by her intimate partner (Hastings, 2014). As she was being abused, she placed her baby inside a toilet and covered the infant with her body. Her intentions were likely to protect the child, who survived but had a traumatic head injury. Under normal circumstances, placing an infant in a toilet may be life threatening; and, in this case, it may have caused a head injury. However, in this circumstance, the mother did not act maliciously. Malicious punishment or willful torture may be aggravated abuse. Some jurisdictions do not protect family members from psychological abuse or mental injury. In jurisdictions where children are protected from mental injury, the government may require evidence of substantial impairment to prove injury. Aggravated child abuse is a first-degree felony; willfully abusing a child without causing great harm is often a third-degree felony.

When child abuse is reported to a tip hotline, hotline operators notify staff of whether a protective investigation must promptly be conducted onsite. Allegations of abuse are also reported to local law enforcement. If allegations of abuse are substantiated and investigators have probable cause, then the accused party will be charged. The allegedly abused child will be placed in state custody or with a temporary guardian; a great deal of evidence is required for removal (*Nicholas v. Scoppetta*, 2004). The department may offer services to families who have been cleared of any serious allegations of mistreatment. For example, families may receive therapy; transportation; clothing; and food.

When intimate partners and children have been abused, they may need to flee their homes (Hardesty, 2011). Research among lesbian couples shows that decisions to report abuse and seek formal help correlate with victims' connections with informal networks. These findings are generalizable to all kinds of victims of domestic violence; but same-sex couples may experience greater difficulty protecting their children due to stigmatization of homosexual parents.

Fetuses under State Control

States have some interest in fetal health and well-being. A Wisconsin court held that a viable fetus is a person who cannot be abused (*State v. Kruzicki*, 1995). The court discussed dicta from *Roe v. Wade* (1973), explaining that the state's legitimate interest in protecting fetal life becomes sufficiently compelling when a fetus is viable. Wisconsin law protects at-risk children. Wisconsin's court said that in light of the government's interest in protecting potential children, Wisconsin law applied to viable fetuses; and, that the government has an interest in making the womb a safe environment for viable fetuses. Fetuses are not legal persons, but they may be assigned a guardian *ad litem* by the court. The court also discussed *State v. Black* (1994), where a defendant committed feticide in violation of a statute prohibiting anyone other than a mother from intentionally killing an unborn child. The *Black* court held that the government had an interest in protecting all unborn children from being killed by anyone other than the mother, who may legally terminate a pregnancy using a medical procedure. The court also discussed *Puhl v. Milwaukee* (1959), where a pre-viable fetus was injured in a car collision. In either *Black* or *Puhl,* one way to limit the state's interest could be to determine whether a fetus was injured post-viability; the other way is to invoke the state's interest if the injured child is born alive irrespective of when the injury occurred. The court highlighted public policy, stating that injured fetuses should not be deprived of their ability to be born. Thus, each jurisdiction may delimit when the state's interest is sufficiently compelling.

A juvenile court may have jurisdiction over a viable fetus for a few reasons; however, government custody may place fetuses, infants, and mothers at risk. First, the state may have jurisdiction if a juvenile is adjudicated delinquent (*In re K.E.A.,* 2012). Delinquent environments threaten fetuses' well-being, but juvenile detention also increases risk; thus, juvenile court should not assume control of fetuses unless their health and safety are at serious risk of harm. A fetus that is in an unsafe environment or is substantially at risk warrants governmental assumption of guardianship. At-risk environments may include unstable and violent environments. A juvenile's refusal to follow a guardian's or parent's advice may indicate instability; however, minors are emancipated from their parents with respect to medical decisions for fetuses. Some states require minors to seek permission from their parents to abort unless seeking permission would result in harm (e.g., domestic violence) (Wood, 2014). In some cases, judicial bypass may permit abortions when guardians or parents cannot be asked for consent. Thus, a second way that a court may have jurisdiction over a fetus is judicial bypass. Judicial bypass may be denied if minors are insufficiently mature to have abortions; yet, pregnancy may result in foster parents surrendering foster children to the state. Thus, a third way is when a minor mother lives in state care. Children born to minor mothers may be forced to live in state custody with their mothers. In general, children in foster care and state custody are targeted for sexual exploitation; thus, infants are at increased risk for abuse irrespective of whether the entry point is delinquency or state custody (*State v. Steer,* 1986).

A mother's threat against a fetus may lead to a state taking custody of a baby. In one case, a mother required medication due to severe mental problems that included seizures, narcissism, bipolar disorder, and explosive disorder (*In re D.W.M., Jr.,* 2014). The baby's father was mentally retarded and was incarcerated for manslaughter and aggravated child rape. The mother stopped taking medication during pregnancy; thus, she began resisting medical advice and threatening self-harm and harm to the fetus. She threatened to drown herself if doctors did not deliver her baby prematurely. Because she was a high risk, doctors institutionalized her and delivered the baby three weeks early. The Department of Children's Services (DCS) was notified, and they investigated the parents' home, which was filthy, cluttered, and infested. The mother neglected to feed her newborn and to keep the infant healthy. DCS filed a petition for dependency and neglect in juvenile court. When the child was four days old, DCS removed the baby and placed the infant in foster care. The infant was ordered to be a dependent of the state. DCS planned to adopt the child or reunify him with his parents. Reunification required parents to maintain a stable home environment; complete parenting classes; adhere to a mental health treatment plan; and submit to supervised therapeutic parenting sessions. Even though both parents complied with the parenting plan, DCS filed a petition to terminate parental rights due to parental mental incompetence.

Neglect and Abandonment

Neglect results when a parent or caregiver fails to provide care, supervision, or means to maintain a child's well-being (Fla. Stat. § 827.03, 2014). This may include failure to provide food, clothing, health care, shelter, or supervision; or to prevent a child from being abused or neglected by another person. Generally, abandonment may result when a parent fails to contact a child or provide any money to the minor for a specified amount of time (e.g., one year). Neglect may traumatize children. Some of the most violent members of society attempt to mitigate their crimes by claiming that they were abused or neglected as children; or their mothers used intoxicating substances during pregnancy (Brendel and Soulier, 2009; *Sochor v. State*, 2004). Thus, some serious effects of neglect are not localized to families; they are diffused onto society at large.

A study of 400 women in Appalachian New York State and 1,139 in Memphis, Tennessee measured whether certain demographic characteristics are prevalent among postpartum mothers who develop conduct disorders and antisocial behavior (Olds et al., 1998). Researchers found that among New Yorkers, 85 percent of them were either minors, unmarried, or of low income. In Memphis, 65 percent were low-income minors. Participation in the research program reduced risk in three capacities. First, mothers were less likely to abuse substances during pregnancy. This is discussed further in Chapter 13. Second, mothers were less likely to maltreat their children. Third, persistent reliance on government aid, family size, and closely timed pregnancies were reduced. The presence of a single factor increased risk for antisocial behavior and conduct disorders, but co-occurrence significantly increased risks for delinquency, violence, and crime. Prenatal and early childhood programs that include home visitation may also reduce risks.

Criminal justice system responses and situational factors may affect outcomes of neglect. Researchers found that women with cocaine dependence who neglect their children, but retain custody, are different from cocaine-addicted mothers who lose custody (Brogan, 2013). Poor, urban, cocaine-addicted mothers who lost custody of their infants experienced greater postpartum impairment, including psychological and functional impairment. Non-custodial mothers were likelier to have risky sex, employment problems, and experience homelessness. Yet, one reason that mothers neglect children is the difficulty of both working and caring for children; thus, women who lost custody also found it difficult to attend drug treatment programs while caring for their children. Thus, custodial mothers were less likely to have received any drug treatment. More than mothers who retained custody, mothers who lost custody experienced somatoform and affective disorders, psychosis, distress, and childhood trauma. Traumatic experiences included neglect and physical abuse; thus, neglect, like abuse, may be a cycle in some women's lives. For example, a 10-month-old infant was abandoned at a train station (AOL, 2014, July 8). Her mother was a prostitute who drove a stolen Mercedes and was facing charges on numerous prostitution arrests. The baby was examined by doctors, but they found that the child suffered no trauma. However, the child's father, who was unaware that his child had been abandoned, indicated that the child's mother had a history of trauma. He attributed her actions to trauma, saying "I think it's because she had a tragic past. . . . She was holding all of that in."

CHAPTER 13

Pregnant on Drugs

Delivery

Over the past 20 years, approximately 90 percent of female drug abusers have been of childbearing age (Saloum, Epstein, and Frost, 2012). Anesthesiologists may encounter drug users or abusers who are entering labor or during emergencies (e.g., fetal distress or placental abruption). Because drug use and drug abuse are possible, and increase risk to patients, anesthesiologists may screen patients for risk factors, including premature labor, absence of prenatal care, and alcohol use. Risk factors could correlate with use of cocaine, opioids, amphetamines, and marijuana. Pregnant patients who use or abuse substances are very likely to lie or play down their substance consumption. Suspiciousness may be appropriate and demonstrate best practices. Nonjudgmental questioning may be necessary to verify suspicions. If patients disclose drug use or abuse, but anesthesiologists do not respond appropriately, then criminal charges may be brought, depending on the level of negligence. In some jurisdictions, doctors can face some of the same charges used to prosecute mothers who harm fetuses in utero. Civil remedies may also be permitted under wrongful-death statutes. Civil recovery for wrongful death may be possible if patients die due to anesthesia, irrespective of their personal drug use (*Glenn v. Performance Anesthesia,* 2011). Doctors are not liable for fetal death if termination was intended and lawful; but doctors may be liable if patients die due to negligently or recklessly administered anesthesia that departs from the professional standard of care. Doctors need not be incompetent to be grossly negligent (*Kearl v. Board of Medical Quality Assurance*, 1986).

In the past, especially before abortion was legal, numerous criminal and civil actions were brought on behalf of patients who died as the result of illegal abortions. Doctors, anesthesiologists, and unlicensed practitioners have been charged with murder, attempted illegal abortion, and other related charges. In some cases, courts were tasked to decide whether illegal abortions or anesthesia were the proximate cause of patients' deaths. Jurors in one case found that the precise cause of death was unknowable; thus, reducing the charge to aggravated battery. In another case, a victim was anesthetized with sodium pentothal (*People v. Jackson*, 1963). The defendant began the abortion and likely internally punctured the victim. The defendant administered atropine and Dilaudid, and then gave the victim sodium pentothal. The victim stopped breathing, but rather than take her to a nearby hospital or contact the police, the offender attempted to revive the victim for more than one hour. The victim died from bilateral pulmonary congestion caused by sodium pentothal. Death was unforeseeable and accidental in this case, even though sodium pentothal is a strong and dangerous drug that should only be administered in hospitals when nurses may attend to patients. The defendant claimed that the anesthesia was an intervening and superseding cause; and that the puncture wound was not the proximate cause of death. If the puncture wound, created during a felonious illegal abortion, would have caused the victim to die, then the defendant would have been guilty of second-degree murder. However, if the anesthesia killed the victim, then the defendant would have been guilty of manslaughter because the sodium pentothal superseded the causation of the puncture wound. In another case, a defendant was tried for murder (*Huntington v. San Francisco*, 1907). The victim likely died from anesthesia administered during a surgical operation. The defendant denied having knowledge of the victim's pregnancy. The defendant also denied intending to perform an abortion. The prosecution contended that an instruction for manslaughter was inappropriate because the defendant had knowledge of the pregnancy and intended to perform an abortion. Thus, the victim was murdered. However, the defendant was convicted of manslaughter.

Addicted Mothers

In the past 25 years, several hundred mothers in more than 30 states have been prosecuted for harming fetuses with substances (Ala. Code § 26-15-3.2, 2011; Alaska Stat. § 11.51.110, 2011; Del. Code Ann. tit. 11, § 1102, 2011; Haw. Rev. Stat. § 709-904, 2011; Idaho Code Ann. § 37-2737A,

2011; Ky. Rev. Stat. Ann. § 218A.1441-1443, 2011; La. Rev. Stat. Ann. § 14:93, 2011; Minn. Stat. Ann § 609.378, 2011; Murphy, 2014; N.D. Cent. Code § 19-03.1-22.2, 2011; Nev. Rev. Stat. § 453.3325, 2011; Ohio Rev. Code Ann. § 2919.22, 2011; Or. Rev. Stat. § 163.575, 2011; Utah Code Ann. § 76-5-112.5, 2011; Wyo. Stat. Ann. § 6-4-405, 2011). Laws vary about whether women may be prosecuted for using alcohol or drugs during pregnancy; or whether use must be extreme or result in harm to fetuses. Some laws mandate women cannot knowingly consume substances or excessive quantities of some substances that result in harm to fetuses; but other laws require women to avoid any recreational substance use during certain months (Gonzalez, 2014; Mohney, 2014). The legality of substance use or substance abuse during pregnancy may turn on a few issues (*Collins v. State*, 1994; *Commonwealth v. Welch*, 1993; *Herron v. State*, 2000; *Hillman v. State*, 1998; *Johnson v. State*, 1992; *Kilmon v. State*, 2006; *People v. Bedenkop*, 1993; *People v. Hardy*, 1991; *Reyes v. Superior Court*, 1977; *State v. Aiwohi*, 2005; *State v. Ashley*, 1997; *State v. Deborah J.Z.*, 1999; *State v. Dunn*, 1996; *State v. Eagle Hawk*, 1987; *State v. Gethers*, 1991; *State v. Gray*, 1992; *State v. Luster*, 1992; *State v. Reinesto*, 1995; *Ward v. State*, 2006; *Washoe County v. Encoe*, 1994).

Drug-using mothers in various jurisdictions may experience significantly different outcomes. First, states' treatment of fetuses as legal persons may affect whether mothers' substance use can be held by statute to harm fetuses (Neil, 2014). If fetuses are not persons, then they may not be protected under specific statutes protecting people from harm. Even when personhood is not granted to viable fetuses, though, legislatures may or may not specifically protect them from particular forms of abuse (e.g., murder or criminal recklessness) (Miss. Code Ann. § 97-3-19, 2006; *State v. McKnight*, 2003). Second, drug use may be distinguishable from addiction. Addiction may not be criminalized, but possession may be prosecuted; and addiction may be treated. Third, jurisdictions may distinguish between substances (e.g., alcohol, Schedule 1 drugs, and Schedule 2 drugs). Schedule 1 drugs include illegal drugs (e.g., cocaine, and methamphetamines). Schedule 2 drugs include highly addictive prescription drugs (e.g., OxyContin) and other prescription medication. Fourth, cases may turn on degree or intent of exposure. Mothers have been prosecuted for exposing fetuses to controlled substances (Ala. Code § 26-15-3.2, 2011; Murphy, 2014). Chemical endangerment laws mainly relate to exposure of children to fumes or byproducts of drug production, but statutes can be applied to a variety of scenarios. If children die after being exposed to controlled substances, then mothers may face felony charges and ten years' incarceration (Ala. Code § 13A-5-6(a)(1), 2011; Murphy, 2014).

Pregnant women may produce, possess, and consume alcohol moderately in public in certain jurisdictions (Fentiman, 2009). Several jurisdictions (e.g., South Dakota, South Carolina, and Wisconsin) criminalize alcohol consumption by pregnant women (Stogner, 2010). Some legislatures have addressed the problem after courts found that existing statutes could not protect fetuses from mothers' alcohol abuse because fetuses were not humans (*State v. Deborah J.Z.*, 1999; Wis. Stat. Ann. § 48.193, 2008). Under some laws, women must know that they are pregnant to be held liable. Other statutes may require that women be offered voluntary treatment prior to legal intervention.

Pregnant addicts may prioritize addiction over motherhood (Mohapatra, 2011; Murphy, 2014; Player, 2014). In some cases, addiction causes women to fear legal repercussions more than health repercussions. Thus, they avoid disclosing addiction to health care providers because they fear that disclosure may serve as an entry point into the criminal justice system. For example, an alcoholic woman in Wisconsin was charged with attempted first-degree intentional homicide and first-degree reckless injury because she went into labor while drinking at a bar. She reported alcoholism to a nurse at the hospital. She was convicted by the lower court, but the Wisconsin Court of Appeals overturned the case because they found that, at that time, a fetus was not a person protected by Wisconsin's criminal statutes under which the woman was charged and convicted. It is estimated that approximately 25 percent of women consume alcohol while pregnant; thus, it is probably likely that women underreport consumption to avoid potential entanglements with the law. However, in some cases, health care providers warn addicted mothers and encourage them to control addictions or to seek treatment (*Reyes v. Superior Court of San Bernardino County*, 1977). Reporting may only result after warnings fail, but women may not be aware of legal nuances before they disclose.

Mental illness may cause women to abuse substances. Mental illness and pregnancy are discussed further in Chapter 16. Expectant mothers may self-medicate depression. In some cases, women may become depressed, delusional, or suffer from mental illness related to substance abuse. Women who attempt to commit suicide during pregnancy by consuming poison or substances may be charged in some cases. In one case, a woman in Indiana swallowed poison and was charged with murder and attempted feticide after her child was born alive but died shortly thereafter (*Shuai v. State*, 2012). However, she pled to a lesser charge of criminal recklessness.

Civil commitment is typically reserved for persons with mental illness, but addicted mothers who cannot control addictions during pregnancy may be civilly committed. Mothers who are addicted to alcohol may be no exception to these statutes (Stogner, 2010). Addiction alone does not qualify as mental illness. However, many states permit civil commitment of addicted persons. Some proponents argue that civil commitment is a positive alternative to incapacitation through incarceration. Critics argue that this measure inappropriately labels or stigmatizes addiction as mental illness. In Indiana, the applicable statute defines mental illness as "a psychiatric disorder that substantially disturbs an individual's thinking, feeling, or behavior and impairs the individual's ability to function . . . [including] alcoholism, and addiction to narcotics or dangerous drugs" (Ind. Code § 12-7-2-130, 2014). Thus, the statute specifically includes addiction for any persons, and does not inappropriately label or civilly commit addicts (Derringer, 2010). In Minnesota, civil commitment statutes are narrowed because the legislature delimits certain drugs to which a qualifying "chemically dependent person" may be addicted (Fitzpatrick, 2012). The list includes alcohol, opiates, cocaine, PCP, amphetamines, and marijuana. Civil commitment is not a criminal measure, it is a civil remedy; thus, it does not violate *stare decisis* holding that defendants cannot be singled out and prosecuted because they are substance abusers (*Robinson v. California*, 1962).

In many states, substance use and substance abuse could be grounds for child removal in family court. Mothers who are unable to provide proper care for infants may be ordered to participate in programs for drug treatment; may lose custody; and may have parental rights terminated, in addition to facing criminal charges (*Kilmon v. State*, 2006). However, criminal remedies are not available in every jurisdiction; and the court may be limited to civil remedies (*Cochran v. Commonwealth*, 2010).

Critics have argued that fathers should be held responsible in civil and criminal cases if they were intoxicated or addicted to drugs (e.g., cocaine) that passed through sperm into embryos contributing to birth defects (Pacillo, 1997). Birth defects are discussed in Chapter 10. Others argue that consequences should be imposed on fathers who knowingly impregnated a drug-addicted woman. Though these arguments raise important gender equality issues, in some legal contexts they may be considered to be specious. The law mainly addresses child abuse and neglect resulting from fathers' actions after children are born, and reserves control over and responsibility for fetuses to women (Daniels, 1997).

Addicted Infants

Black Letter Law regarding women's rights and obligations during pregnancy is not well synthesized. A woman seems to be under no obligation to care for an early pregnancy (Dolgin, 1991). In some jurisdictions, pregnant women may have the right to damage an embryo through the legal use of alcohol, caffeine, tobacco, and other drugs that could potentially cause lifelong deficiencies to fetuses. If a woman decides to carry a child to term, then she may no longer be free to consume substances that could endanger her pregnancy at any point. Moreover, some commentators have suggested that a woman who has the right to abort does not automatically have a fundamental right to engage in embryo abuse, which could manifest as a defect later (*Gonzales v. Carhart*, 2007; *Roe v. Wade*, 1973). The greater power to kill the fetus may not necessarily include the lesser power to injure it. Case law seems to show that as long as the infant's injuries or deficiencies are not evident near the time of birth a mother will not likely be held liable when defects manifest later (Dolgin, 1991). If any defect (e.g., addiction) is noticeable at birth, the state may attempt to causally link the mother's drug use during pregnancy to the deficiency and prosecute her. The loss of viable pregnancies (e.g., stillbirths) due to the consumption of substances during pregnancy has also been prosecuted in some states (Cusack, 2011; Mills, 1998; Vestal, 2007).

Many laws designed to protect fetuses from addiction and harm were formulated in response to the "crack baby" scare of the 1980s and 1990s (Reese and Burry, 2004). The scare caused the public and legislatures to believe that fetuses exposed to drugs in utero would be born as "little junkies" who suffer long-term predisposition to addiction, permanent brain damage, and impeded development (Shannon and Walker, 2008). "Crack babies" are somewhat mythical, but some effects of drug exposure may be serious and can be long term. Schedule 1 drugs include illegal drugs (e.g., cocaine and methamphetamines) that have been linked to abnormalities in infants. These drugs have been the main ones blamed for "crack babies"; however, myths about the long-term physical effects of drug use on persons born to mothers who abused drugs (e.g., "meth babies" and "crack babies") have been dispelled in recent years.

Infants who suffer from Neonatal Abstinence Syndrome experience withdrawal symptoms (Tennessee Department of Health, 2014). Withdrawal may be immediate and may continue for as long as a similarly addicted adult would experience withdrawal. Infants may be addicted to opiates or drugs prescribed to treat addiction. For example, mothers treated for heroin addiction may deliver infants addicted to methadone. Thus, attempts to treat pregnant drug addicts can result in separate addictions. Tennessee's legislature recently criminalized substance use by pregnant mothers to protect fetuses and deter abuse (Pub. Ch. 820, 2014). In 2013 in Tennessee, 921 infants were born drug-addicted; at midyear in 2014, 253 infants had been born addicted (Gonzalez, 2014). Many of these infants were addicted to Schedule 2 painkillers. Addiction not only results from abuse of highly addictive Schedule 1 and Schedule 2 drugs (Tennessee Department of Health, 2014). Infants may also become addicted when mothers use prescribed medicine as directed.

Though the "crack baby" scare has passed, many mothers now give birth to infants who are addicted to prescription drugs, which are Schedule 2 drugs. In South Florida, the epidemic is particularly inflamed. Pain clinics in that region supply individual addicts with hundreds of pain pills each week; and addicts' children are born addicted to oxycodone and other heavy medications. Infants suffer from withdrawal and other serious health complications. Pharmaceutical drugs are classified according to their potential level of risk to fetuses when used as directed by a doctor; pregnancy categories are A, B, C, D, and X, ranging from least risky to most risky. Oxycodone taken during early pregnancy pertains to Pregnancy Category B, meaning that it may have some adverse effects but no truly harmful effects to fetuses will result. Later-term use may be designated Category C because risks of fetal withdrawal may increase. Some critics suggest that these highly addictive drugs should undergo greater clinical trials because dosages prescribed at pain clinics are much higher than dosages in clinical trials. Thus, previous studies underestimate risk to fetuses when mothers take drugs as prescribed.

Differences between opiate and cocaine addiction, infants' gender, and environmental factors have helped to tease apart generalized pandemonium about "crack babies." Sequelae of cocaine exposure among infants and toddlers, including anthropometric growth, neurobehavior, sensory functioning, language development, cognitive development, and motor skills, has been be less severe than among opioid-exposed infants in some studies (Bandstra et al., 2010; Best, Segal, and Day, 2009).

Opioid-exposed infants may suffer from Neonatal Abstinence Syndrome and more neurobehavioral deficits in comparison to cocaine-exposed infants, whose decrements may be more subtle. The month during which particular drugs are administered also effect behavioral and cognitive outcomes for infants (Dow-Edwards, 2010). Heroin-addicted mothers may be more amenable to addiction treatment after month six of pregnancy through to the month following birth. Women who can be detoxified from heroin prior to giving birth may have nonaddicted infants (Comer and Annitto, 2004). Mothers addicted to cocaine may be less predictable in their habits. In some sense, that unpredictability may pose a greater threat to society and contribute to the stigmatization of "crack babies." Babies born addicted to heroin are likelier than nonaddicted infants to experience trauma (Carroll et al., 1995; Emanuel, 1996). Trauma may result from withdrawal, as well as from being in medical isolation and treatment during early infancy juxtaposed with neglectful parenting later on. Trauma may later correlate with inability to meaningfully process emotional experiences, self-medication, mental illness, cycles of abuse, and encounters with the criminal justice system. Caregiving environments clearly play a role in how the effects of drug exposure limit or are overcome by children. Learned behavior, social challenges, and academic deficiencies may stymie development and wellness of drug-exposed infants during their teen years. Environment may affect genders differently. Females may become hyperresponsive to stressed environments, even though several studies indicate that male fetuses are more affected than female fetuses by cocaine use.

In several states, prosecutors have attempted to prosecute mothers under statutes designed to protect children when children have been born addicted to drugs. Some courts have held that the definition of "child" in child protection statutes does not include fetuses; and that the harms affecting fetuses do not meet statutory elements (*State v. Geiser*, 2009; *State v. Wade*, 2007). Alleged harms inflicted on fetuses during pregnancy or on children before they were born do not satisfy certain statutes designed to protect children after they have been born. For example, child endangerment may be an inapplicable charge (*Kilmon v. State*, 2006; *State v. Martinez*, 2006). In some jurisdictions, prosecution for reckless endangerment has succeeded; but, in other jurisdictions, it has failed (*Ward v. State*, 2006). Courts may find that endangerment results when mothers are reckless irrespective of whether children have been born. Depending on statutes' wording, transferring drugs to a child may result when children consume or absorb drugs in utero (*State v. Aiwohi*, 2005). Many states implicitly analogize miscarriages to fetal overdose and specifically permit parents to be charged with manslaughter; however, other states have overturned convictions for manslaughter unless infants die from harm inflicted after birth (*Collins v. State*, 1994; *Reinesto v. Superior Court*, 1995; *State v. Dunn*, 1996). Courts and legislatures may define "victim" or "person" in applicable statutes to include fetuses. In one case, a mother was convicted based on drug use during her pregnancy, but her conviction was overturned. The infant died days after birth, but the Hawaii Supreme Court held that at the time of the allegedly criminal conduct, the fetus was not a person protected by the statute (*Reyes v. Superior Ct.*, 1977; *State v. Aiwohi*, 2005).

Drug Treatment and Rehabilitation

Drug abuse is linked with approximately two million arrests annually (Brendel and Soulier, 2009; Brogan, 2013). This represents approximately 14 percent of all arrests. Approximately 80 percent of drug-related arrests are for possession; and of those, almost half are for marijuana possession. Mishandling prescription drugs has become a leading cause of incarceration and death (*Prison Legal News*, 2013). Women are arrested and incarcerated for drug-related offenses at much lower rates than men; and women's crimes are often less violent. Most incarcerated women have committed nonviolent drug crimes, such as taking drugs not prescribed to them. Yet, retrospective data analysis demonstrates that over the past few decades women may be disproportionately incarcerated for drug crimes. Thus, drug treatment programs to divert women from prison may be necessary. A couple of states mandate prenatal screening for substance abuse; but most women are not obligated to undergo pregnancy or drug testing during criminal proceedings. Thus, identifying pregnant substance abusers can be difficult or limited by court authority and the scope of charges.

In general, drug abuse and child neglect have high rates of comorbidity. Of 513 children exposed in utero to drugs, 30 percent were later involved in tips about child abuse or neglect; and authorities substantiated nearly 20 percent of the reports (Brendel and Soulier, 2009). Almost three quarters, 72.6 percent, of reports were about toddlers. Among families served by child protective services, substance abuse correlates with sexual abuse and child mistreatment in between 33 percent and 66 percent of families. Cycles of drug abuse potentially can result if mothers' addictions are untreated (Brendel and Soulier, 2009). Mothers who expose infants to their drug addiction likely demonstrate poor judgment and poor coping skills. Children exposed to drug-addicted mothers may tend to experience behavioral misconduct and attention deficiency. If children do not receive adequate environmental feedback, they may also develop poor coping skills and insufficient decision-making skills that lead to risky behavior and self-medication to alleviate trauma. Children who experience maternal drug abuse in utero are also more likely to be placed in state custody or out-of-home care due to their mothers' arrests; convictions; drug abuse by mothers' intimate partners; pregnancy complications; lack of prenatal medical service; mental illness; and trauma from drug exposure and environmental factors. Addicted mothers in need of addiction treatment may lack housing, education, employment, or any network of support. This is also discussed in Chapter 12.

Some jurisdictions may attempt to treat substance abuse rather than punish it. Women's treatment may be emphasized by courts during pregnancy because the government has an interest in protecting fetuses and families whenever possible (Brendel and Soulier, 2009). The state's interest in protecting fetuses may be met through incapacitation, but treatment promises to work in children's best interest after birth. To ensure compliance, women may be held in noncriminal, institutional settings before delivery. Women may be restricted to hospitals, but may not receive substance abuse treatment prior to delivery. Mental illness and institutionalization are discussed in Chapter 16.

Courts, legislatures, and organizations struggle to strike a balance between tough-on-crime attitudes, policies that serve the community, considerations about the best interests of children, equal protection of men and women, and how to most efficiently prevent or significantly reduce recidivism risks (Brendel and Soulier, 2009). Some courts feel that treatment programs aid the court by providing greater information and insights about offenders' past substance treatment, mental illness, prognoses, and family history. Mixed-gender facilities may offer less intensive treatment programs than programs designed exclusively for women.

Programming designed for women may be targeted and comprehensive (Brendel and Soulier, 2009). Specific programming aims to identify women's greatest motivators; and thus, improve their chances for success. Women's motivation tends to predicate completion of drug abuse treatment programs. Completion of programs indicates to courts that women are working to remove obstacles, responsibly care for children, overcome stigmatization, and better manage resources. More than half of states have funded substance abuse treatment programs designed for pregnant women. Some facilities involved only treat women or may offer child care service. More often than not, women who receive these services tend to be substance free six months following program completion. Family involvement in therapy and treatment programs increases success because it provides a network for continued and long-term rehabilitation, and because it decreases stigmatization.

In drug court, defendants may be diverted into treatment (Brendel and Soulier, 2009; Cusack, 2013). Courts establish conditions for diversion, for example, whether to include certain misdemeanants, recidivists, or felony offenders. Diversion and compliance are usually voluntary. Yet, incarceration may result if participants fail to participate and stay clean. Patients are supervised throughout treatment, and progress is reported to the drug court. Treatment may be long term (e.g., one year). Treatment may address patients' comorbid issues (e.g., mental illness).

Child welfare needs may be integrated into programming (Conly, 1998). Community-based responses can be beneficial if they coordinate multitiered programming and support systems, including services for participants' GED, transportation, children's school needs, child care, clothing, counseling, and food. Drug courts may act as program liaisons and record keepers. Programs may steer the focus from drug abuse to family therapy and community reintegration. Likelihood of sobriety increases when intimate partners and local relatives support recovering addicts.

In diversion programs, frequency of drug testing may increase as pregnancy progresses (Marchand, Waller, Carey, 2006). For example, a program treatment in Kalamazoo, Michigan tests twice each week, but increases testing to three times each week during later phases of programming for pregnant women. Pregnant women in phases two and three of the program are tested with phase one participants. Additional testing of patients increases pressure and accountability to protect fetuses, and permits staff to discover sooner whether fetuses are at risk for damage.

In Brooklyn, New York, the Kings County Drug Treatment Alternative to Prison (DTAP) program has successfully reduced drug abuse, improved public safety, and efficiently managed resources (Swern, 2007). First, DTAP participants plead guilty to a felony. Then, a plea is drafted that includes a prison term to be imposed if substance abuse treatment fails. Some exceptions permit readmission for low-risk participants because relapse is recognized as being a part of recovery for some addicts. Program completion entitles defendants to withdraw guilty pleas and to have charges dismissed. A five-year longitudinal study of DTAP found that within two years after completing treatment, participants were 67 percent less likely to encounter the criminal justice system than those who had not been treated (Correctional Association of New York, 2012). The program seems to be fiscally efficient. Likelihood of employment increased by 350 percent for recovering addicts after program completion, and DTAP costs half the average rate of incarceration. DTAP saves money each year; between approximately $30,000 and $60,000 is saved for each participant who is diverted from serving one year of jail. Residential treatment is the most expensive treatment, and yet it costs several thousands of dollars less than the lowest average cost of incarceration. New York's Office of Alcoholism and Substance Abuse Services (OASAS) offers several drug treatment programs, including a few residential programs. More than half, 55 percent, of women in correction facilities in New York lived in New York's low-income suburbs prior to incarceration. More than three-quarters, 88 percent, of female inmates self-reported substance abuse, including alcoholism. One survey found that approximately 62 percent of women using OASAS programs were pregnant during treatment or had children. However, only 2.5 percent of OASAS-certified programs offered parents residential care. Thus, residential care for families is likely insufficient, which may affect incarceration rates.

Problematically, OASAS has certified less than 10 percent of its drug treatment programs specifically to help women. This figure may represent a general need for women-centered drug treatment programming nationwide. One study found that approximately 62 percent of females admitted to OASAS-certified programs in 2006 were mothers or were pregnant. Programs designed for male addicts may be ineffective for women, especially mothers or expectant mothers, because many females who abuse substances engage in self-medication to treat past trauma and abuse. Almost three-quarters, 70 percent, of female inmates in New York self-reported history of abuse during childhood. This rate is significantly higher than reports of abuse among male inmates. Only 12 percent of men reported that they had been abused as children. In New York state prisons in 2008, 2,821 women and 59,823 men were incarcerated. Of these, 905 women and 12,520 men committed drug offenses. Thus, OASAS certification focuses on male offenders because they are more numerous; yet, many jurisdictions, including New York, could likely increase holistic and targeted programs for women for greater success.

CHAPTER 14

Parents

Child Support Debts

Child support is a debt owed to a child. The right to receive child support is a right held by a child. Parents are obligated to pay child support. Like alimony, student loans, and taxes, child support is not dischargeable (Landry and Mardis, 2006). Child support is a civil matter. However, parents who disobey court orders to pay support can be incarcerated under a civil contempt charge (James, 2002). Courts do not punitively send parents who are in contempt to "debtors' prison" because the government cannot incarcerate people for failure to pay debts (Weinberg, 2012). However, contempt charges can be used coercively (James, 2002). Almost all states permit some form of incarceration for failure to repay money to the state; and many permit incarceration for child support arrearages. Penologically, the state's reasons for incarcerating debtors who fail to pay child support and comply with court orders may be distinguishable from incarcerating persons who have unpaid private debt.

Paying minimums may be acceptable before parents are incarcerated, but it may be unsatisfactory after incarceration if parents have flouted orders. Parents who are incarcerated may be required to pay lump sums or balances before they can be released; some definite incarceration terms may be imposed for defying orders. Scholars argue, and some courts have held, that indefinite incarceration pending repayment amounts to debtors' prison, which was abolished (*Chadwick v. Janecka*, 2002; James, 2002). Yet, incarceration may be indefinite for failure to pay, not only because child support is owed to a child, but because child support payments and compliance with the law is a debt owed to society under the social contract (Cusack, 2014; *U.S. v. Ballek*, 1999). Prison inmates work, but these jobs do not necessarily sufficiently serve to repay child support debts (Levingston and Turetsky, 2007).

In addition to state-level coercion, federal laws may also be coercive. For example, debtors with more than $2,500 in arrearages may be denied passports, have passports revoked, or be limited in their uses of passports (42 U.S. Code § 652, 2014). This law had been challenged, but was upheld because, although it restricts interstate travel, it does not violate Due Process (*Eunique v. Powell*, 2002). Willful interstate arrearages of more than $5,000 or unpaid debt for more than one year can result in a federal fine and incarceration for up to six months; and more than $10,000 in arrearages or more than two years of interstate unpaid child support can result in federal imprisonment for up to two years and a fine (18 U.S. Code § 228, 2014). Convicted offenders will be ordered to pay restitution in the total amount owed to children.

Incarceration correlates with open child support cases. Relationships between incarceration and child support arrears can be cyclical. For example, in Massachusetts one study found that among all parolees sampled almost all of the inmates, approximately 94 percent, had at least one open child support case (Thoennes, 2002). Arrears may accrue before and during incarceration. Inmates' debt to society is compounded and complicated by the fact that they are poor. The sampled population owed approximately $15 million to custodial parents and $15 million to the State of Massachusetts. On average, 40 percent of the cases in Thoennes' study involved public assistance; and 66 percent previously involved public assistance; but only between 8 and 13 percent never involved public assistance. Most active orders are for $200-$400 per month. This group of 2,191 prisoners, 806 parolees, and 354 inmates living in a house of corrections typically owed interest between $4,000 and $5,000; and the average penalty debt was approximately $2,000. Due to poverty, limited income, and, possibly, limited habilitation among incarcerated samples, parolees were much less likely to be able to repay debts and make payments at higher sums. Thirty percent of house of corrections populations paid; and 40 percent of parolees made voluntary payments that included wage assignments, direct payment, and unemployment intercepts. Eighty-nine percent of prisoners made no payments within a year of the study. Most inmates who entered prison already had child support arrearages; were unmarried; and had histories of domestic violence. Thus, cycles of violence may interrelate to cycles of poverty, debt, arrearages, and incarceration, which could likely affect or perpetuate into successive generations (Patterson, 2008).

DNA

DNA evidence has law, policies, and procedures. Paternity and DNA tests can be administered during criminal investigations, casework, or post-conviction. Evidence may help determine guilty parties or identify victims (DDC, n.d.). Despite the merits of forensic evidence, one study found that forensic evidence in rape cases is auxiliary, nondeterminative, and inconsistent (Sommers and Baskin, 2013). From the time that a victim files a report to the final disposition of a case, a victim's injuries and willingness to testify correlate most strongly with case outcome.

DNA testing is accepted by the criminal justice system as reliable evidence. However, chain of custody issues, contamination, or faulty testing can lead to false convictions. It is widely known that routine DNA testing has caused backlog in forensic labs. Many forensic labs are understaffed to deal with the rise in DNA requests (Cantillon, Kopiec, and Clawson, 2009). Some forensic units attempt to reduce backlog by outsourcing; in fact, all but a small fraction of labs outsource DNA testing. Most outsourced DNA testing relates to post-conviction cases as opposed to casework. It has been proposed that backlog could be resolved if parties who are interested in expediting particular cases paid for forensic testing. One study found that 28 percent of investigators at Miami-Dade Police Crime Laboratory Bureau, Minnesota Bureau of Criminal Apprehension Forensic Science Service, Pennsylvania State Bureau of Forensic Services, Philadelphia Police Forensic Science Bureau, Phoenix Forensic Crime Laboratory, St. Louis Metropolitan Police Department Crime Laboratory, Virginia Department of Forensic Science, and Washington State Patrol Forensic Laboratory Services wish to outsource backlogged criminal post-conviction paternity DNA tests; and 21 percent would like to outsource paternity DNA tests in open criminal cases. However, many times, they cannot afford it. Between 40 and 60 percent of labs require federal assistance to process, within 90 days, DNA requests relating to violent crimes. States continue to demand more DNA evidence, thus thousands of outsourced samples are likely to continue being outsourced at once. This strain could diminish accuracy or the value of timely results in criminal and appellate cases. Chain of custody is extremely important, especially because overworked labs could potentially switch samples leading to false conviction (Cusack, 2014).

Defendants have argued that some expert testimony regarding DNA results violates the Confrontation Clause if the expert who conducted the tests is not present in court. Experts who submit DNA results to the courts may be used as witnesses against the defendant. When cases are outsourced, it can be costly to bring the analyst into court to deliver expert testimony; thus, the prosecution may use expert witnesses other than those who analyzed the DNA samples. Under the Sixth Amendment, the Confrontation Clause guarantees the accused the right to cross-examine witnesses brought against them. In Indiana, the state supreme court held that results of DNA testing conducted by experts may be presented in court by an expert's colleague (*Criminal Law Reporter,* 2009). In *Pendergrass v. State,* a child victim aborted a fetus; and the state performed DNA tests on the aborted fetus (2009). Victims of sexual assault almost always abort fetuses conceived during rape (Reshef et al., 2011). Fetuses, placentas, or other materials may be sent to forensic laboratories for paternity testing. Maternal contamination of placental tissues, the fetus's age, and the condition of the tissue are factors in successful DNA testing. The defendant in *Pendergrass* was convicted of child molestation after DNA evidence demonstrated that he fathered the aborted fetus (*Pendergrass v. State,* 2009). The *Pendergrass* court held that a qualified expert delivered the testimony in a reliable and professional manner, which satisfied Sixth Amendment requirements (*Pendergrass v. State,* 2009).

When a victim has been killed, maggots may be collected from the corpse (Chávez-Briones et al., 2013). Frequently, researchers can determine from the rate of maggot growth the time of a victim's death. DNA analysis may be performed on the contents of maggots' stomachs. When a victim's remains are unidentifiable, then DNA retrieved from maggots' stomachs can be compared to people believed to be the suspected victim's parents. In some cases, findings could exonerate parents, or give them peace of mind; but in other cases, it could further incriminate them. However, this under-studied technique could be subject to attack for unreliability until it is better established.

The Michigan Supreme Court decided *People v. Zajaczkowski* (2012). In that case, DNA evidence demonstrated that two people who engaged in intercourse were unrelated by blood; the pair was previously believed to be half-siblings through their father. The defendant was under the care of their legal father for two years during the 1970s. His biological mother divorced his legal father; and the next child was born long after, in the 1990s. The pair never lived together; and they did not believe that they were related at the time they had intercourse. The state held that a blood relationship was not required to convict for incest. The government argued that civil presumption of legitimacy satisfied the elements. The lower court sentenced the defendant to between 11 and 35 years in prison. The Supreme Court held that the pair was not related by blood; and legal fiction could not override how the pair viewed their relationship (i.e., unrelated by affinity). Civil presumption of paternity could not establish the blood relationship required by the statute.

One court found that significant likelihood of paternity established by a DNA test can prove that a defendant had sex with a victim. The defendant in *Butcher v. Commonwealth* (2002) cohabited with his intimate partner. The intimate partner was the mother of a seven-year-old; and the coupled bore twin girls together. When the twins were born, the defendant began sodomizing, penetrating, and fondling the older daughter, who was at the time ten years old. Regular abuse continued for five years until the victim conceived at fourteen, and subsequently gave birth. DNA testing found that the defendant was 388 times more likely than a random male in the defendant's race to be the father (i.e., 99.74 percent). The defendant argued that using a paternity DNA test to prove that intercourse occurred amounted to bootstrapping. The defendant argued that administration of the test erroneously presumes that sex occurred. The court explained that DNA tests begin with a 50/50 presumption that intercourse occurred. DNA tests compare a defendant's sample to other members of a defendant's race. The test determines the chance that a defendant is the father instead of any other randomly selected person. Neither the defendant nor randomly selected people are specifically presumed to have had sex with a victim by the test. If the court followed the defendant's logic, and began with a zero percent chance of sexual intercourse to presume his innocence, then there would be no likelihood that the defendant committed the crime. The court found that Constitutional presumption of innocence does not require a factfinder to presume impossibility. It only requires the jury to believe that the defendant did not commit the crime until they have heard all of the facts.

DNA paternity testing in civil cases can be used as evidence in criminal cases. In Michigan, a man who had a vasectomy believed that he impregnated his girlfriend (*People v. Nugent*, 2007). He signed an affidavit of paternity, but later discovered that his 14-year-old son fathered his girlfriend's child. The court held that the affidavit could be voidable because the man was mistaken about the fact that he was the father, which caused him to sign the affidavit. However, the court also held that equities could require him to remain the child's legal father in the best interest of the child. Because the child's biological father was only 14 years old, the girlfriend was charged with, and pleaded no contest to, criminal sexual conduct. She chose to terminate parental rights to the child. Paternity and statutory rape is discussed in Chapter 14. In Missouri, a putative father was ordered by a family court to submit to paternity DNA testing in a child support case (*Sanders v. Sauer*, 2006). On several occasions, he refused to submit to testing. A judgment was entered presuming his parentage, which legitimated the child. The legal process of legitimation was later questioned by the defendant in a criminal non-support case. The criminal court relied on the family court's findings to prove that the defendant was the child's father and satisfy the elements of the crime. The defendant claimed that reliance on the family court's order deprived him of Due Process because a criminal court should have used a reasonable-doubt standard rather than the civil court's order. Missouri's Supreme Court held that the court's findings could be relied on because the criminal matter arose from failure to obey the family court's order. Furthermore, the defendant had numerous opportunities to submit to a DNA test for the child support case.

Rape, Visitation, and Child Support

Rapists are likely to have parental rights to visit children conceived from rape. Congressional Representative Debbie Wasserman Schultz sponsored federal legislation to incentivize states to pass legislation terminating parental rights of rapists who conceived children through rape (H.R. 2772, 2013). The Rape Survivor Child Custody Act cites studies showing that approximately 25,000 to 32,000 pregnancies result from rape each year in the United States. The Act points to studies demonstrating that among women who become pregnant from rape, approximately one-third to two-thirds will keep and raise their children. Civil findings of rape may be more effective than criminal findings because only five percent of rapes are successfully prosecuted. In family law, a standard of clear and convincing evidence is used by most states to terminate parental rights; and it has passed the court's muster (*Santosky v. Kramer*, 1982). Schultz's legislation points out that only six states permit rape victims to petition the court to terminate rapists' parental rights. These states require clear and convincing evidence, not the proof beyond a reasonable-doubt threshold required for rape convictions. Clear and convincing evidence is a standard used to terminate parental rights for child abuse, neglect, or abandonment. Best-interest factors may be considered. One factor includes domestic violence between parents or sexual abuse. However, a single incident of sexual abuse between parents may be insufficient to terminate parental rights. Yet, rape between persons uninvolved in domestic situations may be a special case. Nonconsensual insemination, reproductive coercion, intimate partner rape, and marital rape are no less serious than stranger rape or date rape, but the totality of the circumstances may more clearly call for termination of parental rights for cases of stranger rape or date rape. Nonconsensual insemination is discussed in Chapter 15.

The Rape Survivor Child Custody Act cites legislative intent to protect victims from psychological trauma, which can negatively influence children and impact maternal abilities. Schultz also states that legislation is necessary to prevent rapists from blackmailing victims to remain silent at the threat of increased or total parental custody modifications. The bill would authorize the Attorney General to provide participating states with grants. The bill does not specify whether rape would be defined to include forcible rape, nonconsensual sex, sexual assault, and statutory rape. State definitions vary, and based on some states' definitions it seems that women who voluntarily conceived, but were victims of statutory rape, could take advantage of the Act. Furthermore, the legislation only requires states to terminate fathers' parental rights, which completely denies the possibility that women rape men and conceive children; or that female rapists should be treated equally with men. However, many states acknowledge that female offenders may force males to penetrate them. This form of victimization is discussed in Chapter 15. The Rape Survivor Child Custody Act does not affect a biological father's duty to pay child support. Public policy holds that rapists owe child support to children. Children's rights to child support are discussed in Chapter 14. However, men who are statutorily raped, and cause pregnancy voluntarily or involuntarily, also owe a duty of child support to children. The duty is owed to children, not to violators, thus critics have pointed to potential inequity in state laws obligating victims to pay child support and in Schultz's legislation.

Emancipation

"Babies having babies" describes unemancipated minors becoming parents. Emancipation is a technical and somewhat unsettled area of family law that may overlap with criminal law. Generally, minors become legal adults at 18 years old. However, they may not be viewed by the government as being emancipated until they are young adults (e.g., 21 years old or 19 years old) for some matters, like duty to provide medical care or child support.

Children who are independent, self-sufficient, and demonstrate a history of being abused may be emancipated by court order. In general, termination of parental rights in cases of abuse, abandonment, and neglect does not automatically emancipate children. Evidence in emancipation petitions must sufficiently demonstrate that parental rights are not in the best interest of a child and a child does not need to become a dependent of the state. The court may consider best-interest factors and other relevant factors, which may include a minor's age; a child's mental health; a child's medical needs and physical health; parents' ability and willingness to feed, shelter, and clothe a child; parents' providence of medical care; parents' mental illness; and parents' physical health. Typically, minors become emancipated when facts show that they can care for themselves and parents have breached their roles or are unable sufficiently to care for children due to circumstances beyond their control. A minor's independence is usually insufficient for legal emancipation without a showing that parental rights should be terminated. When children are independent, but parental rights should not be terminated, then courts may order implied partial emancipation. Parents must support children, but children can retain their own employment wages.

Many states permit unemancipated children to consent to sex prior to adulthood (e.g., 17 years old). However, these statutes do not emancipate minors. Emancipation and statutory rape are discussed in Chapter 1 and Chapter 14. There is no particular age required by the Constitution at which states must recognize minors' consent to have sex; however, courts may consider a child victim's age to determine whether a victim was capable of knowingly consenting to sex acts (*People v. Lloyd*, 2011). When child rape is alleged, courts may consider a victim's age as one factor for determining whether sex was knowing or unknowing (i.e., voluntary or involuntary). A victim may be so young as to give notice that sex is unknowing. Thus, sex may be rape, not statutory rape. For example, a

13-year-old victim willingly went for a drive with a defendant. The defendant and victim engaged in intercourse, but at trial, they disagreed about whether sex was voluntary. The victim hid details about the incident from her mother until she discovered that she was pregnant and required an abortion. In that case, the court held that a child's age, 13 years old, was insufficient to prove a defendant's knowledge because the victim's age alone did not necessarily inform the defendant that the victim was unable to knowingly consent (*People v. Lloyd*, 2011; *People v. White*, 2012).

Generally, minors are emancipated by marriage. Some prepubescent children may be emancipated by marriage when legal marriages performed abroad are recognized in the United States (10 U.S.C. § 920 - Art. 120, 2014). Minors who are 17 years old become emancipated if they are permitted to serve in the military by parental consent (10 U.S.C. §505(a), 2014). However, their home states may not consider them to be emancipated adults for all purposes. If children are independent and self-sufficient, then they may be emancipated by their home states (*Bradford v. Futrell*, 1961). Courts may not agree that entering a military academy emancipates a minor like entering service (*Howard v. Howard*, 1992). Yet, some courts have decided that enrollment in a military academy is the same as entering active duty with the military (*Porath v. McVey*, 1994; *Zuckerman v. Zuckerman*, 1989). Nevertheless, military cadets cannot be married, have children, or be pregnant without special authorization. Each state delimits ages for marital consent. Many states delimit marital consent between 15 and 17 years old (Md. Code Family Law §2-301, 2014). Judicial waiver can allow minors over a certain age (e.g., 13 years old) to marry. Many jurisdictions permit pregnant minors to be married or permit marriage with parental consent. In some cases, marriages may not be valid. For example, marriage may be invalid when a foreign minor wed in a polygamous marriage enters the country as a second wife. To determine whether a minor is emancipated, courts may question whether minors are self-supporting. Married minors may consent to medical treatment. Emancipated and unemancipated minors may consent to psychological treatment depending on the jurisdiction; but, in some cases, they cannot refuse psychological treatment if their parents consent to it (Cusack, 2013; Md. Code Health-General §20-104). Unemancipated minors can consent to medical treatment for their own children. Parental consent is typically not required for unemancipated children to test for sexually transmitted diseases (STDs). Minors may receive emergency treatment for sexual assault injuries without parental consent; however, parents may be notified. Medical practitioners may be required to disclose some information, but some information may be protected (Md. Code Health-General §20-102, 2014).

Pregnancy does not emancipate minors because it does not demonstrate that a minor can independently provide for herself. However, marriage implies that a spouse, whether male or female, will honor his or her duty to support a pregnant wife if necessary. In certain jurisdictions, minors may consent to prenatal medical decisions if they have achieved the legal age for consent; this age may be the same as the legal age for sexual consent. In some states, minors are legally emancipated for limited purposes, such as medical decisions relating to pregnancy (i.e., prenatal care); this may or may not include decisions about abortions (*In re Smith*, 1972). Some states may require parental notification or consent for medical decisions (e.g., abortion or pregnancy). Minors in several states are not required to notify parents or obtain consent. Parental notification statutes may require that one parent is notified before minors perform abortive procedures. Criminal charges against physicians could result when consent is not obtained. Physicians performing abortions may be required to notify parents of minors' wishes. Some jurisdictions may permit physicians to perform abortions without parental notification if minors are constructively emancipated (e.g., do not live with a parent or guardian); or when diligent efforts have failed to notify parents (Md. Code Health-General §20-103, 2014). Jurisdictions may permit doctors to perform abortions without notification if minors would be physically or emotionally abused by parents as a result of notifying them; if minors are sufficiently mature and capable to grant informed consent; or when notification is not in a minor's best interest.

Notification requirements can pose an undue burden on women (*Planned Parenthood v. Danforth*, 1976). Thus, judicial bypass can be granted in jurisdictions where doctors are not permitted to bypass notification or consent requirements. Independent minors who can understand the decisions to abort may be granted bypass. These policies imply that minors who are not mature enough to understand a decision to abort may be required to give birth. Minors as young as 13 years old have been held to be mature enough to abort in the third trimester, while older teens with early pregnancies have been held to be too immature to abort (Ertelt, 2014). A minor who lives in the custody of and under the care of a nonparental adult, who is not the child's legal guardian, may receive authorization for abortive procedures under certain circumstances depending on jurisdictional variations (Md. Code Health-General §20-105, 2014). Parents and guardians may not force emancipated or unemancipated minors to undergo abortive procedures or to place their children for adoption. Emancipated and unemancipated minors may independently place children for adoption. Parents of unemancipated minors may be notified of proceedings to terminate parental rights.

Among certain populations, pregnancy rates may vary. Where employment rates, availability of parents' insurance, and social stability are higher (e.g., children in military families), pregnancy rates may be drastically lower than among the general population (Burr et al., 2013; Muram et al., 1995). Typically, childbearing among teenagers highly correlates with poverty, social and family instability, poor education, substance use, and unemployment. Thus, many of these minors may not be stable enough to be emancipated or seek judicial waiver for an abortion. Many may rely on their parents for support, and their children will rely on their grandparents for support. Yet, Guttmacher Institute reports that a relatively high percentage of unwed teenage pregnancies may be intended (1998). Sexual or physical abuse is common among childbearing teenagers. Thus, if their parents' rights are terminated or they are removed from their homes while they are pregnant, then they may become dependents of the state.

Pregnant juvenile delinquents or juveniles who perpetrate sex crimes that result in pregnancy may be waived into criminal court if offenses are sufficiently serious (e.g., crimes that carry a life term or capital crimes); and their children may be removed. The doctrine of parental immunity holds that parents and children may not sue each other for tort damages for negligence arising within parental duties. Public policy prohibits interference with parental control. For example, placing a child in "time out" cannot be claimed as false imprisonment (*Hewlett v. George*, 1891). However, the doctrine may not apply if parents committed personal injuries against the minor during sexual assault, abuse, or exploitation. Severely abusive acts are punished by the criminal justice system; and impermissible conduct can make parents liable in torts (Hollister, 1982). The doctrine does not apply to emancipated children (*Baker v. Baker*, 1953; *Grant v. Norwich Discount Liquor*, 2011; *Henderson v. Woolley*, 1994).

CHAPTER 15

Physical Violence

Infanticide

Infanticide is usually committed by mentally ill mothers, violent fathers, or poor families. Some parents commit suicide after committing filicide. One researcher reported that 10 percent of parents who committed filicide had histories of substance abuse (Eliason, 2009). Some experts believe that this figure may be a low estimate. Substance abuse correlates with poverty, depression, trauma, and suicide. Drugs and alcohol significantly correlate with crime in numerous studies, yet filicide does not have a high correlation with history of criminal behavior. Only 25 percent of fathers and 10 percent of mothers who committed filicide had any criminal history. In general, murder-suicide tends to correlate with people involved in lawsuits; typically older couples. More than three-quarters of people who commit murder-suicide are employed full time. However, researchers found that, within populations that committed filicide-suicide, 90 percent of fathers and 30 percent of mothers were employed. Thus, among mothers who commit filicide-suicide, traditional suicide predictors may not be present; but fathers' criminal history, poverty, and other factors may be more predictive (Nau, McNiel, and Binder, 2012). Older perpetrators may be more likely to be afflicted with mental illness. Younger women who are unmarried may be more likely to be motivated by emotional, spiritual, and social problems. When women with no history of mental illness commit infanticide at any point during the first year, they may have attempted to mother the child; but then, for no relational or socioeconomic reason, they fail to cope with motherhood. Suicide rates are extremely low among mothers who commit neonaticide. Approximately 2 percent of mothers and 11 percent of fathers commit suicide after committing infanticide. The average age of women who commit suicide after neonaticide is 29 years old. The average age of women who do not commit suicide after committing neonaticide is 22 years old.

In one study in the United States, half of all child murders and all infant murders were committed by parents (D'Argenio, Catania, and Marchetti, 2013). Between 16 and 29 percent of mothers and 40 to 60 percent of fathers are believed to commit suicide after committing filicide. In some countries, where economic filicide is not routine, fathers tend to murder their wives after committing filicide, but mothers mostly commit filicide-suicide. Fathers are more likely to be violent and tend to kill the whole family. Mothers are likelier to kill children who are younger, while the risk of being killed by a father increases with a child's age. However, in certain countries, fathers are far likelier to kill newborns for financial reasons.

Several research studies indicate that nationality and culture correlate with significant differences in demographic characteristics among parents who commit homicide-suicide (D'Argenio, Catania, and Marchetti, 2013). One difference is that in some cultures, it is more prevalent for a mother exclusively to perpetrate neonaticide during or immediately after delivery, due to her perception that she has been abandoned morally or spiritually. In some countries, filicide is more commonly performed 48 hours after delivery. Either parent may commit aggravated homicide. Some of these cultural particularities are discussed in Chapter 17.

Among depressed mothers in one study, 41 percent thought of harming their children (Friedman and Sorrentino, 2012). Over three years, only 7 percent of control group mothers wanted to harm their children. However, 70 percent of mothers in the general population had explicit aggressive thoughts about colicky infants; and 26 percent thought about infanticide during infants' colic episodes. A study of hospitalized Indian women found that psychotic beliefs about a baby correlated with post-partum infanticide behavior. Negative maternal reaction also correlated with infanticidal behavior among Indian women with postpartum illness. Infanticide in India is discussed in Chapter 17. A pattern may exist among women who kill their infants when mothers experience powerlessness, alienation, and poverty. Gender and economic prejudice may lead to women being executed for postpartum psychosis-related infanticide in countries that routinely practice gender-selective filicide.

Dozens of nations (e.g., Italy and Canada) punish neonaticide differently from filicide; and excuse infanticide with lesser charges and lower sentences (Friedman and Sorrentino, 2012; Nau, McNiel, and Binder, 2012). Countries will charge mothers with manslaughter rather than homicide if mothers suffered from mental illness at the time of the crime. Laws that lower charges for mothers who kill during postpartum psychosis may be based on the 1922 British Infanticide Act (Nau, McNiel, and Binder, 2012). Jurisdictional variations within nations may affect the outcomes of cases. For example, criminal justice responses to infanticide in Australia vary by states (de Bortoli, Coles, and Dolan, 2013). Legislation generally provides a defense for mothers who kill children within one year of birth if mothers are mentally imbalanced due to the effects of childbirth or lactation. Laws apply equally to indigenous and nonindigenous populations, though greater research is needed. In some cases, infanticide results from chronic abuse or neglect that results in fatal maltreatment (Nau, McNiel, and Binder, 2012). It may also result from altruism and belief that death is in the child's best interest. Altruistic motives may be common, especially in filicide-suicide. These beliefs may be related to abuse, poverty, acute psychosis, or other factors. Thus, infanticide relating to delusions can only be exculpated if mothers had not knowingly abused or neglected the infant. In cases where mothers' drug abuse results in delusions or mothers repeatedly murder infants on subsequent occasions, courts are far likelier to charge women with murder even when their behavior relates to delusional thinking because that behavior likely demonstrates knowledge, willfulness, and depraved selfishness rather than momentary inability to conform to the law (NBC, 2014).

In the United States, laws do not address postpartum psychosis and infanticide. Yet, many women who kill during postpartum psychosis prevail on a theory of Not Guilty by Reason of Insanity because women do not know the wrongfulness of their actions during a delusion; and they cannot conform their behavior to the law. However, some defendants struggle to defend themselves if courts focus on the importance of the Diagnostic and Statistical Manual of Mental Disorders, fifth edition (DSMV). Postpartum psychosis is not listed as an illness in DSMV, but it is specified as an onset for psychosis. Following the case of Andrea Yates, in which she believed that the devil would possess her children if she did not murder them, Texas introduced a bill that was widely criticized. Yates' case is also discussed in Chapter 6. Women may be sentenced to as little as a term of probation and mental health treatment. Some factors fueling opposition were gender bias; prejudice against persons with mental illness; and claims that postpartum mothers could find justice in insanity defenses.

In one study of postpartum cases in the United States using the Model Penal Code definition and the *M'Naughten* test definition of criminal insanity, 39 cases of filicide were analyzed in which women prevailed on a theory of Not Guilty by Reason of Insanity (NGRI). Among the defendants, 72 percent had received mental health treatment in the past; 56 percent planned to commit suicide with or after filicide; 49 percent suffered from depression at the time that they killed their children; more than half were psychotic; 74 percent were delusional; 69 percent experienced hallucination (i.e., auditory hallucinations); 82 percent were diagnosed with mood disorder involving psychosis or with a psychotic disorder. More than half, 54 percent, had altruistic motives; 33 percent had motives that were acutely psychotic; 5 percent of filicide resulted from maltreatment; and 2 percent of mothers did not want their children. Even when court evaluations determined that mothers did not want their children, a verdict of NGRI may be found. In some cases, mothers may be intellectually handicapped, but not criminally insane. They may be sentenced for capital offenses. However, mentally ill individuals cannot be executed under the Eighth Amendment and *Atkins v. Virginia* (2002) because penological aims would not met. Low IQ (e.g., below 70 IQ) cannot be the only measure of mental retardation; but low IQ may be one factor in why women kill infants (*Hall v. Florida*, 2013).

In another study of 24 U.S. cases of postpartum psychosis and infanticide, 33 percent of defendants were found NGRI; 17 percent received terms of probation; 42 percent were incarcerated; but fewer than 10 percent received life sentences. NGRI defenses are only raised in 1 percent of felony cases, and they are unsuccessful in 90 percent of cases; but they are more successful among cases involving infanticide (Friedman and Sorrentino, 2012). Approximately one-third of NGRI pleas among postpartum women were successful in one study; and approximately one-half were adjudicated NGRI by agreement between opposing counsels. However, some postpartum mothers have been sentenced to death. There is much greater variability in the outcome of U.S. cases than in jurisdictions with infanticide laws (Spinelli, 2004). For example, England's Infanticide Law requires probation and psychiatric treatment. This is a strong reason for why the DSMV should list postpartum psychosis. Incarceration may fail to treat women and may plant criminal tendencies where none existed previously (Pansarasa, 2004).

Pregnant Battery Victims

Battery and sexual battery of a pregnant woman may aggravate charges. Additional charges may result depending on factors like, gestational weeks, injury to a fetus, and offender's knowledge of a victim's pregnancy. Generally, sexual assault is aggravated when an offender threatens to use or uses a deadly weapon (Conn. Gen. Stat. § 53a-70a, 2013). The law may require that offenders intended to seriously or permanently disfigure the victim. The elements of aggravation may be met when an offender destroys or injures a victim's organs, psyche, or other parts of a victim's body. Aggravation may also result when offenders demonstrate extreme indifference to human life or conduct that is so reckless that it creates a risk of death. This could apply to threats or actual transmission of sexually transmitted diseases (STDs). Use of deadly instrument may include destructive liquids (e.g., HIV-infected semen) (Idaho Code § 18-907, 2012). However, caustic chemicals (e.g., acid) used to irritate or poison a pregnant victim are not considered to be "chemical weapons" (i.e., weapons of war) (*Bond v. U.S*, 2014; Robinson, 2014). A person may commit aggravated battery against a victim if the criminal act causes great bodily harm or permanent disfigurement to an embryo, fetus, or pregnant victim. Pregnancy may result from sexual assault or may exist at the time of sexual assault.

> The mere fact that a fetus is not a permanent part of the mother's body does not lead to the conclusion that it is not a part of her body, within the meaning of [aggravated sexual assault statutes] Conn. Gen. Stat. §§ 53a-70a(a)(2)and 53a-59(a)(2), at least for the period of time that it is attached to and dependent upon the mother (*State v. Sandoval*, 2003, p. 524).

Embryonic tissues from a five-week pregnancy were considered by a court to be part of a victim's body; and, therefore, a "member" of the victim's body because they are attached to the victim's body (*State v. Sandoval*, 2003, p. 524).

Law enforcement and volunteer-based crisis intervention may be ill equipped to respond to aggravated assault involving pregnancy. Participants may be unaware of the applicability of jurisdictional laws because injuries involving conception or harm to fetuses may not be visible. Yet, pregnant victims of intimate partner violence (IPV) may be more likely to receive volunteer-based victim services. In one study victims' reports of IPV to police were analyzed to determine whether police activated volunteer-based crisis intervention (Kernic and Bonomi, 2007). The sample included 2,092 adult females who had been attacked by male intimate partners. In 415 incidents, approximately 20 percent, police activated victims' services. Crisis intervention services were more likely when victims were married to abusers or were pregnant. Victims in certain precincts were more likely than others to receive crisis intervention services. This finding reinforces variability of criminal justice responses to criminal impregnation and pregnant women. Nonconsensual insemination and similar violations are discussed in Chapter 15.

Pregnant Transgressors

Pregnant women may be charged with crimes against fetuses if they instigate attacks or engage in reckless behavior while pregnant. Though not intending to hurt their pregnancies, women may be charged for domestic violence or for batteries against unborn children even if no harm results (720 ILCS 5/12-3.2, 2014). In several states, statutes designed to protect fetuses from illegal abortions could be used to prosecute women who self-harm (Rovner, 2012). For example, a pregnant woman intentionally ingested rat poison during an attempt to commit suicide and feticide. The child was surgically delivered, but died a few days later. The woman was charged with attempted feticide and murder. The case raised questions about federal law and states' laws in the majority of states criminalizing fetal injury and death. Many laws fail to distinguish between harm arising from third-party conduct and injury caused by pregnant mothers. Legislation in Utah proposed to include reckless behavior from conception to delivery resulting in stillbirth or miscarriage (Paltrow, 2010). Legislation could have included prosecution of women who knowingly remained in abusive relationships or failed to receive prenatal care. Prenatal duties and lack of maternal obligation to embryos is discussed in Chapter 12. Legislators allegedly intended to target illegal abortions, but the bill was written in response to a case in which a minor female hired an attacker to induce a miscarriage. The teen and fetus survived the attack.

Normally, self-harm is considered to be a public health issue, but when pregnant women self-harm, it may be a criminal justice issue (Rovner, 2012). For example, in South Dakota assaulting a pregnant woman may lead to criminal battery charges for assaulting an unborn child if a fetus is born alive after an assault (S.D. Ann. § 22-18-1.3, 2014). The government may argue that laws are necessary or important to protect government interests in fetal health. However, laws should be narrowly tailored to only protect viable fetuses, and not to impose duties on women to care for embryos that impinge in rights to privacy found under the Fourteenth Amendment and *Roe v. Wade* (1973). For example, in Kansas, Alexa's Law protects all human life beginning at gestation. However, the law specifically excludes acts committed by pregnant women (Kan. Stat. 21-5419, 2014). Several states have narrowed legislation to punish physical attacks against pregnant women, but do not exclude self-harm. In Iowa, a woman was arrested after she received emergency care following a fall down stairs. Hospital staff alerted police after the woman disclosed that she fought with her husband and then became light-headed and fell. Hospital staff believed that she attempted suicide and feticide. She was held in police custody for two days. Prosecutors could not proceed with the case because she was not in a sufficiently advanced stage of pregnancy to satisfy statutory requirements. On one hand, Iowa failed to treat potential self-harm as a public health issue; but on another hand, they drew an appropriate legal line to protect fetuses while not limiting women's rights.

The case in Iowa raises questions about the extent that initial police investigation and prosecution should rely on emergency medical staffs' opinions that contradict witness testimony (Cusack, 2014). If states continue to apply fetal injury statutes to reckless behavior, then they ought to consider natural changes experienced by pregnant women that may cause them to become more prone to injury during pregnancy. However, public policy does not permit punishing pregnant women for automobile accidents or restricting pregnant women from driving. Ample anecdotal evidence demonstrates that some women become clumsier during pregnancy due to rapid physical transformations. Public policy does not support punishing women who are accident prone. One study found that women in late stages of pregnancy may be more prone to car accidents (Redelmeier, May, Thiruchelvam, and Barrett, 2014). Among 507,262 women who gave birth during the three-year longitudinal study period, 6,922 drivers were in automobile accidents. During the second trimester, 757 pregnant drivers crashed, which was a 42 percent increase. Notably, risk increased most steeply early in the second trimester, and leveled by the third trimester. However, increases were not noted among pregnant passengers or pedestrians involved in accidents, intentional self-harm, falling accidents, or self-reported risky behavior. Furthermore, relative to the general population, risk decreases for poisoning, burns, and depression-related intentional self-harm (Redelmeier et al., 2014; Yadav et al., 2013). Laws targeting fetal harm could refer suspected violence to child protective services prior to escalating to criminal charges (Hallam, 2013). Investigators may handle incidents as family issues and refer many pregnant women to appropriate services rather than prosecute.

Aggravated Battery and Manslaughter

Murder and manslaughter of a pregnant woman may result in murder or attempted murder charges for unborn fetuses depending on statutes, case law, and fetal development. Feticide may be charged. Some jurisdictions actively prosecute, while other jurisdictions seem to reserve prosecution for particularly egregious or high-profile cases. Charges can depend on fetal gestational stage; and whether a child is born alive, dies in utero, or dies subsequent to birth; or whether a mother was murdered with or without malicious intent; and other relevant factors (*Inquisitr*, 2014; *Police Department Disciplinary Bulletin*, 2008).

Some jurisdictions do not codify fetal murder. Where jurisdictions are silent, the doctrine of transferred intent may apply. In one case, a young man killed his intimate partner and his six-month-old child (*People v. Singh*, 2003). He shot his child three times in the head and once in the heart, causing four fatal wounds. He challenged paternity of this, his first child, but he had recently and definitely learned the child was his. He believed that a second child would sidetrack his career plans. While parked in a car with his family, he aimed downward and shot his intimate partner three times in the top of her head. She remained alive during at least one shot because she inhaled some blood before death. A two-inch fetus with well-defined body parts and organs was in her uterus. Investigators specified that the tissue had advanced beyond the embryonic stage. Because the mother died, the fetus died from lack of oxygen. The court held that the doctrine of transferred intent applied because the intended target was murdered (*People v. Bland*, 2002). Generally, completed murder of the intended target may not be required to apply the doctrine of transferred intent. Attempted murder of an intended target mistakenly resulting in murder of an unintended target may be prosecuted as murder in the first degree rather than murder in the second degree under the doctrine of transferred intent because the offender possessed intent to commit homicide and killed the second person. Thus, in states where statutes include fetuses in murder statutes, doctrine of transferred intent may apply.

Courts may mitigate feticide, or feticide may enhance charges. Feticide may not influence courts' sentencing for murder charges. Feticide may be a separate charge not included in murder charges (10 U.S. Code § 919a-Art. 119a, 2014). In one case, an offender was convicted of murdering his parents, his pregnant wife, and his wife's fetus (*Baird v. Indiana*, 1992). He was convicted of unlawfully terminating a pregnancy. The jury recommended the death sentence for the murder of his parents, but not of his wife. The trial court held that his wife's murder was an aggravating circumstance justifying the death sentence for murdering his parents. Many mitigating circumstances outweighed the aggravating circumstance. Mitigating factors include clean criminal history; law abiding and civil conduct; church participation; steady employment; caring for his family; and military service. The offender's crime against his wife was mitigated by the fact that he was under extreme mental or emotional strain, which impaired his ability to conform his conduct to the law. The appellate court found that mental conditions influenced his decision to murder his parents. The defendant was operating under a grandiose delusion about becoming wealthy and feared that his fantasy would be exposed as an unfounded belief to his parents and wife. However, the appellate court felt that character evidence only minimally mitigated the defendant's conduct. The value of clean criminal history was weighted as having a medium value. The appellate court held that the aggravating circumstance was very high, and thus outweighed the mitigating circumstances. Feticide was not considered to be a relevant aggravating factor to his parents' or wife's murder. The defendant argued that feticide statutes were enacted to punish illegal abortion. The court reasoned that the statute contemplates other punishments for illegal abortion; thus, it should be interpreted as a feticide statute. The statute is designed to extend homicide statutes to protect fetuses. He argued that the statutes required specific intent to kill a fetus. However, the statute only requires knowledge that termination will result. Knowledge is construed as high probability of certainty. Feticide in this case was a lesser-included offense of his wife's murder. However, feticide is not inherently included in murder. The information for murder of his wife did not list feticide as being included. Unlawful termination of fetal life punished by the feticide statute is not included in murder charges.

Abortion Doctors

Society's willingness to punish abortion doctors is evident. Abortion doctors and their agents are liable for performing abortions illegally; and for harming women or fetuses (e.g., 22-week abortion in a 20-week jurisdiction) (Segal, 2009). This is discussed further in Chapter 3. Even when abortion doctors safely and legally perform abortions, some members of society are willing to punish them by injuring or killing them. For example, a rash of antiabortion sniper shootings struck Canada and western New York during the 1990s (Yardley and Rohde, 1998). Many doctors were murdered through windows in their homes, after years of antiabortion demonstrations outside their homes. Some were provoked and attacked before they were executed. For example, one doctor was confronted on Hanukkah by protesters decrying him a murderer. The doctor, who also delivered hundreds of babies, was accused of attacking a protester with a baseball bat. The doctor was charged with a felony; but that charge was reduced and he was fined $400. Throughout the 1990s, abortion clinic employees were attacked at work. For example, two employees in Boston were killed when a gunman opened fire. The 22-year-old gunman, who also wounded five people, was sentenced to consecutive life sentences. The gunman killed himself in prison. Several bombs exploded outside abortion clinics throughout the United States. For example, at least two bombs were set at abortion clinics in Atlanta, Georgia; and one exploded in Birmingham, Alabama, killing an off-duty police officer. In recent years, violence has subsided significantly and medical patients have received greater protection. This is discussed further in Chapter 2. Yet, fighting continues to occasionally erupt outside abortion clinics.

Baby Rape

Sexual penetration of infants is particularly egregious because infants are often injured and killed. In one case, an offender raped and murdered an 11-month-old child (*Warner v. Workman*, 2011). The infant lived with the offender, his two young children, and her mother; as well as another toddler on occasion. One day, the victim's mother left their house while all the children and the offender remained at home. When she returned, she saw the victim lying on a bed wearing only a diaper, but the child had been dressed when she left. When she went to grab the victim, the offender intervened and mentioned that the victim was not breathing. The mother grabbed the limp victim and screamed. She ordered the offender to drive to the emergency room and performed CPR. The victim was pronounced dead; but a nurse noticed red blood on the victim's anus, accompanied by fresh injuries. Doctors performed X-rays and discovered two skull fractures; a depression; and two jaw fractures. Combined with retinal hemorrhages discovered in the victim's eyes, the injuries likely indicated violent shaking. The doctor diagnosed sexual abuse and physical abuse. An autopsy revealed numerous head, chest, and abdominal injuries; the victim's brain was crushed; her liver was lacerated; and her organs were bruised. Some external bruises were in the shape of adult fingertips (Cusack, 2015; *Warner v. Workman*, 2011). Blunt force penetration likely caused six rectal tears. The victim's death was ruled a homicide. The offender complained of sore knuckles, but denied abusing the victim. He said the victim fell on the floor and bumped her head. His home was searched and pornography was located near a tub of Vaseline and a container aloe vera gel. Video was cued to a clip of adult lovemaking. The offender's son observed him shaking the victim because she was noisy; and attributed her death to his father's violence. The offender presented witnesses who testified that the victim's injuries could have been caused by a fall. However, his young children testified that he often physically abused them (e.g., whipped them with cords). The offender was convicted. Even though 13 witnesses testified to mitigate his sentence, two aggravating circumstances guided the jury. They found him to pose a continuing threat; and they believed that his crime was heinous and atrocious. He was sentenced to death.

Infant as Weapons, Shields, or Hostages

Every so often, criminals use infants as weapons or shields during crimes. Some offenders have launched infants at police, while others have directly used infants as hostages or to shield their bodies (e.g., from being struck by a taser). For example, one 23-year-old woman was suspected of shoplifting clothing worth $261 from a department store (The Smoking Gun, 2013). She hid the clothing in a baby stroller as she shopped. After realizing that police were notified by store security, she jumped into a getaway vehicle driven by her husband. Inside the vehicle were a four-year-old girl and a two-year-old boy. She held her three-month-old daughter in a baby carrier as she fled from police. While fleeing, she shouted "You will have to shoot through the baby to get me!" Then she fled on foot from the car with the carrier, which she tossed several feet in the air toward police. Rather than stop to rescue the baby, who was uninjured, an officer proceeded to apprehend the shoplifter, who had tripped. While bleeding from a head injury, the woman allegedly said, "Now you motherfuckers have my blood all over you, bitches." Later, the shoplifter claimed that she had stolen school clothes for her children, but she actually shoplifted women's clothes. She was charged with felony child abuse, theft, and resisting arrest.

Nonconsensual Insemination

Nonconsensual insemination may occur under a variety of scenarios including the following: (1) initial consent for penetration is conditioned on parties' mutual intent to use the withdrawal method, but one party intentionally fails to withdraw and intentionally causes insemination; (2) consent for penetration is withdrawn during otherwise consensual sex prior to insemination, with sufficient time for withdrawal, but one party intentionally continues to engage in intercourse to cause insemination after consent for penetration has been withdrawn; or (3) one party intentionally misleads the other to cause insemination (Cusack, 2012; Cusack, 2013a; Cusack, 2013b; Cusack, 2013c). Due to jurisdictional variations, only some sexual assault and assault laws may apply to these scenarios. Depending on statutory language, case law, and legislative intent, these scenarios may be prosecuted or tolerated by the criminal justice system, or they may fall into legal gray areas.

In some jurisdictions, consent can be withdrawn during sex (*In re John Z*, 2003). Definitions of "consent," and rules about withdrawal, express consent, express revocation, and other factors may be determinative. Jurisdictions provide various definitions for "consent." For example, one definition is that "'[c]onsent' implies a willingness, voluntariness, free will, reasoned or intelligent choice, physical or moral power of acting, or an active act of concurrence (as opposed to a passive assent) unclouded by fraud, duress, or mistake" (*People v. Whitten*, 1995, p. 104). "[P]ositive cooperation in act or attitude pursuant to the exercise of free will" is another definition of consent (*People v. Williams*, 1992). Thus, earlier consent may be nullified when consent is withdrawn (*People v. Roundtree*, 2000). If consensual sex is occurring, and the victim actively or attitudinally expresses objection or withdrawal of consent, and attempts to stop sex, then continuation by the defendant is forcible. However, some jurisdictions require demonstrations of force, not withdrawal of consent, prior to penetration to prosecute offenders.

Some critics of nonconsensual insemination argue that because state laws do not require seminal emission to complete an act of sexual intercourse, consent for sex does not automatically or presumptively grant consent for insemination (Conn. Gen. Stat. § 53a-65, 2013). Without express or implied consent for insemination, continuing sex to achieve insemination could be considered to be sexual assault. In one case, the court mentioned that it was an act of sex abuse for the defendant to ejaculate inside of another's orifice (*State v. Makekau*, 2007). Ejaculation may be a separate form of penetration or intrusion since emission is not required for intrusion to occur (HRS § 707-700, 2013). For example, New Hampshire's sexual assault statute lists ejaculate as an emission capable of causing sexual contact (NH Stat. §632A (4)-(5), 2013).

Bullington v. State (1993) held that consent to sex acts may be implied where the victim is affirmatively discussing the sexual activity and does not verbalize her absence of consent. Consent may be withheld or withdrawn, but consent may need to be communicated or indicated (*Bullington v. State*, 1993; *State v. Rider*, 1984). Thus, express consent for penetration may imply affirmative consent for insemination in some jurisdictions; especially when ejaculation is considered to be part of the same sex act as the original penetrative act. Even when withdrawal of consent is expressed or sufficiently implied, courts could examine whether the victim's actions gave sufficient notice. When a victim communicates revocation of consent following consensual sexual intercourse in a jurisdiction that acknowledges revocation, but the sexual intercourse continues, then the defendant has committed sexual assault in the first degree (*State v. Siering*, 1994). However, the defendant may have a reasonable amount of time to respond to the withdrawal of consent (*State v. Bunyard*, 2003). Thus, depending on when the victim expressed nonconsent for insemination, the defendant's failure to withdraw could constitute rape. Five minutes, for example, is not a reasonable amount of time to continue penetration once consent has been withdrawn. Some critics argue that consent for insemination is implied by non-use of condoms.

Under some circumstances, the defendant can make the inference that consent was constructively withdrawn (*McWatters v. State*, 2010). The existence of consent for a sex act must exist at the relevant time (*State v. Garcia*, 1984). In *State v. Ayala*, the defendant was convicted when the victim asserted that she believed that the defendant knew that she did not consent, even though she verbalized consent out of fear (1994).

State v. Ayala could stand for the proposition that verbalizations may not be as determinative as a victim's belief that the defendant knew that sexual intercourse during insemination was nonconsensual. Consent at the relevant time is an objective fact; nonconsensual sex acts cannot be consented to after the fact (*State v. Garcia*, 1984). Under this law, the court may need to decide whether at the time consent for initial penetration was granted the sex act was anticipated to include insemination; and whether non-consent for penetration during insemination or insemination was expressed, obviated, or implied by the circumstances. Thus, victims should not be blamed for having unprotected sex when they do not expressly consent to insemination (Cusack, 2012; Cusack, 2013a; Buchhandler-Raphael, 2010; Solinas-Saunders, 2007; *State v. Bunyard*, 2003; Subotnik, 2007).

Non-consent may be defined by absence of an agreement or resistance implied or expressed; and sexual assault may be proven by either direct or circumstantial evidence (*State v. Tatum*, 1980; *State v. Holloman*, 1976; *State v. Willis*, 1986; *State v. Hirsch*, 1994). Typically, agreements must be intelligent, knowing, and voluntary (Fla. Stat. § 794.011, 2012). However, consent is a relative term that can be evaluated in light of the circumstances (*Commonwealth v. Ascolillo*, 1989; *Russell v. State*, 1991). A jury must determine whether consent was intelligent, knowing, and voluntary (*Gautreaux v. State*, 1991). The state must prove that the victim did not consent because non-consent is an element of sexual assault; and the state must prove every element of the crime (*Soukup v. State*, 2000; *Khianthalat v. State*, 2006). Consent is a defense. In some jurisdictions, affirmative and freely granted permission for a specific act of penetration (e.g., insemination) can be inferred (*In Interest of M.T.S.*, 1992). Inferences can reasonably be drawn from either acts or statements under the totality of circumstances (*In Interest of M.T.S.*, 1992; *State v. Hilding*, 2009). Express, affirmative permission is not required if a reasonable person would have believed that permission was affirmatively and freely granted for a particular act of penetration (*In Interest of M.T.S.*, 1992). A victim does not need to unequivocally express an absence of desire or a desire to conclude sexual activity. Failure to protest or resist does not transform unwanted contact into consensual contact. Yet, in some jurisdictions sexual assault through nonconsensual insemination only occurs if the force used is greater than the force required to penetrate (*Commonwealth v. Wallace*, 2010). This is the extrinsic force standard. Under *State v. Sedia* (1993) and numerous other cases, courts recognize an intrinsic force standard. Intrinsic force standards require no greater force than the force necessary to penetrate. Several jurisdictions have adopted this standard.

Fraud in fact occurs when an act is different from what the defendant said he or she would do (*State v. Bolsinger*, 2006). Fraud in fact vitiates consent. Fraud in the inducement, whereby the promised act occurs for an ulterior purpose, does not vitiate consent. In *State v. Bolsinger* (2006), boys agreed to give semen for a research study, but no such study existed. This vitiated their consent because they agreed to ejaculate under one set of reasoning, but not under the condition that actually occurred. Nonconsensual insemination can result from fraud in fact. If a person agrees to have sex pursuant to the withdrawal method, but the defendant does not withdraw, then consent is vitiated because the defendant promised one type of sexual activity but performed another. A victim of nonconsensual insemination does not experience fraud in the inducement if the defendant's motives for insemination (e.g., ulterior or forthright) are immaterial or irrelevant.

In jurisdictions where sexual assault statutes are inapplicable to nonconsensual insemination, battery laws may apply. Battery laws vary between jurisdictions (Cusack, 2012). In some jurisdictions, the slightest unwanted, rude, or harmful touching can constitute a battery. Nonconsensual insemination may qualify as a battery in jurisdictions where injury is not required. However, in other jurisdictions, batteries are not sustained unless victims are damaged or injured. Harm may result from disease transmission or pregnancy during sexual assault; thus, perhaps these kinds of harms would result in the requisite damage under battery laws.

Nonconsensual insemination is a legal, social, and interpersonal problem that may primarily affect women, but likely also victimizes men. In a pilot study, no men reported having been inseminated by partners, but 60 percent of male respondents had committed nonconsensual insemination (Cusack, 2013c). However, 20 percent of males had been forced by female partners to inseminate. Approximately 10 percent of female respondents admitted to committing nonconsensual insemination; but approximately two-thirds of females reported being victims of nonconsensual insemination. Only about one-quarter had never been victims of nonconsensual insemination. Only a single female respondent had been victimized and committed nonconsensual insemination. No respondents had ever reported nonconsensual insemination to police or health care providers or been asked about it by health care providers. Despite its prevalence, 100 percent of male respondents and 86 percent of female respondents reportedly felt that nonconsensual insemination is "wrong." A study of state-level prosecutors throughout the United States asked whether prosecutors would prosecute nonconsensual insemination if a health care provider and a patient reported the event to police, and police arrested a perpetrator (Cusack, 2014). Seventy-five percent of female respondents and 19 percent of male respondents reported that they would prosecute. More than half, approximately 57 percent, of total respondents reported that they would not prosecute based on the given scenario. Thus, criminal justice response to nonconsensual insemination may be gendered. Responses may reflect traditional gender norms imposed on victims, perpetrators, and members of the criminal justice system.

Criminal Insemination

The government has an interest in preventing the effects of unwanted pregnancy resulting from sexual violations (*Griffin v. Warden*, 1982). Some statutes provide legal consequences for reproductive coercion or unintended pregnancy resulting from sexual assault. For example, first-degree sexual assault may occur when nonconsensual penetration causes pregnancy or great bodily harm (Wis. Stat. Ann. § 940.225, 2013). Pregnancy may be sufficient to show bodily harm (§ 720 ILCS 5/11-1.30, 2013; *People v. Bishop*, 2006; *People v. Mays*, 2011). In *People v. Bishop*, the victim's pregnancy was aborted, yet the aggravation occurred with the pregnancy in itself (*People v. Bishop*, 2006; *People v. Haywood*, 1987). However, neither pregnancy nor injury is required to prove sexual assault (*People v. Trail*, 1990; *People v. Bowen*, 1993). Nonconsensual contact may be prosecuted more harshly when contact results in any illness; disease, injury, or impairment of a sexual or reproductive organ; or mental anguish requiring medical care (MCLS § 750.520a, 2013; Nev. Rev. Stat. Ann. § 0.060, 2012; *People v. Cathey*, 2004; R.R.S. Neb. § 28-318, 2012; *State v. Martin*, 1989).

Sexually transmitted disease (STD) transmission may be illegal in some jurisdictions under certain circumstances (Cusack, 2013d). When STD transmission is caused by sexual assault, then aggravated sexual assault and battery statutes apply. However, when nonconsensual transmission of STDs results during consensual sexual activity, then transmission may be criminalized. Depending on the circumstances, HIV transmission is a crime in approximately half of U.S. states (Ala. Stat. § 22-11A-21(c), 2011; Alaska Stat. § 12.55.155 (c)(33), 2011; Cal. Code 120290, 2011; Cal Stat. § 12022.85, 2011; Miss. Stat. § 97-27-14, 2011; Okla. Stat. 21 § 1031, 1192, 2011; §191.677 R.S. Mo., 2012; N.Y. Code PBH 2307, 2011; S.D. Stat. § 22-18-31-34, 2011; Tenn. Stat. §§ 39-13-109 -516, 2011; Tenn. Stat. § 68-10-107, 2011; Utah Stat. § 76-5-102.6, 2011; Utah Stat. § 76-10-1309, 2013). Nonconsensual HIV transmission may specifically be criminalized when HIV transmission is intentional or knowing (Kan. Stat. § 21-3435, 2011; Nev. Stat. § 201.205, 2011; N.J. Stat. § 2C:34-5, 2011; Va. Stat. § 18.2:67.4, 2011; Va. Stat. § 32.1-289.2, 2011). Exposing a victim to HIV or causing a victim to fear HIV transmission may also be a crime (Wash Stat. § 9A.36.011, 2011). Consent may be a defense to intentional HIV transmission (Ohio Stat. §§ 2903.11 - 2927.13, 2011).

Nonconsensual transmission of other STDs may also be criminal (Mo. Stat. § 191.677, 2011; S.C. Stat. §§ 44-29-60 -145, 2011; R.I. Stat. § 23-11-1, 2011). Informed consent, including affirmative consent or express consent, may be a defense against transmission (Ark. Stat. § 5-14-123, 2011; S.C. Stat. § 44-29-60 -145, 2011; S.D. Stat. § 22-18-31-34, 2011). In some jurisdictions, consenting to sex implies consent for STD transmission (Burns Ind. Code Ann. § 35-42-2-6, 2013; Idaho Stat. § 39-601; 39-608, 2011; § 720 IL 5-16.2, 2011; Iowa Stat. § 709C.1, 2011; Mich. Stat. § 333.5210, 2013).

A 50-state survey provided prosecutors with a hypothetical scenario in which a gender-neutral victim disclosed nonconsensual insemination to a health care provider who reported it to police as a crime (Cusack, 2014). Police investigated and referred it for prosecution. Without specific details about the crime (e.g., reproductive coercion or STD transmission), prosecutors were asked whether they would prosecute nonconsensual insemination as sexual abuse, battery, intimate partner violence, or another crime. Roughly 43 percent of prosecutors reported that they would prosecute. Slightly more than 40 percent of respondents were female; and slightly less than 60 percent were male. Of the total affirmative decisions to prosecute, 75 percent were made by female prosecutors; and 81 percent of prosecutors who elected not to prosecute were male. These findings could have implications about how criminality is understood and labeled; and how insemination is contextualized within gender politics and perceptions of sex roles.

CHAPTER 16

Illness

Mental Illness

Historically, women's criminal responsibility was considered in light of mental illness, which, in part, was attributable to menstruation, pregnancy, and childbirth (Kelly, 2009). Insanity and mental defect were considered to be similar to weakness in some cases (Meggendorfer, 1931). Explanations for criminal behavior were mainly biological. Heredity was used to explain why psychiatric treatment failed in some cases. Theories of social Darwinism explained that mental illness was proportionate to effective medicine. As medicine became more reliable, unfit genes were more likely to survive. Eugenicists believed that prescreenings prior to marriage for hereditary mental illness could improve breeding and consequently lower crime. Divorce reform was sought on behalf of individuals married to partners with mental defects. Birth control was also suggested for criminally insane individuals. Institutionalization, and resultant incapacitation, became a form of eugenic birth control for a period in history. Throughout the nineteenth and twentieth centuries, eugenically oriented sterilization was practiced. In 1965, a survey of administrators at 105 state mental hospitals and 48 schools for mentally retarded students found that illegitimate pregnancies within these populations occurred at one-fifth the rate of the general population (Wignall and Meredith, 1968). This low but substantial figure was likely central to institutions' respective decisions in favor of and contrary to contraceptive prescription, depending on their opinions about this population and the management of associated risks.

In the 1980s, researchers studied a group of women who were of child-bearing age, between 13 years old and 42 years old, who were admitted to inpatient treatment for psychiatric disorders (Shapiro, 1983). The disorders related to abortions and pregnancy. Approximately two-thirds of the sample had experienced prior psychotic episodes that required hospitalization. Onset of illness varied between gestational and postpartum periods. Schizophrenia, chronic psychotic disturbances, and borderline personality states were prevalent. Though medicine is capable of treating these illnesses so that many patients are able to manage and live normal lives, in general, women are much more likely to participate in cycles of crime if they suffer from any severe mental illness. Women with severe mental illness who do not receive treatment are at much greater risks for incarceration (Brendel and Soulier, 2009).

Among incarcerated women, 6 to 10 percent are pregnant (*Journal of Obstetric, Gynecologic, and Neonatal Nursing*, 2010). Pregnancies within this population are typically unintended and of high risk. A large percentage of psychotic women become pregnant (Gentile, 2006). Thus, unintended pregnancy among inmates with psychiatric disorders is also high. In general, prior to encountering the criminal justice system, pregnant women are unlikely to have received any prenatal care; and they are likely to have been involved in intimate partner violence and traumatic experiences (*Journal of Obstetric, Gynecologic, and Neonatal Nursing*, 2010). In addition to drug addiction and mental illness, they are also likely to suffer from poor nutrition, infectious diseases, and chronic diseases. These problems likely contribute to mental illness, drug addiction, and crime cycles to some extent.

Treatment in correctional settings for psychiatric disorders may include treatment for substance abuse, personality disorders, behavioral disorders, trauma, suicidality, and posttraumatic stress disorder (Brendel and Soulier, 2009). Trauma-informed and trauma-specific services may require integration of behavioral, cognitive, psychological, and pharmacological strategies and treatments (Veysey, 1998). For example, security staff spending several hours each day with women in institutional settings should receive sensitivity training to appropriately respond to traumatized pregnant women. Treatment may also include protocols for HIV- or AIDS-exposed pregnancies. Inmates may receive therapeutic treatment designed to habilitate and educate about motherhood. Seventy-five percent of women in jail exhibit a mental disorder (Veysey, 1998). Most arrested women test positive for drugs; however, only one-quarter have received outpatient treatment for drugs. Mental health treatment, drug treatment, and habitability should continue after inpatient care; and women in therapy should expect to receive integrated outpatient care and treatment also. For example, in a study among primiparous women in England, 7 percent were admitted to state inpatient care for one month or more (Wolkind, 1977). Admitted patients were likely to be unmarried teenagers living in poor housing conditions. They reported that their health deteriorated during pregnancy, and they scored higher on a malaise inventory. In addition to treatment for habitability and mood, some pregnant women may require treatment for specific kinds of self-harming disorders (e.g., bulimia) (McKnight, 2010). Holistic treatments help women avoid criminal justice encounters because they may integrate biopsychosocial treatments (Ghaemi, 2009; Hatala, 2012; Veysey, 1998).

Institutionalized pregnant or puerperium women may be treated with psychotropic drugs (Gentile, 2006). They may require combinations of psychotropic drugs if their illnesses are capricious. Some debate exists about the safety of newer psychotropic drugs in comparison to older psychotropic drugs, and sometimes patients must make important decisions about treatment and risk. Their psychopharmacological needs may be distinct from other patients due to relationships between treatment and breastfeeding in adverse medical conditions (American Psychiatric Publishing, 2012; Gentile, 2006; *In re K.E.A.*, 2012). Pregnant patients may be institutionalized after failing to take prescribed medication for mental disorders. In one case, a woman with bipolar disorder was institutionalized after she stopped taking medicine and threatened that if she could not immediately and prematurely deliver, then she would commit suicide and feticide by drowning; swallow abortifacients to induce labor or to abort the fetus; or incise her abdomen to surgically remove the child (*In re D.W.M., Jr.*, 2014). After giving birth, she wanted to retain custody of her child and dismissed her threats as being empty. Following delivery, mentally ill women are at high risk of relapse following mother-baby bonding (Gentile, 2006). Thus, appropriate treatment is imperative during the early postpartum period. Mother-baby hospital units may likely be the best place to treat psychotic women; however, these units may not be available, especially in small or rural communities (Gentile, 2006).

In some cases, women may not want to bond with newborns or receive certain treatment. Some treatments (e.g., experimental drugs) may require informed consent (Constantine, 2008). In the general population, researchers have found that informed consent is only sought for half of treatments requiring informed consent if patients believe that procedures are routine and do not require consent. Among psychiatric populations, care providers may not adequately inform patients about informed consent. While health care providers may believe that patients have a right to refuse treatment, few patients may know their rights (Cusack, 2013). For example, a study in Finland measured inpatients' self-determination and perceptions of decision-making rights and rights to refuse treatment (Valimaki, Leino-Kilpi, and Helenius, 1996). Researchers found that 75 percent of respondents believed that they had rights, but only 39 percent believed that they could refuse treatment; and 8 percent did not believe that they had a right to express their opinions. Even when patients are skeptical about treatment plans requiring informed consent, health care providers may manipulate their options or information, or they may manipulate patients psychologically.

Some institutions may use non-pharmacologic approaches to manage pregnant women's mental disorders (Brogan, 2013). Immune modulation, toxicity, vitamin D, folate, and fatty acids may be managed. Doses of SAMe that are safe for pregnant women and bright-light therapy may also be useful. In some institutions, cranial electrical stimulators may be self-administered by patients to help regulate endorphins, neurotransmitters, and cortisol to reduce anxiety, depression, and insomnia. Social and environmental factors may likely contribute to postpartum depression or moodiness (Seward, 1972). Formulating desirable attitudes and mental perspectives among patients' relatives prior to delivery and making arrangements for family assistance following birth may aid postpartum recovery.

Children born to institutionalized mothers will be at increased risk for delinquency and crime due to possible genetic tendencies, absence of one or both parental figures, high-risk pregnancy, and experiencing custodial care for any period of time. In a longitudinal study over 20 years, 86 female and 121 male Danes were studied beginning at approximately 15 years old (Silverton, Finello, and Mednick, 1983). Their risk for schizophrenia was much higher than others in their age cohort. Using the Current and Past Psychopathology Scales and the Present State Examination, infancy temperament, perinatal complications, institutionalization, and early separation were analyzed as predictors for schizophrenia later in life. Pregnancy and birth complications prevalent in high-risk pregnancies among institutionalized women correlated with schizophrenia. In that study, early separation correlated with schizophrenia among high-risk males, but not high-risk females. Traumatic pregnancies and births, maternal psychopathology, early state care, or extended-family custody may produce pathogenic and intergenerational institutionalization.

Amount of time spent in custodial care, environmental stability, quality of care, adequacy of medical care, and racial similarity between the child and people in the custodial environment may also affect risk (Mullin, 2012).

HIV

Vertical transmission of HIV between mothers and infants may be criminalized in some jurisdictions depending on how transmission occurs. Pregnant women are not required to consent to HIV blood testing (*Doe v. Division of Youth & Family Services*, 2001; *In re J.M. and L.N.*, 2013; Ulrich, 2012). However, HIV-positive pregnant women may elect to take medication that reduces likelihood of in utero vertical transmission. To reduce the likelihood of HIV transmission, some prophylactic interventions (e.g., antiretroviral therapy and C-section surgery) may be performed prior to membrane rupture (Kaplan, 2010). Courts may not order pregnant women to undergo prophylactic measures. Transmission of HIV is a crime in approximately half of states, but HIV laws may not apply to in utero transmission. For example, any conduct that can be reasonably calculated to result in transference of HIV-positive bodily fluids is a crime in Oklahoma unless the uninfected person grants informed consent (Oklahoma §21–1192.1, 2013). In utero transmission is excluded from prosecution; however, postpartum transmission is not excluded. Courts may order newborn infants to be placed into child protective services (CPS) custody in a hospital hold to be tested for drug addiction and HIV exposure or infection (Kaplan, 2010). Mothers may be required to administer HIV medication to infants and submit to supervision by CPS. Mothers who fail to take or administer medication ordered for infants' well-being can be charged with abuse and neglect (HIV Justice Network, 2008). Criminal sanctions have been imposed against some parents who knowingly, willfully, or negligently stop providing necessary medicine to HIV-exposed or HIV-positive infants.

Some estimates show that one-quarter of pregnant HIV-positive women transmit HIV in utero (McGowan and Shah, 2000). Studies show that enhanced interventions are necessary to reduce transmission, achieve compliance with strategic protocols, and build comprehension among infected mothers (Richter et al., 2014). Enhanced interventions may include several antenatal and postnatal small group meetings. Globally, organizational focus has been placed on reducing vertical transmission through education and destigmatization (PEPFAR.Gov, 2011). Achieving comprehension among target populations may be somewhat difficult because information about transmission changes as studies' findings emerge. For example, definitive information about the likelihood of transmission during mixed breastfeeding and exclusive breastfeeding is lacking, despite hundreds of thousands of documented cases of transmission through breastfeeding annually (De Cock et al., 2000; Rossenkhan et al., 2012; Shapiro, 2003). Worldwide, HIV-positive mothers have been criticized, and they may feel stigmatized (Nutman, Mckee, and Khoshnood, 2013). Stigmatization reduces overall benefits because it discourages women from seeking education, being self-efficacious, and adhering to treatment plans (Turan and Nyblade, 2013). Preventive steps successively build and dropping out disrupts progress. For example, mothers who feel stigmatized may be less willing to ask partners about their HIV status or follow mother-child transmission-prevention feeding strategies. However, stigmatization may also play an important role in deterring women from engaging in behaviors that transmit disease. Stigmatization could help pressure mothers to prevent mother-child transmission. For example, stigmatization may deter women from engaging in risky sex or pregnancies while using drugs. However, some intravenous drug users are unaware that they are HIV-positive until after they become pregnant (Thorne, Semenenko, and Malyuta, 2012). Thus, some groups who are likely to transmit HIV, such as poor women, drug users, and women with poor hygiene, may be stigmatized for reasons in addition to HIV-positive status (Hassan, 2012; Meier and Labbok, 2010). When these factors are coupled with clinicians' lack of training, knowledge, and understanding, HIV-positive mothers may receive little support, become likely to drop out of treatment programs, and increase their likelihood of transmitting HIV knowingly, willfully, or negligently.

Postpartum Psychiatric Disorders

Postpartum anxiety, depression, and psychosis have been blamed for or linked to crime. The Diagnostic and Statistical Manual, fifth edition (DSMV), does not classify postpartum illnesses separately, but it does specify postpartum onset for psychosis. Infanticide is the most common crime associated with postpartum illnesses. Infanticide is discussed further in Chapter 15 and Chapter 17. When postpartum mothers kill infants, they may not be charged with murder if they can prove that they suffered from diminished responsibility or insanity (Gosselin and Bury, 1969). For example, in one case, a mother believed that prescribed antidepressants would enter her children's bloodstreams through her breast milk. She feared that if she breastfed her children, then child protective services (CPS) would remove her children. She suffocated her children. Because she suffered from a perinatal psychiatric condition, her charges were reduced from murder to manslaughter. Another woman suffering from postpartum mental illness suddenly became confused and dissociative. She sprinkled talcum powder on her infant's face, which caused asphyxiation and death. Postpartum psychosis is present in almost all successful defenses for Not Guilty by Reason of Insanity (NGRI) (Friedman and Sorrentino, 2012). However, postpartum depression is insufficient to succeed on an NGRI defense.

Postpartum psychosis may result in hallucinations, disorganization, delirium, confusion, mood swings, dissociative behavior, and possibly insomnia (Friedman and Sorrentino, 2012). Postpartum psychosis onsets within weeks of birth. Postpartum depression is likely to relate to bipolar disorder either through the mother's family history or personal history (Friedman and Sorrentino, 2012; Monzon, di Scalea, and Pearlstein, 2014). Dysphoric mania may rapidly shift manic and depressive symptoms, or permit the symptoms to coexist. Hallucinations during postpartum psychosis are similar to hallucinations caused by other disorders; however, delusions progress quickly and tend to focus on the infant, motherhood, or the mother's life. Mothers are at greater risk for perpetrating violence if delusions center on her infant's evilness or a belief that the infant is not her child. Untreated, postpartum psychosis increases risk of infanticide 4 percent and risk for suicide 5 percent (Friedman and Sorrentino, 2012).

Postpartum psychosis is somewhat rare, but postpartum depression is somewhat common. Postpartum psychosis is present in approximately two of every 100,000 births (Friedman and Sorrentino, 2012). Postpartum depression, which is like major depression and anxiety, affects 10 to 20 percent of mothers. Women with family or personal history of depression, heavy stress, low emotional support, and poor sleep are at greater risk. Women who suffer from schizophrenia are at an increased risk of 25 percent (Monzon, di Scalea, and Pearlstein, 2014). Despite the relatively low rates, postpartum is when women are generally at highest risk for mental illness (Monzon, di Scalea, and Pearlstein, 2014). Mental illness may onset immediately after birth or within a year after birth;

depression may possibly onset further than psychosis from the time of birth. However, approximately one-quarter of women who suffer from postpartum psychosis are symptomatic one year after initiating medical treatment. A mother who has experienced postpartum psychosis is highly likely to experience subsequent postpartum mental conditions, like blues or depressions, with another child. Postpartum blues are not depression, but may contribute to attitudinal changes that result in crime. Postpartum blues reportedly affect 50 percent to 75 percent of women.

Young fathers are not immune from postpartum depression and baby blues (Lee, Fagan, and Chen, 2012). In a longitudinal study of 1,403 young fathers with toddlers, 46 percent were African American, 27 percent were White, 23 percent were Latino, and 4 percent were another ethnicity or race. The Composite International Diagnostic Interview-Short Form (CIDI-SF) was used to measure depressive symptoms. Late-adolescent fatherhood and irregular pay significantly correlated with depressive symptoms during the third year of fatherhood, but not the fifth year. Fathers with low social support were likely to be depressed at the third and fifth years. Fathers who experienced stress because of encounters with the criminal justice system (i.e., being booked or charged with crimes) also experienced fifth-year depressive symptoms, but not third-year symptoms. First-year symptoms did not predict depressive symptoms during the third or fifth years. These findings emphasize situational and environmental factors in postpartum depression and blues, as well as biological factors in postpartum psychosis that affect women.

CHAPTER 17

International and Comparative

Europe

Legal issues relating to pregnancy and infants throughout Europe are as complex and wide-ranging as problems in the United States. Widespread child abandonment has correlated with economic despair throughout Europe. Abandonment is discussed in Chapter 5 and Chapter 12. Child abandonment in Greece has crested due to economic hardship (Carassava, 2014). It mirrors abandonment in Romania during the 1980s, as parents abandon newborns wrapped inside pillowcases, cardboard boxes, and towels at orphanages, hospitals, clinics, and charities. Some estimates describe spikes in abandonment as being between 300 and 1,000 percent.

England's Infanticide Law, discussed in Chapter 15, led other nations to consider the relevance of psychological disorders to postpartum manslaughter of child victims. Yet, infanticide among Europeans has increased over the past 20 years. Some nations, such as Hungary, have maintained high rates; but these figures, as well as increases in other nations, are attributed to economic fluctuations (i.e., poverty), not mental illness (Journeyman Pictures, 2007). Figures became alarmingly high during the collapse of the world economy between 2005 and 2011; and in some nations, Ireland for example, filicide-suicide rates soared (Connolly, 2007).

Infants being born and living inside penal colonies is on the rise throughout Europe (e.g., Russia and Italy) (Jail Babies, 2013). In her memoir, Amanda Knox describes her time in an Italian prison with a little girl named Mina (Knox, 2013). Her mother, Gregora, was uncertain of Mina's age because she lived in prison throughout her life. After some years, prison officials guesstimated that Mina was three years old; so, she was moved into an orphanage. Mina was permitted to visit her mother for one hour each month. Of the day that Mina was forced to leave the maternity ward to live in an orphanage, Knox said, "prison tore families apart, and they could never be stitched back together."

Corporate criminal charges were brought in Germany for birth defects resulting from birth control. In 1968, an extensive criminal trial was held to determine whether Grünenthal agents were culpable of negligent homicide and injury. The company was found not guilty by the criminal court; and they settled with victims. The settlement required them to pay 100 million deutsche marks into a foundation, which paid victims; and they were fined another 320 million deutsche marks by the government. In 2008, the corporation paid 50 million Euros to the foundation.

Canada and Australia

In Australia and Canada one of the most serious issues with pregnancy and infants resulted from racial conflicts between Whites and Natives. Since the beginning of European settlement in Australia, Europeans removed Indigenous children and employed them to inculcate them and benefit from their labor (Australian Government, 2009). In 1814, a school for Aboriginal children was founded that appealed to Indigenous families; yet the school was actually designed to separate children psychologically and culturally from their traditions and families. After voluntarily sending their children at first, Aboriginal communities eventually became hostile toward the school. Settlers began to systematically remove and inculcate Indigenous children. Children were placed at reform schools, stations, and industrial schools. First, children were removed as toddlers and sent to dormitories; and then, as teens they were sent to work at settlements or missions. There, at least 10 percent of girls were sexually abused; and boys' heads were shaved and they were divested of their possessions. Children were treated as prison inmates without due process or identity and subject to constant surveillance. Assimilation policies and practices ostracized and discriminated against Natives; thus, the government reformed assimilation practices, making assimilation optional in 1967. Following inquiry by the Human Rights and Equal Opportunity Commission, Australia began to officially recognize harm caused by assimilation.

In Canada, a truth-and-reconciliation commission was formed to discuss stolen generations (Cusack, 2015; Karpenchuk, 2011). More than 1,000 victims and relatives shared accounts of how Native children in Canada were forced to assimilate into White society. They were required to attend religious boarding schools financed by the Canadian government beginning in the late 1800s. Like Aboriginal children in Australia, Canadian Natives were deprived of their language and traditions; and thousands suffered sexual, psychological, and physical abuse (Lyons, n.d.). The schools were not phased out until the 1960s; and the government refrained from apologizing until 1998. Controversy in Canada continues as skeptics of procreative rights allege that Planned Parenthood and other abortion providers target Natives (Mosher and Mason, 2008). Critics have compared low-cost abortion services to genocide because of historical connections between abortion, sterilization, and eugenics in North America, including among Native North Americans (Rutecki, 2010; Wabie and Morgan, 2012). Planned Parenthood defends its practices by maintaining that it serves less-affluent communities; and some poor communities have Native constituents. The Native Women's Association of Canada (2004) indicates that Aboriginal women continue to lack any access to reproductive health care clinics or telemedicine providing emergency contraception and abortion.

Africa

Several nations in Africa routinely experience human rights violations involving rape and impregnation. One example is corrective rape and impregnation of lesbians in South Africa. In South Africa, as many as one in four men have nonconsensual sex with women; but, corrective rape is a practice that targets lesbians to shame them (Carter, 2013). Rapists believe that women are supposed to want men sexually; or that lesbians believe that they are males. Thus, raping them may be perceived as an educational or enlightening experience. Some victims are brutally gang raped and murdered. In some cases, women who are merely suspected of being lesbians are raped. In one case, a woman was seen at a bar with a friend. After she was raped, her attacker shattered her skull; gouged her eyes out; and stabbed her repeatedly with shards of glass. Families have assisted rapists, and in some cases, arranged marriages to convert lesbians into heteronormative wives. Victims are regularly met with apathy by religious institutions and the criminal justice system, even when they contract HIV or are impregnated. In one case, a lesbian woman was raped by her uncle when she was a child. He later tried to sell her to one of his friends. She became impregnated by her uncle's friend and contracted HIV from her uncle. The victim carried the pregnancy to term; and was impregnated again by a priest who raped her. She bore the child and filed a complaint against the priest; but she was ignored. Some lesbian children have been kidnapped because their mothers are gay. It is difficult for lesbian mothers to exercise parental rights because the system is apathetic toward them.

Fetal Alcohol Spectrum Disorder (FASD) affects a disproportionally high percentage of South African children (Crawford, 2013). Since 2002, South Africans have experienced the highest rates of FASD worldwide. Some South African women have begun participating in child abuse to manipulate the child welfare system. Pregnant patrons drink with the goal of injuring fetuses because children suffering from Fetal Alcohol Syndrome receive financial assistance from the state. Speakeasies sell highly toxic moonshine to pregnant women. Police attempt to shutdown speakeasies, but they cannot be stamped out because they are clandestine and easy to operate. One study of pregnant women in South Africa found that those with histories of trauma are more likely to drink during pregnancy even if they were less likely to drink before pregnancy (Choi et al., 2014). Drinking before pregnancy does not predict drinking during pregnancy as much as traumatic experiences do.

Asia

Due to sex-selective female feticide, infanticide (i.e., gendercide), abuse, and neglect, approximately 25 percent of girls in India die before puberty (Davis, 2012; Freed and Freed, 1989). The mortality rate of girls between the ages of one and five is 40 percent higher than that of boys in part because of son preference and daughter avoidance. Factors for why women are considered to be a burden include patriarchy, poverty, and the dowry system. Men may force their wives to have male children first, because a male child is assumed to better protect siblings and family prosperity. Approximately 200 million women may be missing from the world due to gendercide. India and China kill more girls annually than the number of girls born in the United States annually. Sex-determination tests are illegal in India because they are used for sex-selective abortion. Pre-Conception and Pre-Natal Diagnostic Techniques (PCPNDT) ultrasounds are not permitted to reveal gender. The PCPNDT Act of 1994 prohibits gender identification during sonograms; yet many doctors are bribed and ignore the law. In addition to willful violations, there is little governmental enforcement. Women who choose to carry female fetuses unwanted by their husband or husband's family may be physically abused to induce abortion. Women's families may be supportive of female children, but wives may not disclose abuse to their families. Some women in India voluntarily participate in sex-selective abortions and infanticide. For the first time in India's history, a mother was convicted of infanticide in 1997 and sentenced to life in prison.

In China, a one-child policy was implemented in 1979. In 1999, rural families were permitted to have two children if their first child was a daughter (*Zheng v. Mukasey*, 2009). Previously, parents could have two children if neither parent had siblings; but the law was recently eased so that parents may have two children if either one is an only child. Financial punishments for attempting to have a third child (i.e., a son) result in a 10 percent income tax for parents for several years. Due to severe consequences, sex-selective abortions are practiced. However, sex-selective abortions are explicitly banned. Despite worldwide condemnation of Chinese reproductive policies, sex-selective abortions are not banned in many countries, including the United States, where most jurisdictions permit it (Wang, 2014). In China, paid informants may disclose illegal pregnancies to the family planning office. Sweeps for illegal pregnancies in neighborhoods have resulted in forced abortions after the family planning police raid homes and round up women. Ample anecdotal evidence demonstrates that late-term abortions have been perfunctorily performed; and involuntary sterilization has been utilized in some cases. Women have been forced to undergo regular gynecological exams and use intrauterine devices against their wills. One woman who was pregnant in her final trimester claimed that officials broke into her home and dragged her into a car (*Zheng v. Mukasey*, 2009). She was taken to a clinic and given an abortifacient shot. The injection caused a sharp pain in her abdomen, and within one hour she delivered a stillborn child. Police threatened to arrest her husband and he went into hiding. The one-child policy is designed to help reduce poverty and modernize the nation, but impoverished parents have resorted to selling children and infants rather than using birth control (Ying, 2012). In one recent case, Chinese officials made 802 arrests relating to two infant trafficking gangs who were attempting to sell 181 abducted children. Some are mothers who have trafficked their own children. Newborns are worth approximately $150 to $300 to parents; but newborns retail at a 500 percent markup. The business is not risky because infants are undocumented and disposable. Thousands of infants are also trafficked into China from Vietnam and other areas. Female infants are abducted and sold to men in rural areas.

The buyers are unable to reproduce with local women due to a lack of brides, a result of the sex imbalance in the population (*The Huffington Post*, 2011). Hundreds of offenders have been arrested in connection with human trafficking into China.

Latin America

Numerous social and legal issues have developed as a result of pregnancy among migrant women. The infant mortality rate among Mexican migrants is low; so, the rate of infants with Mexican parents being born in the United States is high (Hummer et al., 2007). Most migrant infants are not crossing the border within the first few hours or days of life; however, when Mexican women cross the border with infants, they often lack diapers, food, and basic necessities (Potter, 2014). Normally, fetuses are being transported with their mothers, often to anchor families to the United States. The term "anchor baby" is used to describe the phenomenon of pregnant women crossing the U.S. border to deliver children who will be entitled to U.S. citizenship. However, the phenomenon is especially intriguing to researchers because mortality rates are approximately 10 percent lower than for non-Hispanic, White children born in the United States. Anchoring may not be a well-supported motive for birthing children in the United States because children cannot legally claim their parents until after they are 21 years old; and under some circumstances, people who are discovered to be illegally living in the United States will be deported (Jacobson, 2010). The law prohibits them from legally reentering the country for at least ten years. Anecdotal evidence demonstrates that the motive may be payment of health care expenses. Some women may secure temporary U.S. addresses and utility services in their names to qualify for birth-related aid. Some wealthy drug lords in Mexico are alleged to pay for premium birth-related health care services in the United States; and have anchor babies who will live in the United States (Judicial Watch, 2012). For example, a daughter of the kingpin running the Sinaloa Cartel was caught illegally entering the country to give birth. Her father is among the most-wanted drug lords in the world; yet, his daughter was attempting to enter to receive free health care benefits. She was charged with fraud and misuse of legal documents. Another cartel leader's wife delivered twins in California the year before.

A serious problem involving children entering the country without much government oversight occurs when children from Guatemala are adopted (Merino, 2010). Russia, China, and Guatemala provide the most adopted children to the United States. An absence of adoption laws in Guatemala offends the Hague Convention, yet 98 percent of such adoptions are international. Canada, Spain, and Germany are a few nations that have criticized and discouraged adoption of children from Guatemala, but the United States is the main destination for all adopted Guatemalan children. One percent of all children born in Guatemala are adopted by American families. This is approximately 270 children each month. Most of the population is poor, and more than one-third of pregnancies are unintended. Adoption is privately arranged and lacks any government oversight. The average international adoption takes three years and costs $29,000. Guatemalan mothers are paid between $200 and $2,000 for infants. Thus, while private arrangements help solve the problem of unintended children, poor families may be motivated by money to conceive and sell children. Lawyers, *uotarios* who broker babies, foster parents, and pediatricians arrange adoptions without judges or governmental agencies. Governmental oversight would normally verify that birth parents and adoptive parents are not participating in human trafficking. Thus, ethical and practical distinctions between adoption and human trafficking may be somewhat unclear.

Bibliography

Abcarian, R. (2014, May 5). After Supreme Court prayer decision, Satanist offers his own prayer. *Los Angeles Times*. Retrieved from http://www.latimes.com/local/abcarian/la-me-ra-abcarian-scotus-20140505-column.html

Arredondo, T. N. L. (2008). Toward a viable policing model for closed religious communities. *American Journal of Criminal Law, 35*(2), 107–144.

Bannon, C. (1994). Recovered memories of childhood sexual abuse: Should the courts get involved when mental health professionals disagree? *Arizona State Law Journal* 26, 835.

Barness, S. (2014, September 17). Trained rescue dog ruins fun time by saving kid who doesn't need saving. *The Huffington Post*. Retrieved from http://www.huffingtonpost.com/2014/09/17/rescue-dog-kid-doesnt-need-saving_n_5836040.html

Beckham, D. B. (2006). Criminal law: Thrashing pecans and other non-pc crimes. *Texas Bar Journal* 69, 262.

Belt, D. (2014, May 30). Toddler in coma after police grenade detonates in crib. *Dallas-Hiram Patch*. http://dallas-hiram.patch.com/groups/police-and-fire/p/toddler-in-coma-after-police-grenade-detonates-in-crib68443

Bobo, J. (2013, August 26). Couple sentenced for faking baby miscarriage to bilk donations. *Kingsport Times-News*. Retrieved from http://www.timesnews.net/article/9066660/couple-sentenced-for-faking-baby-miscarriage-to-bilk-donations#ixzz35Tg8YyNT

Brantner-Smith, B. (2014). Pregnancy and policing. *Officer.Com*.

Brogan, K. (2013). Perinatal depression and anxiety: Beyond psychopharmacology. *Psychiatric Clinics of North America, 36*(1), 183–188.

Brownstein, A. (2006). Taking free exercise rights seriously. *Case Western Reserve University* 57, 55.

Buck, T. (2012). From big love to the big house: Justifying anti-polygamy laws in an age of expanding rights. *Emory International Law Review* 26, 939.

Burk, D. L. (1997). The milk free zone: Federal and local interests in regulating recombinant bST. *Columbia Journal of Environmental Law* 22, 227.

Candland, D. K. (1993). *Feral Children and Clever Animals: Reflections on Human Nature*. New York, NY: Oxford University Press.

Carassava, A. (2014, February 14). Greece grapples with soaring numbers of abandoned children and babies. *The Washington Post*. Retrieved from http://www.washingtonpost.com/blogs/she-the-people/wp/2014/02/14/greece-grapples-with-soaring-numbers-of-abandoned-children-and-babies/

Carlson, K. (2010). Strong medicine: Toward effective sentencing of child pornography offenders. *Mich. L. Rev. First Impressions* 109, 27.

Carpenter, K. A. (2012). Limiting principles and empowering practices in American Indian religious freedoms. *Connecticut Law Review* 45, 387.

Carter, C. (2013, July 27). The brutality of 'corrective rape'. *The New York Times*. Retrieved from http://www.nytimes.com/interactive/2013/07/26/opinion/26corrective-rape.html?_r=0

Chang, D. (2011, April 21). Woman smuggles drugs with baby's diaper: Cops. *NBC Philadelphia*. Retrieved from http://www.nbcphiladelphia.com/news/local/Woman-Smuggles-Drugs-With-Babys-Diaper-Cops--120356129.html#ixzz36q63nc3O

Chung-Park, M. (2008). Emergency contraception knowledge, attitudes, practices, and barriers among providers at a military treatment facility. *Military Medicine, 173*(3) 305.

Collins, N. (2011, July 25). Premature baby survives after doctors advised abortion. *Telegraph*. Retrieved from http://www.telegraph.co.uk/health/healthnews/8660450/Premature-baby-survives-after-doctors-advised-abortion.html

Conly, C. (n.d.) The women's prison association: Supporting women offenders and their families. *U.S. Department of Justice (DOJ), Office of Justice Programs: National Institute of Justice*. Retrieved from https://www.ncjrs.gov/pdffiles/172858.pdf

Connelly, L. (2011, June 24). Pregnancy and policing. *Police Magazine*. Retrieved from http://www.policemag.com/blog/women-in-law-enforcement/story/2011/06/pregnancy-and-policing.aspx

Connolly, J. (2007). Murder-suicide. *Crisis: The Journal of Crisis Intervention and Suicide Prevention, 28*(3), 111–112.

Constantine, M. L. (2008). The effect of the institutionalization of medical care on quality of patient's informed consent. (Order No. AAI3295682). *Dissertation Abstracts International: Section B: The Sciences and Engineering*, 255.

Cowley, A. D. (2014). "Let's get drunk and have sex": The complex relationship of alcohol, gender, and sexual victimization. *Journal of Interpersonal Violence, 29*(7), 1258–1278.

Crawford, C. (2000). Criminal penalties for creating a toxic environment: Mens rea, environmental criminal liability standards, and the neurotoxicity hypothesis. *Boston College Environmental Affairs Law Review* 27, 341.

Crawford, A. (2013, January 6). South Africa: Women drinking to harm babies. *Sky News.* Retrieved from http://news.sky.com/story/1033939/south-africa-women-drinking-to-harm-babies

Crossley, L. (2014, February 15). The maternity military: How nearly 100 female soldiers have been sent home from the Afghan front line after getting pregnant. *Daily Mail.* Retrieved from http://www.dailymail.co.uk/news/article-2560032/The-maternity-military-How-nearly-100-female-soldiers-sent-home-Afghan-frontline-getting-pregnant.html#ixzz32aUv0tja

Cusack, C. M. (2011). Placentaphagy and embryophagy: An analysis of social deviance within gender, family, or the home (*etude* 1). *J. L. & Soc. Deviance* 1, 112.

Cusack, C. M. (2012). Boob laws: An analysis of social deviance with in gender, family, or the home (etudes 2). *Women's Rights Law Reporter* 33, 197.

Cusack, C. M. (2012). Death revolution: Eating the dead to save our world. *Journal Envtl. & Animal Law* 4, 37.

Cusack, C. M. (2012). Nonconsensual insemination: Battery. *Journal of Law and Social Deviance* 3, 78.

Cusack, C. M. (2012). Tit-for-tat about tats on tots: An analysis of social deviance with in gender, family, or the home (etudes 3). *Children's Legal Rights Journal* 32, 50.

Cusack, C. M. (2012). Two films, one law. *EASL Journal, 23*(3), 62.

Cusack, C. M. (2013). A feminist inquiry into intimate partner violence law, policy, policing, and possible prejudices in Alaska. *Journal of Law & Conflict Resolution* 5, 24.

Cusack, C. M. (2013). Comparative sexology: nonconsensual insemination in the United States and the European Union. *Sexologies* 23, e19.

Cusack C. M. (2013). Feminism and husbandry: Drawing the fine line between mine and bovine. *Journal for Critical Animal Studies, 11*(1), 24.

Cusack, C. M. (2013). How the content of online pornography depicts expressed consent for insemination. *Online J Commun & Media Technol (OJCMT)* 3, 3.

Cusack, C. M. (2013). Kent make-up their minds: Juveniles, mental illness, and the need for continued implementation of therapeutic justice within the juvenile justice and criminal justice systems. *Am. U. J. Gender, Soc. Pol'y & L.* 22, 149.

Cusack, C. M. (2013). Nonconsensual insemination: A pilot study. *Online J Soc Sci Res* 2, 61–72.

Cusack, C. M. (2013). Nonconsensual seminal transmission. *Criminal Law Bulletin* 49, 1.

Cusack, C. M. (2013). To-get her forEVEr: A man hater's right to same-sex marriage. *Journal of Law & Public Policy* 10, 63.

Cusack, C. M. (2014). 50 state survey of prosecutors' willingness to prosecute nonconsensual insemination. *Family & Intimate Partner Violence Quarterly* 26, 7.

Cusack, C. M. (2014). Does size matter in the field?: Qualitative investigation of the portrayal of body size in TLC's police women of Broward County. *The Qualitative Report* 19, 35.

Cusack, C. M. (2014). No stroking in the pokey: Promulgating penological policies prohibiting masturbation among inmate populations. *J. L. & Soc. Deviance* 7, 80–124.

Cusack, C. M. (2014). *Pornography and the Criminal Justice System.* CRC/ Francis & Taylor: Boca Raton, FL.

Cusack, C. M. (2015). *Animals and Criminal Justice.* Transaction Publishers: Piscataway, New Jersey.

Cusack, C. M. (2015). *Criminal Justice Handbook on Masculinity, Male Aggression, and Sexuality.* Springfield, IL: Charles C Thomas, Publisher.

Daniels, C. R. (1997). Between fathers and fetuses: The social construction of male reproduction and the politics of fetal harm. *Signs, 22*(3), 579–616.

Daniels, R. (2009). The gay religion. *Southern California Interdisciplinary Law Journal* 19, 129.

Davis, E. G. (Director). (2012). *It's a girl.* Shadowline Films.

Dennis, W. (1941). The significance of feral man. *The American Journal of Psychology, 54*(3), 425.

Derringer, M. (2010). If addiction is a mental disease, let's start treating it like one: An additional recommendation for the Indiana general assembly's prenatal substance abuse commission. *Indiana Health Law Review* 8, 141.

Dixon, K. (2014, May 19). Woman sues Sandy Springs over sex toy ordinance. *Sandy Springs Patch.* Retrieved from http://sandysprings.patch.com/groups/police-and-fire/p/woman-sues-sandy-springs-over-sex-toy-ordinance

Dolgin, J. L. (1991). The law's response to parental alcohol and "crack" abuse. *Brooklyn Law Rev.* 56, 1213.

D'Onofrio, E. (2005). Child brides, inegalitarianism, and the fundamentalist polygamous family in the United States. *International Journal of Law, Policy and the Family, 19*(3), 373.

Dow-Edwards, D. (2010). Sex differences in the effects of cocaine abuse across the life span. *Physiology & Behavior, 100*(3), 208–215.

Dunbar, P. (2011, October 16). 300,000 babies stolen from their parents - and sold for adoption: Haunting BBC documentary exposes 50-year scandal of baby trafficking by the Catholic church in Spain. *Daily Mail.* Retrieved from http://www.dailymail.co.uk/news/article-2049647/BBC-documentary-exposes-50-year-scandal-baby-trafficking-Catholic-church-Spain.html#ixzz3FfuluWVY

Dussias, A. M. (2012). Friend, foe, frenemy: The United States and American Indian religious freedom. *Denver University Law Review* 90, 347.

Edwards, A. (2013, September 16). Gang that smuggled £9m of heroin from Pakistan into Britain in baby powder bottles are jailed for total of 109 years. *Daily*

Mail. Retrieved from http://www.dailymail.co.uk/news/article-2421891/Gang-smuggled-9m-heroin-Pakistan-Britain-baby-powder-bottles-jailed-total-109-years.html#ixzz36qB7UjGD

Elder, D. P. (1991). Investigation and prosecution of child sexual abuse cases. *Western State University Law Review* 19, 249.

Eliason, S. (2009). Murder-suicide: A Review of the recent literature. *J Am Acad Psychiatry Law, 37*(3), 371–376.

Elkins, .K. A. (2004). The devil you know!: Should prisoners have the right to practice Satanism? *Houston Law Review* 41, 613.

Emanuel, R. (1996). Psychotherapy with children traumatized in infancy. *Journal of Child Psychotherapy, 22*(2), 214–239.

Ertelt, S. (2014, May 14). Judge rules 13-year-old can abort her 30-week-old unborn baby. *LifeNews.com*. Retrieved from http://www.lifenews.com/2014/05/14/judge-rules-13-year-old-can-abort-her-30-week-old-unborn-baby/

Farrington, B. (2014, February 16). Prisoners' use of smuggled cellphones on the rise. *Yahoo News*. Retrieved from https://news.yahoo.com/prisoners-39-smuggled-cellphones-rise-160421892.html

Fentiman, L. C. (2009). Pursuing the perfect mother: Why America's criminalization of maternal substance abuse is not the answer—a comparative legal analysis. *Michigan Journal of Gender & Law* 15, 389.

Fernandez, M. (2014, January 26). Texas woman is taken off life support after order. *The New York Times*. Retrieved from http://www.nytimes.com/2014/01/27/us/texas-hospital-to-end-life-support-for-pregnant-brain-dead-woman.html?_r=0

Fidrus, M. (2012, September 6). Customs thwart crystal meth smuggled inside baby powder bottles. *The Jakarta Post*. Retrieved from http://www.thejakartapost.com/news/2012/09/06/customs-thwart-crystal-meth-smuggled-inside-baby-powder-bottles.html

Fitzgerald, L. (2011). 'Let's play mummy': Simulacrum babies and reborn mothers. *European Journal of Cultural Studies, 14*(1) 25–39.

Fitzpatrick, E. (2012). *Cochran v. Commonwealth*: Revisiting whether Kentucky should charge, commit, or cure pregnant substance abusers. *University of Louisville Law Review* 50, 551.

Foy, P. (2014, January 14). Thomas Lippert sperm swap scandal attracts 17 calls to Utah fertility clinic hotline. *The Huffington Post*. Retrieved from http://www.huffingtonpost.com/2014/01/14/thomas-lippert-sperm_n_4598263.html

French, R. (2003). Shopping for religion: The change in everyday religious practice and its importance to the law. *Buffalo Law Review* 51, 127.

Galanter, M. (1998). An oil strike in hell: Contemporary legends about the civil justice system. *Arizona Law Review* 40, 717.

Gaskin, I. M. (2012). Has pseudocyesis become an outmoded diagnosis? *Birth: Issues in Perinatal Care, 39*(1), 77–79.

Gecker, J. (2014, August 23). Interpol seeks clues to Thai 'baby factory'. *MSN*. Retrieved from http://news.msn.com/world/interpol-seeks-clues-to-thai-baby -factory

Gentile, S. (2006). Schizoaffective disorder in women with childbearing potential: Focus on treatment with newer and emerging psychotropic agents. In William H. Murray (Ed.), *Schizoaffective disorder: New research* (pp. 187– 220). Hauppauge, NY: Nova Science Publishers.

Ghaemi, S. N. (2009). The rise and fall of the biopsychosocial model. *The British Journal of Psychiatry*, 195, 3–4.

Giannelli, P. C. (2011). *Daubert* and criminal prosecutions. *Criminal Justice* 26, 3.

Gibbons, H. (2004). *De sciuridae et homo sapiens*: The origin of rights and duties. *The Boston University Public Interest Law Journal* 13, 145.

Gonzalez, T. (2014, April 30). Tennessee criminalizes pregnant drug use. *USA Today*. Retrieved from http://www.usatoday.com/story/news/nation-now/2014/ 04/30/tennessee-criminalize-pregnant-drug-use/8502813/

Gorman, R. (2014, October 1). Missing child Sabrina Allen found in Mexico 12 years after disappearance. *AOL*. Retrieved from http://www.aol.com/ article/2014/10/01/missing-child-sabrina-allen-found-12-years-after-dis- appearance/20970557/?icid=maing-grid7%7Cmain5%7Cdl21%7Csec1_ lnk2%26pLid%3D538743

Green, M. D. (1996). *Bendectin and Birth Defects: The Challenges of Mass Toxic Substances Litigation*. Philadelphia, PA.: University of Pennsylvania Press.

Greenwood, K. (2010). The mysteries of pregnancy: the role of law in solving the problem of unknown but knowable maternal-fetal medication risk. *U. Cin. L. Rev.* 79, 267.

Gregorian, D. (2013, November 18). Guard impregnated by cop killer loses custody of baby. *New York Daily News*. Retrieved from http://www.nydailynews.com/ new-york/guard-impregnated-killer-loses-custody-baby-article-1.1521047

Hamilton, M. A. (2009). The Maryland constitutional law schmooze: The rules against scandal and what they mean for the First Amendment's religion clauses. *Maryland Law Review* 69, 115.

Hanson, H. (2014, June 16). Baby needs organ reconstruction after alleged rape. *The Huffington Post*. Retrieved from http://www.huffingtonpost. com/2014/06/16/julio-iturralde-jasmin-davis-baby-rape_n_5500530.html

Hartmann, M. (2011, September 26). Woman wins court order against self-induced abortion ban. *Jezebel*. Retrieved from http://jezebel.com/5843714/ woman-wins-court-order-against-self-induced-abortion-ban

Hastings, D. (2014, September 19). Ga. mother shot in head saves baby by hiding her in a toilet: family. *New York Daily News*. Retrieved from http://www .nydailynews.com/news/national/dying-ga-mom-saves-baby-hiding-toilet -article-1.1946161

Hatala, A. R. (2012). The status of the "biopsychosocial" model in health psychology: Towards an integrated approach and a critique of cultural conceptions. *Open Journal of Medical Psychology*, 1, 51–62.

Held, K. (2011, January 11). Pregnant woman rescued after attack by dogs. *KSDK News*. Retrieved from http://origin.ksdk.com/news/world/story.aspx?storyid=237860

Hershberger, G. L. (2014, January 20). Report on information request for restraint use of pregnant women. *Department of Public Safety and Correctional Services*. Retrieved from http://dlslibrary.state.md.us/publications/JCR/2013/2013_108.pdf

Hofstetter, J. (2010). Shielding Ohio's newborns: Defending a broad interpretation of "child" within the meaning of O.R.C. § 3113.31. *Clev. St. L. Rev.* 58, 717.

Hollister, G. D. (1982). Parent-child immunity: A doctrine in search of justification. *Fordham Law Review* 50, 1.

Hosch, C. M. (2003). Business Torts. *Southern Methodist University* 56, 1171.

Howle. E. M. (2014). Sterilization of female inmates: Report 2013–2120. *California State Auditor*. Retrieved from https://cbssanfran.files.wordpress.com/2014/06/forced-sterilization-audit.pdf

Jacobs, S. B. (2009). Crises, congress, and cognitive biases: A critical examination of food and drug legislation in the United States. *Food and Drug Law Journal* 64, 599.

Jacobson, L. (2010, August 6). Fact-checking the claims about 'anchor babies' and whether illegal immigrants 'drop and leave'. *Tampa Bay Times*. Retrieved from http://www.politifact.com/truth-o-meter/statements/2010/aug/06/lindsey-graham/illegal-immigrants-anchor-babies-birthright/

James, R. E. (2002). Putting fear back into the law and debtors back into prison: Reforming the debtors' prison system. *Washburn Law Journal* 42, 143.

Jensen, C. L. (2014, March 24). Pa. woman charged with surrogate scam. *Washington Times*. Retrieved from http://www.washingtontimes.com/news/2014/mar/24/pa-woman-charged-with-surrogate-scam/#ixzz34uj46Qx5

Johnson, A. A. (2010). Ninth circuit says setting on taser is important in evaluating use of force. *Criminal Law Reporter, 87*(2), 45.

Johnson, K. (2014, May 15). Clandestine websites fuel 'alarming' increase in child porn. *Detroit Free Press*. Retrieved from http://www.freep.com/usatoday/article/5184485

Johnston, A. (2014, May 23). Lawsuit: Inmate in solitary confinement says jail ignored birth, leading to baby's death. *Independent Mail*. Retrieved from http://www.independentmail.com/news/lawsuit-inmate-solitary-confinement-says-jail-igno

Kaplan, M. (2010). "A special class of persons": Pregnant women's right to refuse medical treatment after Gonzales v. Carhart. *University of Pennsylvania Journal of Constitutional Law* 13, 145.

Karpenchuk, D. (2011, July 18). Canada's stolen generations speak out. *ABC*. Retrieved from http://www.abc.net.au/news/2011-07-19/canada-stolen-gene ration-speaks-out/2799630

Kelly, B. D. (2009). Criminal insanity in 19th-century Ireland, Europe and the United States: Cases, contexts and controversies. *International Journal of Law and Psychiatry 32*(6), 362–368.

Kent, S. A. (2006). A matter of principle: Fundamentalist mormon polygamy, children, and human rights debates. *Nova Religio, 10*(1), 7–29.

Kisch, W. J. (1996). From the couch to the bench: How should the legal system respond to recovered memories of childhood sexual abuse? *The American University Journal of Gender & the Law 5*, 207.

Knox, A. (2013). *Waiting to be Heard: A Memoir*. New York, NY: Harper.

Kruger, K. J. (2006). Pregnancy policy: Law and philosophy. *The Police Chief 73*(3).

Kuruvilla, C. (2014, September 5). Teen Maine mom fights to reverse baby's do-not-resuscitate order after child comes out of coma. *New York Daily News*. Retrieved from http://www.nydailynews.com/life-style/health/teen-momwants-lift-brain-damaged-baby-dnr-order-miraculous-recovery-article-1.1929404

Lake, P. F. (1999). Boys, bad men, and bad case law: Re-examining the historical foundations of no-duty-to-rescue rules. *New York Law School Law Review 43*, 385.

Laly, G. P. (2004). Baby is born in police station. *Women Police, 38*(1), 6.

Larner, A. J. (2013). Delusion of pregnancy: A case revisited. *Behavioural Neurology, 27*(3), 293–294.

LaVey, A. S. (1967). The eleven satanic rules of the Earth. *Church of Satan*. Retrieved from http://www.churchofsatan.com/eleven-rules-of-earth.php

LaVey, A. S. (1988). Pentagonal revisionism: A five-point program. *The Satanic Bible*. Retrieved from http://www.churchofsatan.com/pentagonal-revision-ism.php

Leblanc, S. M. (2007). Cruelty to the mentally ill: An Eighth Amendment challenge to the abolition of the insanity defense. *American University Law Review 56*, 1281.

Leo, R. A. (1997). "Recovered Memory" and the law: The social and legal construction of repressed memory. *Law and Social Inquiry 22*, 653.

Lim, S. Y. (2008). Protecting the unborn as modern day eugenics. *Health Matrix 18*, 127.

Locke, F. (2014, March 15). This Utah mommy blogger plagued by fake revenge porn proves that no one is safe. *Mommyish*. Retrieved from http://www.mommyish.com/2014/03/15/mommy-blogger-revenge-porn/#ixzz34aOr0JMM

Lonon, S. (2014, June 25). Vegan mom refused care for dehydrated newborn, cops say. *South Tampa-Hyde Park Patch*. Retrieved from http://

southtampa.patch.com/groups/police-and-fire/p/vegan-mom-refused-care-for-dehydrated-newborn-cops-say

Lopez, P. (2014, January 4). Hong Kong customs officials say they have arrested 64 people for unlicensed baby milk powder exports ahead of Chinese New Year. *ABC News*. Retrieved from http://www.abc.net.au/news/2014-01-04/an-hkong-baby-formula/5184486

Lowe, L. (2014, May 22). Air Force captain opens up about leaving the military and being pregnant on active duty. *Parade*. Retrieved from http://parade.condenast.com/297245/linzlowe/air-force-captain-opens-up-about-leaving-the-military-and-being-pregnant-on-active-duty/

Lyons, K. (2014, February 16). A glimpse of hell: Traumatised survivors relive public executions, rape and forced abortions inside North Korea's prison camps. *Daily Mail*. Retrieved from http://www.dailymail.co.uk/news/article-2560933/It-make-hair-stand-end-Brutal-executions-hard-labour-forced-abortions-rape-survivors-tell-life-North-Korean-prison-camps.html#ixzz3FztohRlN

Lyons, T. (n.d.). For more than 20 years, Canada took native children from their homes and placed them with white families. Now a lost generation want its history back. *West Region Child and Family Services*. Retrieved from http://www.wrcfs.org/repat/stolennation.htm

Malm, S. (2012, October 24). Man who attacked his pregnant wife and cut out their unborn baby is charged with feticide. *Daily Mail*. Retrieved from http://www.dailymail.co.uk/news/article-2222328/Jeffrey-Reynolds-Man-attacked-pregnant-wife-cut-unborn-baby-charged-feticide.html#ixzz34b9ZtLrX

Manning, P. (2012, May 30). When the border gets tough, smugglers get creative. *Fox News Latino*. Retrieved from http://latino.foxnews.com/latino/news/2012/05/30/smugglers-get-creative-bringing-drugs-and-people-over-border/

Marzulli , J. (2013, June 28). Ex-prison guard knocked up in jail by cop killer Ronell Wilson to plead guilty. *New York Daily News*. Retrieved from http://www.nydailynews.com/new-york/brooklyn/guilty-plea-ex-prison-guard-knocked-inmate-article-1.1385376

Matsuda, M. J. (1998). Crime and affirmative action. *The Journal of Gender, Race & Justice* 1, 309.

Mayes, S. (2013, June 19). Court rejects appeal from Oregon City faith-healing couple convicted in teenage son's death. *The Oregonian*. Retrieved from http:/;www.oregonlive.com/oregon-city/index.ssf/2013/06/court_rejects_appeal_from_oreg.html

McCrone, J. (2003). Feral children. *The Lancet Neurology, 2*(2), 132.

McLaughlin, E. M. (2014, June 25). Tragic accident or murder in hot-car toddler death? *CNN*. Retrieved from http://www.cnn.com/2014/06/25/justice/georgia-toddler-death/index.html?hpt=hp_t1

McNeill, M. (2014). Mind-witness testimony: The unreliability of first-person accounts in sex trafficking discourse. *Albany Government Law Review* 7, 56.

McKnight, R. (2010). "Bringing new life into psychiatry—Extra": Correction. *The British Journal of Psychiatry, 196*(4), 333.

Meggendorfer, F. (1931). Gerichtliche psychiatrie: Eugenische gesetzgeben. *Fortschritte Der Neurologie, Psychiatrie Und Ihrer Grenzgebiete, 3,* 117–133.

Merino, F. (2010). Facts on file. *Adoption and Surrogate Pregnancy.* Retrieved from https://catalog.wakegov.com/Record/618515/Home

Meyer, S. (2011, May 24). Should I use peyote if; I am pregnant or breastfeeding? *Native Mothering.* Retrieved from http://nativemothering.com/2011/05/should-i-use-peyote-if-i-am-pregnant-or-breastfeeding/

Meyers, J. (2014). Pregnancy FAQs. *Navy Personnel Command.* Retrieved from http://www.public.navy.mil/bupers-npc/organization/bupers/WomensPolicy/Pages/FAQs-Women'sPolicy.aspx;

Mills, M. D. (1998). Fetal abuse prosecutions: The triumph of reaction over reason. *DePaul L. Rev.* 47, 989.

Mohapatra, S. (2011). Unshackling addiction: A public health approach to drug use during pregnancy. *Wisconsin Journal of Law, Gender & Society* 26, 241.

Mohney, G. (2014, August 13). First woman charged on controversial law that criminalizes drug use during pregnancy. *Good Morning America.* Retrieved from https://gma.yahoo.com/first-woman-charged-controversial-law-criminalizes-drug-during-192016548--abc-news-topstories.html

Moore, C. (2012). A two-faced light duty. *Law Enforcement Technology, 39*(8), 54.

Morris, J. F. (2001). RU-486: Perpetuating the myths of abortion. *Kan. J.L. & Pub. Pol'y* 11, 309.

Mullin, B. M. (2012). Caucasian mothers' experiences of raising a transracially adopted child. (Order No. AAI3491605). *Dissertation Abstracts International: Section B: The Sciences and Engineering,* 2546.

Murphy. A. S. (2014). A survey of state fetal homicide laws and their potential applicability to pregnant women who harm their own fetuses. *Indiana Law Journal* 89, 847.

Murphy, W. (2014, February 19). Nancy Gonzalez, ex-prison guard, draws 1-year sentence for having sex with convicted cop killer. *Newsday.* Retrieved from http://www.newsday.com/news/new-york/nancy-gonzalez-ex-prison-guard-draws-1-year-sentence-for-having-sex-with-convicted-cop-killer-1.7134077

Nagareda, R. A. (1998). Outrageous fortune and the criminalization of mass torts. *Michigan Law Review* 96, 1121.

Neil, M. (2014, May 5). Pregnant moms face potential jail terms if their babies are born addicted. *American Bar Association (ABA) Journal.* http://www.abajournal.com/news/article/pregnant_moms_face_potential_jail_terms_if_their_babies_are_born_addicted/

Newling, D. (2011). Giant rats eat two babies in South Africa townships in separate attacks. *Daily Mail.* Retrieved from http://www.dailymail.co.uk/news/article-1393836/Giant-rats-eat-babies-South-Africa-townships-separate-attacks.html#ixzz3GWRr8LTN

Ochs, R. (2013, April 2). Hero dog Louie helps save pregnant woman and her premature baby. *The Huffington Post.* Retrieved from http://www.huffingtonpost.com/2013/04/03/hero-dog-louie_n_3000528.html

Oosterbaan, D. (2011). The fallacy of simple possession: The impact of targeting, charging, and plea bargaining at sentencing. *United States Attorneys' Bulletin: Sexual Exploitation Crimes Against Children, 59*(5), 1–86. Retrieved from http://www.justice.gov/usao/eousa/foia_reading_room/usab5905.pdf

Orovitz, S. (2012). *Free bird*: No right to qualified immunity for police who retaliate against the middle finger gesture. *Journal of Law and Social Deviance* 3, 1.

Osbeck, M. K. (1985). Bad Samaritanism and the duty to render aid: A proposal. *University of Michigan Journal of Law Reform* 19, 315.

Ostas, D. T. (2007). When fraud pays: Executive self-dealing and the failure of self-restraint. *American Business Law Journal* 44, 571.

Pacillo, E. L. (1997). Expanding the feminist imagination: An analysis of reproductive rights. *Am. U. J. Gender & Law* 6, 113.

Paltrow, L. M. (2010, March 6). Utah continues reckless efforts to lock-up pregnant women. *The Huffington Post.* Retrieved from http://www.huffingtonpost.com/lynn-m-paltrow/utah-continues-reckless-e_b_488673.html

Pansarasa, C. L. (2004). Adolescent pregnancy denial, dissociative symptoms and neonaticide: Expanding understanding, furthering treatment and prevention. (Order No. AAI3133416). *Dissertation Abstracts International: Section B: The Sciences and Engineering,* 2645.

Patterson, E. G. (2008). Civil contempt and the indigent child support obligor: The silent return of debtor's prison. *Cornell Journal Law & Public Policy* 18, 95.

Phillis, M. (2014, March 12). Passaic County judge rules pregnant woman does not have to allow father in delivery room. *NorthJersey.com.* Retrieved from http://www.northjersey.com/news/passaic-county-judge-rules-pregnant-woman-does-not-have-to-allow-father-in-delivery-room-1.739682#sthash.itAkJI1S.dpuf

Plastine, L. M. (1993). "In God we trust": When parents refuse medical treatment for their children based upon their sincere religious beliefs. *Seton Hall Const. L.J.* 3, 123.

Player, C. T. (2014). Public assistance, drug testing, and the law: The limits of population-based legal analysis. *American Journal of Law & Medicine* 40, 26.

Potter, M. (2014, June 18). Border agents give migrant moms diapers, baby formula. *NBC News.* Retrieved from http://www.nbcnews.com/news/latino/border-agents-give-migrant-moms-diapers-baby-formula-n134361

Prager, J. (2014, May 9). Florida town must open meeting with Satanic prayer or violate Supreme Court ruling. *Americans against the Tea Party.* Retrieved from http://aattp.org/florida-town-must-open-meeting-with-satanic-prayer-or-violate-supreme-court-ruling/

Price, M. E. (2011, August 18). Are people "naturally" polygamous? *Psychology Today.* Retrieved from http://www.psychologytoday.com/blog/darwin-eternity/201108/are-people-naturally-polygamous-0

Prosser, W. L. (1960). Privacy. *California Law Review* 48.

Przynski, M. (2006). Region 7 News. *Women Police, 40*(3), 17–18.

Ramos, B. (2013, March 28). 12 real pregnant pornos that will scare the uterus out of you. *Mommyish.* Retrieved from http://www.mommyish.com/2014/03/28/pregnant-porn/#ixzz3FuhAU8X1

Rafter, N. H. (2001). Seeing and believing: Images of heredity in biological theories of crime. *Brooklyn Law Review* 67, 71.

Rao, M. (2014, July 15). Japan arrested the 'vagina artist,' but these 5 phallic toys are apparently fine. *The Huffington Post.* Retrieved from http://www.huffingtonpost.com/2014/07/15/vagina-artist-arrest-japan_n_5588664.html?cps=gravity

Rawlinson, K. (2014, August 23). Interpol investigates 'baby factory' as man fathers 16 surrogate children. *The Guardian.* Retrieved from http://www.theguardian.com/lifeandstyle/2014/aug/23/interpol-japanese-baby-factory-man-fathered-16-children

Rapp, G. C. (2008). The wreckage of recklessness. *Washington University Law Review* 86, 111.

Richards, J. (2010). Autonomy, imperfect consent, and polygamist sex rights claims. *California Law Review, 98*(1), 197.

Robinson, W. (2014, April 27). Man blows up woman he got pregnant during one-night stand by tying a gas canister to her and igniting it . . . but now he is fighting for life alongside her in Chinese hospital while the baby is still alive. *Daily Mail.* Retrieved from http://www.dailymail.co.uk/news/article-2614271/Chinese-man-ties-gas-canister-girlfriend-got-pregnant-mistake-ignites-seat-car-Severely-burned-woman-recovering-hospital-attacker.html#ixzz34b8jD5Tf

Rovner, J. (2006, February 21). 'Partial-Birth Abortion:' Separating Fact from Spin. *National Public Radio (NPR).* Retrieved from http://www.npr.org/templates/story/story.php?storyId=5168163.

Rovner, J. (2012, May 18). Woman who tried to commit suicide while pregnant gets bail. *National Public Radio (NPR).* Retrieved from http://www.npr.org/blogs/health/2012/05/18/153026015/bail-granted-for-indiana-woman-charged-in-attempted-feticide

Rustad, M. (1992). In defense of punitive damages in products liability: Testing tort anecdotes with empirical data. *Iowa Law Review* 78, 1.

Rustad, M. (1997). How the common good is served by the remedy of punitive damages. *Tennessee Law Review* 64, 793.

Rutecki, G. W. (2010, October 8). Forced sterilization of Native Americans: Late Twentieth Century physician cooperation with national eugenic policies. *The Center for Bioethics and Human Dignity*. Retrieved from https://cbhd.org/content/forced-sterilization-native-americans-late-twentieth-century-physician-cooperation-national-

Salako, J. (2012, August 7). Fertility doctor "caught in false pregnancy scam"; "sorry, your baby disappeared." *News Rescue*. Retrieved from http://newsrescue.com/fertility-doctor-caught-false-pregnancy-scam-sorry-baby-disappeared/#ixzz35Tbrpjfw

Sanghani, R. (2014, February 14). 'Women get pregnant, even in the army—get over it'. *Telegraph UK*. Retrieved from http://www.telegraph.co.uk/women/womens-politics/10645787/Women-get-pregnant-even-in-the-army-get-over-it.html

Seelinger, K. T. (2010). Violence against women and HIV control in Uganda: A paradox of protection? *Hastings International and Comparative Law Review* 33, 345.

Segal, K. (2009, February 7). Doctor loses license in live birth abortion case. *CNN*. Retrieved from http://www.cnn.com/2009/US/02/06/florida.abortion/

Seldin, H. S. (2013). Circumcision, child fatalities, and Constitutional free exercise in New York. *Journal of Law and Social Deviance* 6, 99–153.

Severson, K. (2014, January 12). As conjugal visits fade, a lifeline to inmates' spouses is lost. *The New York Times*. Retrieved from http://www.nytimes.com/2014/01/13/us/with-conjugal-visits-fading-a-lifeline-to-inmates-spouses-is-lost.html?_r=0

Seward, E. M. (1972). Preventing postpartum psychosis. *The American Journal of Nursing, 72*(3), 520–523.

Sharp, D. (2014, September 19). Maine court dismisses do-not-resuscitate appeal. *Yahoo*. Retrieved from http://news.yahoo.com/maine-court-dismisses-not-resuscitate-appeal-200354159.html

Shenon, P. (1985, August 22). Lily Pleads guilty to Oraflex charges. *N.Y. Times,* p. A16.

Silverberg, E. A. (1994). Looking beyond judicial deference to agency discretion: A fundamental right of access to RU 486? *Brooklyn L. Rev.* 59, 1551.

Shapiro, S. (1983). The pregnant patient on an in-patient psychiatric service. *Journal of Psychiatric Treatment & Evaluation, 5*(4), 363–370.

Shuman, D. W. (1997). Law and psychology: The standard of care in medical malpractice claims, clinical practice guidelines, and managed care: towards a therapeutic harmony? *California Western Law Review* 34, 99.

Solinas-Saunders, M. (2007). Male intimate partner abuse: Drawing upon three theoretical perspectives (dissertation). ProQuest Dissertations and Theses.

Sperling, D. (2004). Maternal brain death. *American Journal of Law & Medicine* 30, 453.

Spindelman, M. (2013). Sexuality's law. *Columbia Journal of Gender and Law* 24, 87.

Spinelli, M. G. (2004). Maternal infanticide associated with mental illness: Prevention and the promise of saved lives. *The American Journal of Psychiatry, 161*(9), 1548–1557.

Spivack, C. (2010). Section II.A: civil law: The law of surrogate motherhood in the United States. *The American Journal of Comparative Law* 58, 97.

Srinath, D. (2012). A new weapon in the obesity battle: Coordinated state attorneys general *parens patriae* consumer protection lawsuits. *Journal of Law and Social Deviance* 4, 40.

Stewart, B. S. (2011). Opening the broom closet: Recognizing the religious rights of wiccans, witches, and other neo-pagans. *Northern Illinois University Law Review* 32, 135.

Stogner, J. (2010). The war on whiskey in the womb: Assessing the merit of challenges to statutes restricting the alcohol intake of pregnant women. *Rutgers Journal of Law & Public Policy* 7, 259.

Stone, J. (2013). Rape, consent and intoxication: A legal practitioner's perspective. [Editorial] *Alcohol and Alcoholism, 48*(4), 384–385.

Subotnik, D. (2007). Hands off": Sex, feminism, affirmative consent, and the law of foreplay. *Southern California Review of Law & Social Justice* 16, 249.

Swern, A. J. (2007). Sixteenth annual report. Drug treatment alternative-to-prison (DTAP). Retrieved from http://www.prisonpolicy.org/scans/DTAP%20Sixteenth%20Annual%20Report.pdf

Swift, A. (2009, February 14). Inmate who lost baby in Collier jail: 'I want them to make changes'. *Naples News*. Retrieved from http://www.naplesnews.com/news/2009/feb/14/inmate-who-lost-baby-collier-jail-i-want-them-make/

Tennyson, E. G. (2012). A "phantom recall" does not comport with FDA's regulatory practice—or does it?: The need for more stringent mandatory reporting in FDA matters. *Iowa Law Review* 97, 1839.

Thoennes, N. W. (2002). Massachusetts incarcerated and paroled parents. *Center for Policy Research, Child Support Profile*. Retrieved from http://cntrpolres.qwestoffice.net/reports/profile%20of%20CS%20among%20incarcerated%20&%20paroled%20parents.pdf

Ulrich, M. (2012). With child, without rights?: Restoring a pregnant woman's right to refuse medical treatment through the HIV lens. *Yale Journal of Law and Feminism* 24, 303.

Underwood-Nunez, J. (2013). How to deal with pregnancy in law enforcement. *Police Magazine*. Retrieved from http://www.policemag.com/blog/women-in-law-enforcement/story/2013/06/female-pregnancy-in-law-enforcement.aspx

Vestal, C. (2007, May 17). Stillborn laws entangled in abortion debate. *State Line*. Retrieved from http://www.stateline.org/live/details/story?contentId=208701

Veysey, B. M. (1998). Specific needs of women diagnosed with mental illnesses in U.S. jails. In Levin, B.L., Blanch, A.K. and Jennings, A. (eds.), *Women's Mental Health Services: A Public Health Perspective*. Thousand Oaks, CA: Sage Publications.

Vorzimer, A. (2011, March 23). Surrogate mother arrested for theft. *Egg Donation, Inc.* Retrieved from http://www.eggdonor.com/blog/2011/03/23/surrogate-mother-arrested-theft/

Waldeck, S. E. (2002). Encouraging a market in human milk. *Columbia Journal of Gender and Law* 11, 361.

Wardle, S. W. (2013). The advance directive statute revisited. *University of Miami Law Review* 67, 861.

Wardell, D. (1980). Margaret Sanger: birth control's successful revolutionary. *Am J Public Health, 70*(7):736–742.

Wang, F. (2014, July 21). Study debunks myths surrounding sex-selective abortion bans. *NBC News*. Retrieved from http://www.nbcnews.com/news/asian-america/study-debunks-myths-surrounding-sex-selective-abortion-bans-n161191

Wayne, B. (2011, March 15). Woman breastfeeding monkey. *Youtube.com*. Retrieved from https://www.youtube.com/watch?v=R6FMb1wHc4g

Weinberg, M. A. (2012). When bankruptcy is not the best option. *Clearinghouse Review: Journal of Poverty Law and Policy* 46, 90.

Whiten, A. (1993). A natural education - feral children and clever animals: Re. (1993). *Nature, 366*(6453), 375.

Witt, L. (1975, October 20). Was Susan Cochran kidnapped or merely being wooed in a strange courtship? *Reproductive Medical Technologies* 4, 16.

Wolkind, S. N. (1977). Women who have been "in care": Psychological and social status during pregnancy. *Child Psychology & Psychiatry & Allied Disciplines, 18*(2), 179–182.

Wood, S. (2006, January 28). Surrogacy agent charged with theft. *Inquirer*. Retrieved from http://articles.philly.com/2006-01-28/news/25410958_1_surrogate-mother-surrogacy-business-bernardi

Wood, K. (2014). A quandary of the legislature's making: Applying parental consent statutes to minors without parents. *In Re Anonymous 5*, 286 Neb. 640 (2013). *Journal of Law and Social Deviance* 7, 242–282.

Yeung, K. (2014, April 8). Phantom pregnancies. *Indonesia Expat*. Retrieved from http://indonesiaexpat.biz/sports-health/phantom-pregnancies/#sthash.E6WWvH4m.dpuf

Ying, Z. (2012, July 12). The mothers who sold their newborns: A tale of child trafficking in China. *Worldcrunch*. Retrieved from http://www.worldcrunch.com/culture-society/the-mothers-who-sold-their-newborns-a-tale-of-child-trafficking-in-china/c3s5832/#.U3lV3NJdVyU

Yoo, K. (2010). Tainted milk: What kind of justice for victims' families in China? *Hastings International and Comparative Law Review* 33, 555.

Index

Lightning Source UK Ltd.
Milton Keynes UK
UKOW06n1645050515

250909UK00005B/86/P